CICELY SAUNDERS

Best wishes,

Cicely Saunders

CICELY SAUNDERS

Founder of the Modern Hospice Movement

Shirley du Boulay

HODDER AND STOUGHTON
LONDON SYDNEY AUCKLAND TORONTO

British Library Cataloguing in Publication Data

Du Boulay, Shirley
  Cicely Saunders: founder of the modern
  hospice movement.
  1. Saunders, *Dame* Cicely   2. Hospices
  (Terminal care) – Great Britain
  I. Title
  362.1'75   R726.8

  ISBN 0 340 39938 4

*For the patients of St Christopher's
past, present and future*

We die with the dying:
See, they depart, and we go with them.
We are born with the dead:
See, they return, and bring us with them.

T. S. Eliot, 'Little Gidding', *Four Quartets*

FOREWORD

by the Right Reverend John Taylor
former Bishop of Winchester

Some biographies are an indispensable duty required by the status of the subject. But this is a story that simply had to be told. For here is someone who, almost single-handed (though she would fiercely deny this), has tackled and overcome one of the greatest unspoken fears that haunt human beings today, the fear of a painful and humiliating death from an incurable disease. The dread that this might befall some beloved relative is often greater than the fear for oneself. Hence the despair that lends such force to the case for euthanasia. And it is this despair that Cicely Saunders has dispelled with the light of a new hope. In 1960 she declared the conviction which she had proved by careful experiment. 'It is my experience in two terminal homes that we can relieve the suffering of ninety per cent of the patients and bring it within their diminishing compass where we cannot relieve it entirely.' 'Suffering is only intolerable when nobody cares and one continually sees that faith in God and his care is made infinitely easier by faith in someone who has shown kindness and sympathy.' The first of those statements is about clinical technique, the second is about a new style of care in terminal illness. Both these breakthroughs were achieved as the result of a remarkable gift for making an intimate friendship with a dying person and learning from it. This new understanding is now being applied to the treatment of terminal patients and their families not only at Dame Cicely's own foundation, St. Christopher's Hospice in Sydenham, London, but also in a growing number of similar units in the United Kingdom and beyond, and is being brought to the attention of medical students from some of the big teaching hospitals through the work of the training centre that has been opened next door to St. Christopher's. So more and more people are seeing for themselves the truth of Cicely Saunders' great affirmation that human beings are capable of dying their own deaths with dignity and at peace.

But very few people beyond her most intimate friends know anything of the personal story of the one who achieved all this. Yet behind every gift of vision, every tenacity of vocation, lie those individual experiences that have twisted 'the sinews of the heart'. With exceptional courage Dame Cicely has allowed the author, Shirley du Boulay, to read her most personal papers and journals in order to tell the story honestly and completely. As the originator of the successful television series, *The Light of Experience*, and script associate for *The Other Side of Me*, she has a talent for bringing privacy to the light with delicacy and perfect respect for her subject. She records the events unpretentiously, letting the story tell itself, and the result is a biography that is both profound and readable. It deserves to be known far and wide, for here is inspiration and here is Good News.

Bishop John Taylor

FOREWORD

by Sir Douglas Black

Past President, Royal College of Physicians

In the post-Strachey era it is refreshing to read a biography whose author clearly likes her subject; and now that Freud has lived and died, it is a comfort to be spared yet another *tractatus* from the woodshed school of mystery and imagination. Also I was quickly won over, first by the narrative skill of the earlier chapters, and then by the sincerity brought to the discussion at various points of the spiritual spring of Dame Cicely's remarkable achievement. I welcome the opportunity to make some comment on the medical aspects of the story, and at the same time to express my own admiration for a very remarkable person.

Cicely Saunders was born into a most interesting family, in which she was exposed to the well-attested perils of wordly success. Competitiveness verging on combativeness was prominent in the home, and any depth of religious feeling rather strikingly absent, at least on the surface – for who can tell what lies in the heart. In spite of the worldly advantages, Cicely apparently managed to attain that prerequisite of future eminence, a not entirely happy childhood and adolescence. Her parents were temperamentally at odds, and their marriage ended in separation; she herself was shy and lonely at school, even though her talents and determination brought her the headship of her house at boarding-school. Later on, though she ultimately became a finder, she spent long years and essayed a number of careers as a seeker for a vocation. She entered Oxford to study PPE, but when war broke out she turned to nursing, and was trained at St. Thomas's Hospital. She loved nursing, and especially the contact with patients, but her back was unequal to the physical strain of heavy lifting, and she had to accept orthopaedic advice to give up nursing. Nevertheless, it was at this time that her caring instinct found practical fulfilment, and she had her first deeply emotional encounters with death and dying. She then trained as an almoner, and ultimately as a doctor.

To this triple professional qualification for her future work she had already added a driving force which in concert with her talents and training would enable her to reach her goal in spite of all difficulties. This critical period in her life is thus described: 'The few months after she left Oxford were a momentous time for Cicely. Between June and September she had got her degree and her diploma, her parents had separated and she was converted to Christianity.' (The diploma referred to was in Public and Social Administration, and was obtained in 1945, at the age of 26.)

While training as an almoner, and following the death of a Polish friend, David Tasma, Cicely did voluntary evening work in St. Luke's Hospital, where she learned the value of giving analgesic drugs in time to prevent pain, rather than when pain had already developed to such a pitch that larger doses would be needed to control it, and still might only be partially effective. And also the value of giving medicines by mouth, so that it would be practical at home as well as in hospital.

So now she had become dedicated to the care of patients approaching death; she had mastered the relevant professional disciplines; and she had gained practical experience of the management of such patients, including a valuable system of medication which was not in wide general use. She was therefore uniquely qualified to bring about a radically new approach to an aspect of care which had hitherto been overshadowed by other aspects of medical and nursing practice.

When she began her work, the very high mortality which was accepted in earlier times had begun to yield to improved social conditions; and what has been described as the therapeutic revolution was under way. The excitement of new treatments, and the challenge of new technologies were paramount in the outlook of both doctors and nurses. Concentration on acute, and particularly on curable illness, was tending to divert attention from the problems of chronic illness, and especially of illness which was shortly going to prove fatal. There is of course no inherent contradiction between 'curing' and 'caring'; and it is very largely the actual clinical situation which determines which of these approaches is possible, and therefore relevant. But for us all there comes a stage of illness, whether sudden or gradual, in which the possibilities of cure have been exhausted, and what remains is to make possible a course of dying which is free from avoidable pain and anxiety. Cicely Saunders' great contribution has been to demonstrate to the caring professions everywhere the importance of caring for terminal illness, and the range of help which can in fact be given. St. Christopher's Hospice is known throughout the world. It has given help to countless individuals directly; and to very many more through those who have first visited it, and then set up comparable homes. St. Christopher's bears the stamp of its creator, and is probably in the narrow sense of the word inimitable, particularly as it is adorned by the pictures painted by her gifted husband, Professor Marian Bohusz. But even if it were possible, slavish imitation is not what is needed – the requirement is that those responsible for medical and nursing care should be infected by the attitude that the dying patient needs and deserves not only compassion and consolation, but also the full deployment of medical and nursing skills which – Christopher-like – can ease their journey. Cicely Saunders has been foremost in forming, proclaiming and confirming this attitude.

Douglas Black

Acknowledgments

I would like to thank all those whose help has made this book possible, especially:

Sir Douglas Allen; Sister Antonia, St. Joseph's Hospice; Dr. Mary Baines, Consultant of St. Christopher's; Sir Douglas Black, Past President, Royal College of Physicians; Dr. Kerry Bluglass, Director of Studies, St. Christopher's Hospice; Dr. A. G. Brown, Specialist in Community Medicine; Mrs. Rosetta Burch; Mrs. Lilian Buss; Hilary Chapman; Mrs. Kitty Cole; Dr. David Cooper; Dr. Chris Dare, St. Luke's Hospice, Cape Town; Mrs. Mary Dempster; Mrs. D. Diamant; Miss Madge Drake; Elisabeth Earnshaw-Smith, Principal Social Worker, St. Christopher's Hospice; Henry R. Erle, Cornell Medical School, New York; Dr. Douglas Farquarson; Dr. Herman Feifel, California School of Medicine; Dr. Gillian Ford, Deputy Chief Medical Officer, Department of Health and Social Security; John E. Fryer, Temple University Health Services Center, Philadelphia, USA; Dr. Robert Fulton, University of Minnesota; Mr. Jack Galton; Mrs. Bridget Gibb; Mrs. Sheila Hanna, Organiser – Volunteers, St. Christopher's Hospice; Dr. Joan Haram, Recorder, St. Christopher's Hospice; Frank Hill, Bursar, St. Christopher's Hospice; Christine Kearney, Personal Assistant to Dr. Saunders; Dr. Samuel C. Klagsbrun, Four Winds Hospital, New York; Avril Knight; Dr. Sylvia Lack, Hospice Inc., New Haven, Connecticut; William M. Lamers, Jr., Director, Hospice Calgary, Alberta; Dr. Richard Lamerton, author *Care of the Dying*; Father Paul Lewis, Chaplain, St. Christopher's; Mrs. Janet L. Lunceford, Public Health Service, Maryland; Lt.-Colonel and Mrs. H. E. Madge; Barbara McNulty; Professor Balfour Mount, Royal Victoria Hospital, Montreal; Peggy Nuttall, former Editor, *Nursing Times*; Dr. Colin Murray Parkes, London

Hospital Medical College; Betty Read; Mary Rous; Mr. and Mrs. Christopher Saunders; Mr. and Mrs. John Saunders; Miss Freda Saunders; The Reverend Canon Dr. and Mrs. Stephen S. Smalley; 'Peter' S. W. Justin Smith; Miss Joan Steel; Harold Stewart, Professor Emeritus, University of London; Miss Dorothy Summers, Deputy Director of Studies (External), St. Christopher's Hospice; The Reverend Carleton J. Sweetser, Chaplain, St. Luke's Hospital Center, New York; The Right Reverend John Taylor, Bishop of Winchester; Dr. Robert Twycross, Consultant Physician, Sir Michael Sobell House; Dr. Thérèse Vanier, Consultant, St. Christopher's Hospice; Mrs. Florence Wald, Associate Clinical Professor, Yale University School of Nursing; Mrs. Jack Wallace; Dr. Thomas D. Walsh, Research Fellow, St. Christopher's Hospice; Mrs. E. S. West; Dr. T. S. West, Deputy Medical Director, St. Christopher's Hospice; Professor Eric Wilkes, Department of Community Medicine, Sheffield; Miss Helen Willans, former Matron, St. Christopher's Hospice; Dame Albertine Winner, DBE; David Winter; Mrs. Paddy Yorkstone, Research Associate, St. Christopher's Hospice.

My warm thanks also to Deborah Crowe, who typed the manuscript most patiently and cheerfully; to my husband John, for his unfailing support and encouragement; and most of all to Cicely, for her total co-operation and disarming honesty.

The extract from 'Little Gidding' from *Four Quartets* by T. S. Eliot is reprinted by permission of Faber and Faber Ltd.

Contents

1

FAMILY AND SCHOOL

Nothing bears fruit without having first been mortified.
Henry Madathanas

Burgersdorp, January 27th, 1900
The Colonel still worse, and at times raving mad, I was
on watch with him from seven till ten this morning. At
times it was quite pathetic the way he talked to me.
Once he said, 'Are we nearly in harbour?' I could not
help thinking he might not be far from harbour, for his
voyage seemed nearly over. Another time he said, 'Let
me feel you, *do* let me feel you', and putting up his two
mangled hands felt all over my face. Then he said,
evidently imagining in his delusion that some dear one
was with him, 'Kiss me, oh do kiss me', and when I
kissed him, tears trickled down his brave face and he
sobbed like a child. I had to restrain myself from joining
my tears with his. I soothed him by rubbing his arms
and soon he was in a peaceful sleep again. Poor man he
is dreadfully ill, may God spare him to his dear ones at
home.

That moving account of a mortally wounded man's last
hours comes from the diary of Frederick Knight, one of the
early settlers in South Africa, written during the year in
which his village was occupied by the Boers. Frederick
Knight was a gentle, charming and handsome man, who
wanted 'to care for people rather than to kill them' and
who had such a feeling for caring that people far and wide
used to seek his advice. This quality was inherited by his
granddaughter Cicely, who, over fifty years later, was to
revolutionise the medical profession's attitude to dying
and death and restore dignity to the terminally ill.

Fred Knight ran the local store at Burgersdorp, where his qualities of tenderness and concern for others were of little help in the running of his business. His kindly instincts led him to oblige people with too much credit, he was incompetent commercially and the Boer War, raging at his doorstep, cannot have helped. Two sons and a daughter, Chrissie, were born into this troubled life, the family being somehow held together by his extremely dominating wife. She consoled herself by preserving the family papers, which spoke of happier – or at least more socially distinguished – times. She could recall, for instance, how one of her ancestors, Sir John Strode, was made famous by the fury of Charles I. Sir John and eight fellow Members of Parliament would not agree to the raising of taxes demanded by their monarch, who stormed into Parliament seeking vengeance only to find they had been warned of his wrath and had absented themselves. It was this incident which from that time on determined that no reigning monarch should enter the House of Commons unannounced. Such memories may have cheered her, but she grew increasingly forbidding as life became harder and eventually had a fairly serious nervous breakdown. By the time Chrissie was thirteen the family had admitted defeat and returned to England.

Chrissie grew up into a woman to whom people reacted in very different ways. Some people found her gentle, thoughtful, charming and considerate – a sweet and loving person. Others found her shallow, irritating and demanding. She was an elegant woman, slim and trim with a wonderful dress sense; she was a perfectionist: 'a meticulous worker, everything she did was perfectly done.' There is something very touching about this well-meaning woman who seems to have found life so difficult. Even her strengths became self-defeating. A perceptive friend of Cicely's describes Chrissie as 'a wonderfully kind shadow doing everything perfectly'.

In marrying Gordon Saunders she found her opposite. Where she was negative, he was positive; where she was fragile, he was strong. He was a man of tremendous vitality – generous, inspiring, hard-working, big, power-ful and rather overbearing. 'Very hale and hearty. The sort of person who makes a party go.' These extrovert qualities do not appeal to everyone; someone who knew him in later life found him an arrogant, successful, bored man, who needed constant entertaining.

Gordon's vulnerable side was less apparent, but Cicely knew his soft centre and realised that he could easily be deflated. This, together with his surprising inability to stand up to opposition, reveals an insecurity that, for the most part, he managed to conceal.

His father must have had something of the enterprise which was Gordon's hallmark, for at a time when the camera was young, he owned a string of photographer's shops in Eton, Oxford, Cambridge, Harrow and Camber-ley. He had married twice, Gordon being the youngest and most brilliant of seventeen children. Old Mr. Saunders died shortly after Gordon's first birthday and his money was soon spent. 'Grabbed or wasted' one of his grand-children claims. Certainly the older children do not seem to have run the family business with their father's acumen and his wife, who was an excellent Victorian water-colourist, seems to have spent most of her time painting; but one can only have sympathy for a widow left with quite so many children in those days before the Welfare State. None-the-less when Gordon was in his early teens money was somehow found to send him to Dauntsey's, an agri-cultural school in Wiltshire. He had two glorious years there – playing in all the school teams, shooting, going out illegally in the middle of the night looking for moths – before he left, determined to restore the family fortunes. Despite the imminence of the First World War, there was no question of active service for Gordon, as he had broken an ankle very badly at school and it had never set proper-ly. He had to find a job, a job that would enable him to make money quickly but that did not need capital to start. He decided on estate agency work, as his training at Dauntsey's gave him a good background, and signed up at night school. After a short spell with Giddy and Giddy he joined John D. Wood, becoming a partner in 1916. There were eight partners at the time and the firm was already well-established, specialising in the upper end of the property market. Business was thriving and Gordon was a welcome addition. Cicely describes him as 'a real buccaneer' and his colleagues would certainly have agreed. He had the knack of seeing the potential of a property immediately and he worked with the unflagging determination of a man who knew exactly where he was going. As John D. Wood and Gordon Saunders suited each other perfectly he did extremely well; he was senior partner for about thirty years, eventually managing affairs for huge estates like the Grosvenor and doing some highly successful speculative buying. And he did what he had set out to do – he made a great deal of money. Endearingly and typically he said to a partner as they were congratulating each other on their success, 'We've done better than that, Algie, we've enjoyed it.'

The Knights and the Saunders came together in North London just before the First World War. Both families were going down in the world socially and Gordon's dynamism and determination to change this state of affairs must have been very attractive to the ineffectual, if charming, Knights. Chrissie's mother made a dead set at him for her daughter and, though Chrissie resisted for a while, when he proposed for the third time she eventually accepted him. Doubtless this resistance attracted and encouraged Gordon, who claimed later that he didn't stand a chance. It is hard to believe that such an extrovert, ebullient man did not have the courage to resist a scheming mother, but though he was confident in his profession he had had little experience of the world and felt socially inadequate. He was only twenty-two, had grown up with sixteen brothers and sisters, like puppies in a basket, and had all the company he needed at home without testing the waters of the outside world. Besides, Chrissie was on the spot and beautiful. They were engaged for four years – long engagements were common in those days and Gordon would have wished to be established in his profession

before he set up home – but years later he admitted to
Cicely that by the time they married he felt sorry for her
and couldn't possibly break it off. Since pity, however
honourable an emotion, is not a good basis for marriage,
there were trying times ahead. Though Gordon and Chrissie never stopped loving each other, they found it hard to
live together.

Cicely was the first of their three children and was born
on June 22nd, 1918. She was christened Cicely Mary
Strode Saunders – Strode of course being a reminder of
her distinguished seventeenth-century ancestor. The two
boys followed: John, born in 1920 and Christopher six
years later. For the twenty-eight years they were together
Gordon and Chrissie lived in Barnet, in houses that
reflected Gordon's increasing prosperity. Their first married home was Linden Lodge, a fairly ordinary suburban
house, then, in 1922, they moved to Monkenholt, a large
period house on Hadley Green. There they acquired servants, a normal part of middle-class life in the 1920s, and
the children hardly knew a time when there was not a
nanny or a companion around to help Chrissie. There was
Emily, then a Miss Morrison, and 'Stocky', who was to be
a great favourite, came when Christopher was born. There
were also Mr. and Mrs. Read, who worked as cook and
butler.

Cicely went to a kindergarten school in a house run by
the Misses Smythe, which she enjoyed, and then to a day
school, which she hated. She was taken to and from school
in a horse-drawn vehicle with several of the other girls
and used to return home pathetically eager to escape from
them. She was mystified by her unpopularity and helpless
to do anything about it. Perhaps it was her height, for she
was already very tall for her age; perhaps her sharp
intelligence was already showing, to the disadvantage of
the other girls. At all events her parents decided that this
should not continue and when she was ten she was sent to
Southlands, a boarding school in Seaford. There she was
perpetually in trouble for talking too much, or at least,
with the gaucheness of the very shy, for talking at the

wrong time and getting caught: however she now had an ally in the Matron, who was her aunt and godmother, her father's sister Daisy. Aunt Daisy, who was to be an important figure in Cicely's life for many years, used to help her out of trouble in a tactful, unobtrusive way and would come up and see her if she was sent to bed for the day, as sometimes happened. She was there for four years and was happy enough.

By the time Cicely was fourteen, Gordon felt that she was not being sufficiently extended and sent her to Roedean, the fashionable girls' boarding school near Brighton. She was furious at being treated in such an arbitrary fashion and still sounds outraged at this paternal liberty. 'He never even discussed it with me. I should have thought that at the age of fourteen I should have been taken into my father's confidence.' She was thoroughly miserable and lonely. She hated it so much that she used to refuse to go in the school train and had to be driven down. One term the car wouldn't start and another had to be hired, so determined was she not to anticipate the horrors of school by so much as a train journey. She even lost the one friend she had, a girl from Southlands who had come on to Roedean with her. They shared a double room, were caught 'talking after lights out' in a time-honoured tradition, and were promptly separated and put in single rooms. She was shy, so shy that she remembers going a whole term without mid-morning cocoa because there was no table she felt able to join. Chapel was preferable if only because she sang in the choir and therefore had somewhere to sit.

After two or three years one of those seemingly insignificant incidents turned the tide of Cicely's misery. 'Somebody stole something of mine. A registered parcel should have arrived, it was a gold bangle, and I'd written home to say it hadn't come. So my father wrote to the housemistress and it turned out that another girl had taken it. I didn't tell anybody else about it, partly because I hadn't got any friends to tell anyway – and the parents of this girl and the housemistress were so pleased that I'd been so amazingly discreet that I got tremendous kudos for that. Actually I made friends with the girl, who was just another lost lonely girl who didn't know what to do with herself.'

It was a turning-point. From that moment something changed. She became a sub-prefect, rather late, and shot up to the head of her house. She took on this role with some apprehension because her predecessor had been very popular, very good at games, very good at everything she touched. In fact Cicely was so apprehensive that she went to see her former housemistress about it. Miss Mellanby was one of the few good things about Roedean for Cicely (the headmistress Miss Tanner was the other) and Cicely valued what she said so much that she wrote telling her father of the advice she'd been given. Miss Mellanby had said to her, 'After a person has gone they are remembered for themselves and not for the job that they do. They will not compare you with her as head of the house, you will step in and do it on your own. They won't forget Liz, but they won't think of her as head of the house.' Armed with this advice, Cicely quite enjoyed her last year and when she left the headmistress was able to write, 'Although not a natural leader, she has been a good head of house.' Cicely did not feel she had been particularly well educated at Roedean, but she had acquired something else – a feeling for the underdog 'because I felt I'd been an underdog fairly frequently myself'.

If school was an unhappy time for Cicely, home was not much better. Materially Gordon's dreams had been realised. He had worked hard, he *had* restored the family fortunes, and now he was determined to have the best of everything; schools (he really felt he was giving Cicely the best in sending her to Roedean), cars, hotels, clothes, and of course houses. Soon after Cicely went to Roedean they moved to Hadley Hurst, a vast and impressive William and Mary house on the other side of Hadley Common. There were three cottages, a large garden, a small dairy with one cow, two grass tennis courts, a hard court, a squash court, a walled garden, a fig tree, peach trees, nectarines and greenhouses. And there was a staff to match; a cook, a kitchen-maid, a butler, a house-maid, three gardeners and a chauffeur to look after Gordon's Rolls and Chrissie's Morris. He even employed a man part-time to make his model trains, for which he had such a passion that they were given the run of the entire top floor of Hadley Hurst; holes were bored in the walls so that the trains could shunt from room to room.

But the marriage was not working, and though the Saunders never quarrelled in public, it showed. Visiting friends found the atmosphere terrible. Gordon and Chrissie irritated each other and were growing increasingly apart. Gordon's dynamic, ebullient nature demanded people and activity, and his enthusiasms met no response from his wife, who would disappear upstairs for a day, sometimes two days, at a time. The extent of their non-communication is illustrated by an occasion when she persuaded an embarrassed third party to come with her when she had to admit to her husband that she had an overdraft of £200 – the sort of encounter most couples would prefer to take place in private. There were various little incidents which burned in Cicely's mind. 'I never forget a day when my parents were meant to be going to a high-powered reception and my mother had got a new dress and new shoes and had her hair done and everything and when it came to the point she refused to go. They had actually got in the car and driven to London and she absolutely refused to go in. I was so sorry for them both for that sort of thing. My father didn't know how to cope with it and she really didn't know how to cope with him.'

In fact Chrissie couldn't really cope at all. She seems to have had an ambivalent attitude to the large house and all that went with it. On the one hand she was a snob. Cicely remembers falling about in helpless laughter when a railway porter let the children through to the train, but stopped Chrissie, fur coat and all, saying, 'Only first class beyond here, Madam.' They probably were travelling first class, Cicely admits, 'But to pick on *Mummy* to say that to and not us!' On another occasion, a hot day, Chrissie was wearing a hat. Cicely asked her, with the persistence of children, why was she wearing a hat? Wasn't she uncomfortable wearing a hat on such a hot day? To which her mother replied, 'You seem to forget, Cicely, that I am Mrs. Saunders of Hadley Hurst.' But though she enjoyed the position she held as Gordon's wife, neither her background nor her temperament had equipped her to deal with the attendant responsibilities, in particular with servants, a problem peculiar to the rich, and previously quite outside her experience. She did not know how to recruit them or how to manage them. Christopher thinks it was this more than anything else that wore her down.

One of the bright spots in this grey landscape was Lilian Gardner. She was young, only twenty-one, when she joined the household, she was positive, warm, outgoing and beautiful. She came to help Chrissie look after Christopher, but in no time she found herself running the house – in fact she took over everything, doing the shopping, mending the children's clothes, supervising the servants, even buying the wine for Gordon. She took to the children immediately, from the moment young Christopher greeted her with 'Hello – do come to the greenhouse and I'll show you how dragonflies mate' – and they to her. In fact, says Christopher, 'Life changed dramatically for the better. Lilian rapidly took over the mother position, especially for me.' She quickly spotted that he had no friends and made it her business to get to know other mother's helps and their charges. To Cicely, only seven years younger than her, she became a friend, an elder sister, and someone who 'always made things fun'.

Despite the underlying tensions, there was plenty of activity in the Saunders household. There was tennis, squash and riding – Chrissie gave Lilian ten lessons for an Easter present so that she could keep Cicely company; there were Christmas dances and there were parties. Once a year Cicely and Lilian would organise 'the aunts' party' for Gordon's numerous brothers and sisters and their

children and they would play games; there were fishing
holidays in Scotland and summer holidays at the Treloyan
Manor Hotel in St. Ives, where the stuffy atmosphere was
shattered by the children coming downstairs on a tea-tray
during the nine o'clock news – a time sacrosanct to the
middle-aged residents. Cicely turned out to be an excellent surfer, and a family friend enshrined her talent in
verse.

> There was a tall girl from Roedean,
> Who of all the surfers was queen.
> When she caught the best wave
> You just had to rave,
> As she flashed by so sylphlike and lean.

There was even a Mediterranean cruise to Gibraltar and
Madeira, for Christopher 'a bitter thing' as he was consid-
ered too young to go, but a great excitement for John and
Cicely.

The family were, however, never alone and the children
hardly knew what it was like to be just a family. There
were parties of people at the fishing lodge in Scotland,
countless friends came to Cornwall with them – the faded
photos show a dozen or more on the beach together –
Gordon's friends the Diamants and Percy Deas accompanied them on the Mediterranean cruise; when Gordon and
Chrissie went on holiday to Egypt, even then they took
friends with them. It was no accident. Perpetual company
was orchestrated deliberately. This was partly to keep
Gordon happy. He liked to have people around, he liked to
dominate and hold court; he was also extremely generous
and used to take people under his wing, paying their hotel
bills if necessary. But it was also an unconscious conspir-
acy which served to paper over the cracks in the marriage.
And it worked – in a way. Cicely feels that they, the
children, 'weren't very seeing' in that they were for so long
unaware of the tensions. That, however, could also be a
tribute to their parents' efforts to put on a good show in an

attempt to prevent the children suffering too much. If they couldn't give them a happy and loving background, at least they could give them a good time.

They got on quite well, Cicely, John and Christopher – with the friendly unconcern that often exists where there's enough space to lose yourself when you feel like it and when two-thirds of the time is spent at boarding school anyway. John and Cicely, only two years apart, tended to do things together. They made superb dancing partners, so good that people would stop and watch them. Christopher, eight years younger, felt they were not interested in him; predictably, they felt that he, as the youngest, was given things that they weren't. He remembers teasing Cicely by getting himself well-positioned near a door and saying 'Cicely, if you weren't so round-shouldered you'd be even taller, wouldn't you?' and disappearing with haste. They were certainly a formidable family. Somebody once offered the judgment that 'Gordon's brilliant, Cicely's brilliant, Christopher's brilliant. It's just as well John's good at games.' John was indeed more concerned with cars and sport than with intellectual wrangling, but the lowly placing of such an intelligent person (he was later known as 'Sagacity John') sets the other three well above the average, to say the least. John feels that if he is quiet now, it is partly because Cicely talked so much. He used to sit through meals, silently, while Cicely and their father argued, sometimes 'fought like cats' – mostly over principles. As one might expect, Gordon was conservative in his views and there was much he could not tolerate; Cicely's caring, liberal nature which began to show early, led to fierce arguments. If Gordon arrived late at the office his colleagues would ask if he'd had 'another row with Cicely'.

But if they argued, they argued because they stimulated each other, because they both had vitality and idealism and because both, in their ways, were more vulnerable than they appeared. Cicely loved and admired her father and he was devoted to her, as indeed to all his children, proud of her and ambitious for her. As a teenager she was already showing many of his characteristics – his ability, his breadth of interest, his need for constant activity. There were other qualities yet to emerge but already latent, notably his powers of leadership, which were to become so strong in her. She says of him, 'All my father's geese were swans, he was marvellous at inspiring people.' Years later the same was to be said of her.

Gordon tried hard to be a good father; he spent hours teaching them cricket, bowling, tennis – but they did not, naturally enough, share all his interests. Cicely could not summon up much enthusiasm for farming, and as he did a good deal of voluntary work for the Ministry of Agriculture and farmed in Norfolk (he reclaimed acres of the Fens) this – perhaps unreasonably – distressed him. Nor could she muster up any interest for things like bridge. She wrote years later that he tried to teach her bridge but 'I couldn't care enough to concentrate. Poor Dad.' More crucially she failed, for some time, to fulfil his expectations that in whatever she did she would excel. His ambitions for her were going to have to wait.

But all this was the cut and thrust of a real and loving relationship. Cicely's relationship with her mother was another matter altogether. In fact all the children in their various ways found her difficult. Close family friends remarked how they would all be playing happily and the temperature would drop as she came in. Christopher, ironically her favourite, is the most outspoken. He can never remember being intimate with his mother and recalls how she became drawn and lined and grim-visaged, rather like her own mother. But where her mother's grimness was expressing force and determination Chrissie's was more 'withdrawal and resignation and sorrow and unhappiness, to which inevitably we children contributed as we didn't love her'. From the earliest times he remembers trying to escape, wheedling things out of her and getting her to spend money on him, but 'totally cynically, the way children are'. There is an infinitely sad story of Christopher spending hours by a pond at the far end of the garden and when asked why he spent so much time there saying, 'Because it's the farthest I can get from my mother.'

Poor Chrissie. She tried so hard to be a good mother and so totally failed. She came nearest to succeeding with John, who feels she has been maligned. But even he realised how impossible she found it to display any emotion and says that, 'Dancing with her was like dancing with a broomstick, she was so unyielding.' He also realised how difficult she found it to keep up with the rest of them. 'She talked too much, and fatuously. She had a very small brain and was competing with Cicely, Pa and Christopher, all of whom had brilliant minds.' They were all good at something except Chrissie, who wasn't good at the things she wanted to be good at. She *was*, however, good at nursing and 'nursed everyone within sight' and she took a genuine interest in other people, provided it wasn't too challenging. She was at her best meeting someone on a train or talking to her friends' grandchildren. She was – however harsh a word it is – superficial.

Though she was barely aware of it as a child, Cicely found her mother difficult and irritating and there is a real sense in which she was motherless. Or she would have been, had it not been for Aunt Daisy. Aunt Daisy, as one of the older girls of old Mr. Saunders' second family, was used to mothering, though she never married or had children of her own. She always remembered how her father came to tell her Gordon was born and said to her 'He shall be your baby.' She adored Cicely and Cicely adored her. In fact everyone who knew her seemed to love her. Cicely describes her as 'a lovely stalwart warm person. She was soft and kind outside but very strong inside.' When Cicely was born and Chrissie couldn't cope it was Aunt Daisy who came to the rescue and looked after her, but after a few months it was clear that the baby preferred Aunt Daisy to her mother, so Aunt Daisy had to go. Eventually, the air cleared, and by the time Cicely was four she would come and stay every other holidays – there was great excitement when it was her turn to come to Hadley Hurst. She had a strong influence on Cicely – for instance giving her all her favourite books as a child. If she was unfortunate in her mother, at least she was fortunate in her aunt. Cicely said of her, 'If I could have chosen my mother I would have chosen Aunt Daisy.'

2

EDUCATION

The child who is absorbed is utterly relaxed. The adult mind,
also, must be unstriving, receptive, expectant, before there
can be any creative insight. Again and again this is the state
of mind in which new truth dawns. We do not work it out or
think it out; rather, we have the sense of waiting for the
disclosure of something that is already there.

John V. Taylor, *The Go-Between God*

Cicely left Roedean rather put out that she had failed her
Oxford entrance but she was still determined to get there.
She had spent over a year in the sixth form concentrating
on music, only deciding rather late to try for the University. Even so, it seems surprising, considering her later
academic achievements, that she was turned down by both
Lady Margaret Hall and Somerville and was put on the
waiting list at Newnham College, Cambridge. But she
persisted, went to Bendixen's, a crammer in Baker Street,
and was eventually accepted by the Society for Home
Students, later St. Anne's College, Oxford. At first she was
uneasily aware that it was her last choice and that it had
not yet got full collegiate status, but once over the
threshold she was glad to be there. Having given up her
earlier flirtation with the idea of following her father into
estate agency work she decided to read Politics, Philosophy and Economics, thinking she might become secretary to a politician. She was lucky enough to study with
Miss C. V. Butler, the economics tutor who had such
influence over generations of social workers between 1914
and 1945. C.V.'s first comments on Cicely were that she
was 'better grounded in elementary economics than any
first term student I have known.' In fact Cicely's interest
in the subject had grown from her schoolgirl admiration

for a Mademoiselle Lyon, who taught politics and economics at Roedean. However, this early promise was not immediately fulfilled. At the end of her first year her report pronounced that, though she had done industrious and intelligent work, she was 'taking some time to settle into Oxford standards'. A footnote takes a swipe at her old school. 'I don't think Roedean is a good preparation for PPE at present.'

She was successful in her Pass Moderations, which in those days included French and Latin, but after her first year of study, war was declared and life changed at Oxford as everywhere else. Grace Hadow, the Principal of the Society for Home Students at the time, describes war-time Oxford in a letter to the Society's Magazine *The Ship*. 'We are a pleasant jumble of civil servants, of officials and clerks from London offices of various kinds, and of academic Oxford . . . an addition to the strange elements in Oxford are the seething crowds of excited small people with strong Cockney accents . . . and numbers of obviously East End mothers pushing prams rather sadly up and down 'The Corn' obviously thinking it is not a patch on the Mile End Road.' Cicely stayed for one war-time term, increasingly uneasy at studying while the world was at war, and taking her British Red Cross exams in Home Nursing and First Aid. She had first been attracted by the idea of nursing while she was at school but, discouraged by her parents, had not pursued it. Now her inclinations and her sense of duty were working hand in hand. She decided to disregard her family, leave Oxford and become a nurse. Miss Butler approved of this change, saying she felt Cicely would be happier doing practical work and that she was 'in no way a student', but the Acting Principal could not understand anybody preferring anything to Oxford. She wrote curtly, asking Cicely for her tuition fees for the next term as she had not given sufficient notice of her departure. She concluded by saying how sorry she was that Cicely had decided to take up nursing. 'It is a great pity to break off the training you have already undertaken and to take up work which, although extremely useful, can at the present moment be adequately fulfilled by a large number of people. As things are there is even a shortage of work for nurses already trained.' But Cicely was not to be put off. She wrote to St. Thomas's saying, rather loftily, that doing her Red Cross training she had become so interested in nursing that she was anxious to take up this as a career without further delay. Ten days later she wrote again, asking for books on anatomy and physiology so that she could start reading. Alas, the wheels of bureaucracy move slowly; there were references to be taken up, interviews to be nervously endured and vacancies to be waited for. She had to bide her time for nearly a year, impatiently 'pottering about at home doing Red Cross and things' before she could be given a place.

War-time nursing had its own special character. After the war scare in 1938 preparation had been made should a state of emergency arise, and when war was declared the following year, the Nightingale Training School was evacuated to various mental and mental deficiency hospitals in Surrey and Hampshire. The Preliminary Training School was moved to a country house in Shamley Green, near Guildford, and it was there that Cicely, along with some twenty others making up a 'set', reported for their first eight weeks' training on a cold November day in 1940. It was a tough life and a tough training. They lived in unheated rooms, black-out restrictions were in force, they got up at six thirty to wash in water frozen in jugs and do 'household duties' before the main lectures and practical work of the day. These duties had to be meticulously carried out in a way that would have won the approval of Florence Nightingale herself; baths had to be cleaned with the right cloth and the right amount of Gumption, furniture 'wet-dusted' and 'dry-dusted' and all had to bear the subsequent inspection of their superiors. Their training was in the hands of 'Sister PTS', a spirited teacher, who managed to combine strictness with humour. 'Only run in cases of fire and haemorrhage', she would say. And 'Get out of breath at least once a day, it's good for you.'

There was a strong *esprit de corps* among Nightingale nurses. In the course of their training they came across nurses from other hospitals who felt that St. Thomas's nurses considered themselves unique and St. Thomas's to be the only possible place to learn to be a nurse. They could well have been right; Nightingale nurses tended to feel a bit special and they would joke about it a little self-consciously. There was a saying amongst pre-war nurses 'St. Bartholomew's for money, the London for hard work, St. Mary's for sport, Guy's for flirts, St. Thomas's for ladies.' It was true that St. Thomas's at that time only employed 'gentlewomen', who were expected to behave as such. For instance while nurses from Guy's were allowed on duty without stockings – and they were, after all, hard to come by during the war – not so Nightingales, they were expected to get hold of them somehow.

For the next three years Cicely and her set rotated between Hydestile near Godalming, Park Prewett near Basingstoke, and Botley's Park in Chertsey. They were typical of the mental institutions of the time – spartan bleak buildings hastily converted for hospital use. There were bars everywhere, padded cells remained in some of the wards, the windows would only open a few inches, the lavatories did not have locks and the beds were low with hard mattresses and even harder pillows. There was no privacy. In Park Prewett Cicely slept with five others in a room with six doors and no curtains round the beds; there was another group of fourteen and yet another of twenty who all had to go through their room every time they wanted to go to the bathrooms or lavatories. One summer they had to shake earwigs out of their clothes every morning, once there was a plague of fleas and sometimes they would find bugs under the mattresses. The food combined war-time shortages with the lack of imagination common to all institutional cooking and they seemed to have lived largely on pilchards and bread. They earned about fifty pounds a year.

Cicely was happy – marvellously happy. For the first time *she* was the popular girl, the one whose opinion was

sought, who had friends, who was successful. She slotted
in to nursing and its way of life like a book finding its right
place on the shelf. Over forty years later she still glows
with warmth as she remembers the feeling that she had
'come home'.

That Cicely and nursing were compatible was apparent
within weeks, but even so her training was not all plain
sailing. She had to fight a natural shyness and her ward
reports are conflicting. Some describe her as diffident and
say she was 'somewhat handicapped by nervousness' and
that she 'appeared to suffer from an inferiority complex';
one even found her 'quiet and unassuming, rather a negative personality. One feels that she has overgrown her
strength and has no power to assert herself more often or
more firmly.' Yet other reports remark on her determination to overcome the opposition still shown by her parents
and say that she naturally took the lead. Perhaps the key
is in the word 'determined'. Her headmistress, when asked
for a reference by St. Thomas's, had written: 'She is a girl
who might easily have decided to live at home and enjoy
herself as there are no financial reasons for her to earn a
living, but she has always given serious thoughts to her
career, and I should be greatly surprised if anything
deterred her once she had decided to embark on a piece of
work.'

The nursing staff also appreciated her potential; there
was one ward sister, Sister Nuffield, who to start with
gave Cicely a rough time, chasing her up and down the
wards and greeting her requests to go off duty with, 'Yes,
do go.' One day Sister Nuffield caught her doing something silly, ticked her off soundly and said, 'You *can* be
good and you *will* be good. That is why I chase you.'

The conflicting reactions can perhaps be best explained
as the result of her strained home life and her consequent
poor showing and unpopularity at school. Though she was
a gifted person she had not so far received the nourishing
acceptance that fosters confidence and an early blossom-
ing of talents. But she was ambitious and determined to
conquer her own shortcomings and conceal her shyness.

And she succeeded. After the preliminary training at Shamley Green they all went to Park Prewett, newly and proudly 'pros' and Cicely was immediately elected 'set representative', by her fellow students; this meant she was in charge of all the other probationers in her set and sometimes even of those above her. If her superiors detected her problems, they were not apparent to her fellow probationers.

Mary Rous, a friend and contemporary, remembers her well. 'Cicely's ability was striking. Even then she always seemed to have finished every job first. I remember her specially at Hydestile, a gynae ward, under a fearsome and efficient sister who we all admired and feared. It was up to Cicely to see that the probationers' jobs were all done by a certain time, even though she was a probationer herself. There were six or seven of us in each ward and whenever a list went up Cicely's name was always at the top. She had to whizz round to see if there were any little things anyone hadn't got round to and that could be on top of her own work. She always managed to have done her own work and also be around to help people who hadn't finished in time.'

Her contemporaries began to realise Cicely was rather special. They not only liked her, but admired her and enjoyed listening to her articulate accounts of patients, which were dry, amusing and sympathetic. She struck them as an intellectual, who could have been a teacher or a professor; she also seemed a little more mature than most of the others. She was twenty-two and they were in fact a bit younger, mostly eighteen or nineteen. She had a large photo of a handsome RAF pilot standing on her locker, which caused much speculation. (He was, Cicely says, 'quite a real boyfriend', but their friendship did not survive his joining the air force.) She was better off too, as her father was always generous; Cicely's suede boots, ocelot-fur gloves and crocodile handbag were the envy of all and her Elizabeth Arden make-up was regarded as the ultimate in war-time luxury.

She was also tremendous fun and used to tell jokes,

bawdy and risqué by 1940 standards. There is an endearing story about Cicely putting on an end of term show for a visiting Matron. It included a skit about the way probationers, inexperienced, if well-meaning, left their patients feeling thoroughly uncomfortable. In comes a ghostly figure, wearing one of Cicely's dresses which reached her ankles, carrying a lamp and skilfully putting the patients to rights. In the background of this touching scene they all sang, to the tune of Swanee River, a chorus that ended not 'Poor Old Jo' but 'Poor Old Flo'. It did not go down well. Cicely was summoned to Matron and told 'You'll never be a really good nurse, Nurse, if you do not learn that there are some things about which one does not make jokes. If you are really thinking of being a Nightingale Nurse, Nurse, you must not make jokes about Miss Nightingale.' Cicely really thought she was going to be given the sack. But her good name was restored a few months later when she put on a nativity play, which was considered to be 'splendidly in the hospital tradition'. The visiting Matron this time was none other than the famous and internationally known Matron of St. Thomas's, Dame Alicia Lloyd Still. She could not know that the young probationer producing the Christmas Show was herself to become a Dame.

Cicely worked on the medical, surgical, children's and gynaecological wards as well as in the theatre and the Diet Kitchen. She loved it all, even being on night duty in the children's wards where she was particularly stretched. 'I didn't know anything about children and I was in charge and I had somebody who knew even less than I did as my number two and night sister wasn't paediatric trained and two or three babies died and it was really wearing.' She still remembers Reggie, who used to put up a weak little finger and pull off her glasses as she was tube-feeding him. When he died she could not bear the hospital porter taking him up to the mortuary and she carried him there herself.

Then, as now, probationers were marked on everything they did. There were weekly reports on personal qualities; was the nurse in question punctual, quiet, trustworthy, personally neat and clean? Each attribute was marked, as were the professional skills. Ward Management, Dressings, Enemas, Catheters, Helpless Patients, Bandaging, Making bandages, Making beds, Waiting on operations, Preparing patient for operation, Sick cooking, Keeping wards fresh, Cleanliness of utensils, Management of convalescents, Observations on the sick. They worked hard, the hours were long and the training meticulous. Appetising food had to be offered on dainty trays, not just dumped unceremoniously on the patient's lap. They were taught to wipe faces carefully and firmly (practising initially on a dummy called 'George') and they learnt to remember every fact and every symptom about each patient. They had to stand with their backs to the patients and report down half a ward (eighteen beds) with each patient's name and age, what operations or treatment they had had, the drugs they were receiving, temperature, pulse, respiration. Some of them were terrified of this, particularly when the Sister on duty was one known as 'The Green Dragon', but it did not present a serious problem to Cicely.

Some of the things they had to do seemed, even then, strangely out of date. They had to learn to 'tease the tow' and pad splints, though plaster of Paris was already being used, and Cicely remembers warming a linseed poultice on an old Aga and dashing back across the huge ward to the patient, while it was still warm, to ease the pain of angina. She felt it salved the nurses' consciences more than the patients' pain. Sterilising instruments was the responsibility of the nurses then – there were no neat, sterilised packs as there are today. The probationers had to boil the scalpels, kidney dishes, knives, forceps, needles and 'porringers' on a gas burner, pricking holes in the mantle and standing back to light it with a long taper before it went off with a bang. The black-out led to some embarrassing situations. In the winter they would start work while it was still dark, when, of course they could not put on the lights. Working in the half dark led one probationer to collect the patients' false teeth instead of their water glasses. It was just as well, when it came to fitting the right denture to the right jaw, that the patients were good-tempered.

The long hours of nursing were accompanied by almost continual backache. Since her teens Cicely had been dogged by back trouble. Even as a young girl she was tall and lanky and she had a congenital slight curvature of the spine inherited from her mother, who was of a similar build. At Roedean she had been made to lie on the floor for forty minutes every day (no radio, no books, and under the housemistress's eye) and when her headmistress, Miss Tanner, heard of her intention to nurse, she wrote warning her to be sure that her back would stand up to it. Cicely was undeterred, and battled on through continual pain, only surviving the training by spending her off-duty time lying down. It was a real case of mind over matter, for she always appeared full of energy, but the hard physical work compounded the trouble and she put out a spinal disc very early in her nursing life. She staggered on through her three years, taking a little longer than average because of sick leave as she became increasingly run-down with sinus trouble, whitlows, styes and bronchitis – symptoms of her lowered vitality – but by the time she got to the last section of her training at Botley's Park it all became too much. She was then on night duty (twelve nights on, two nights off), and in the mornings could hardly drag herself up the hill back to the nurses' home. She went to the family doctor who sent her to the hospital orthopaedic surgeon. He took one look at her back and said she'd better stop. So that was that. She got her Honours Certificate, Silver Medal Standard (they didn't give medals during the war) but her nursing career was over. She never went on duty as a nurse again.

It was a shock, despite the warnings, to receive such a definite ultimatum, but it is not in Cicely's character to sit around and feel sorry for herself. She had anticipated that her back might prevent her staying the course and had written to St. Anne's asking if she could come back to Oxford to qualify for a job in Public Health. But by the time she was invalided out of nursing, she knew she had to have a job which kept her near patients. So she decided to be an almoner.

Almoners in the 1940s were still known as 'lady almoners' to distinguish them from the almoners who dispensed alms and administered hospitals in the middle ages. The 'lady' was dropped in 1948 with the advent of the National Health Service; in the mid-fifties 'almoners' became 'medical social workers'. The work of an almoner of the forties was very similar to that of today's medical social worker, but there was less emphasis on psychology and more on basic material needs. Old style almoners were very practical people. They arranged convalescent homes for people coming out of hospital and special diets for those who needed them, they found out if people could afford to contribute anything to the hospital, they assessed patients' financial circumstances, where necessary meeting their needs from the Samaritan Funds, endowments from the sixteenth century available for the poor of the twentieth. They did casework when there was time.

Training as an almoner involved both practical and theoretical work and, after writing again to St. Anne's, Cicely was advised to take two 'sections' in the social sciences to complete her degree and the Diploma in Public and Social Administration. So after six months spent helping to teach at St. Thomas's, October 1944 saw Cicely back at her old college, now known as St. Anne's Society, reading for a degree and a diploma at the same time. She settled down quickly and after a few weeks wrote to Miss Turner, who was now the Matron at St. Thomas's, 'Life here is very enjoyable and the work interesting but I miss hospital life and long for more practical work at times.' Cicely has always needed both the practical and the intellectual and sometimes the balance between the two has been difficult to achieve, but she was gratified to find that her mind, far from atrophying as she had half feared it might after three and a half years of nursing, was actually much sharper. After a few months, Miss C. V. Butler, who had previously thought her abilities 'ordinary

second to third class' was predicting that she should get a
distinction. Once more much of her studying was done
lying on her back, but after doing two years' work in one
year she gained distinctions in Political Theory – which
together with another 'section' and her nursing (which
counted as war service) gave her a war degree – and in the
Diploma of Public and Social Administration. There are
advantages in maturing late, if it is only the pleasure of
confounding your tutors.

So Cicely took a room at the Lady Margaret Hall settle-
ment (a centre for social workers living in Lambeth) and
went on to the next stage of her training. She had un-
reserved recommendation from St. Anne's saying 'her
intellectual abilities are distinctly above average . . . she
is quite clear what she wants to do in life', which must
have pleased as well as puzzled her. She was not even sure
she wanted to be an almoner, still less what she wanted to
do with the rest of her life. She was, however, determined
that anything she did she was going to do thoroughly. She
was attached to the Institute of Almoners in Tavistock
Square, doing practical work at a variety of hospitals,
including St. Thomas's, where she was under the aegis of
the famous Miss Deacon, to whom she became devoted.
This year of practical work was arranged by Betty Read,
who, first as tutor at the Institute while Cicely was training, later as Head Social Worker at St. Thomas's while she
was working there as a qualified almoner, came to know
her well. She found her quite brilliant and was amazed at
the ease with which she passed her exams, but never felt
that being an almoner was going to stretch her enough.
'She needed a much broader canvas. She was someone
who had an enormous amount to give in a way which
would be revealed.' She felt that Cicely was still getting
over her disappointment at not being able to nurse;
being an almoner was not likely to last. Cicely shared her
doubts. She wrote again to Miss Turner, telling her that
she was very much enjoying the practical training, 'especially the work for those who are in trouble for medical
reasons. But I don't like it yet as much as nursing.'

Certainly it was being near patients again which satisfied her most. So enthusiastic was she about them that her fellow almoners felt her patients were more exciting than anybody else's. They probably weren't, but perhaps her love for them was greater.

Once again her health interrupted her training and she was forced to take six months off for an operation on her back. This time it was nothing to do with her curvature, but a laminectomy aimed at curing a damaged inter-vertebral disc. There was a ten per cent chance that the operation would make a bad situation worse, but she entered into it with optimism, already considering the new horizons – like medical missions – that would open up if she were free of pain. It was a great success and she felt better than she had done for years. She got her AIMSW (Associate of the Institute of Medical Social Work) and started looking for a job in a teaching hospital, preferably St. Thomas's, longing to stay in one place and see a case through to the end. There were ways in which she had found being a student very tantalising.

So in September 1947, aged twenty-nine, she got her first job on the staff of St. Thomas's Hospital, as an assistant almoner at the Northcote Trust. This was a conscious choice. The Northcote Trust was at that time part of St. Thomas's and it specialised in cancer patients. Cicely had done six weeks of her training at the Royal Cancer Hospital and was already thinking of specialising in that area. But exactly how, she was not yet sure.

3

WATERSHED

The moment of seeing is fraught with immensely important
things. It arrests this man on his way, turns that one back and
bows another to the earth. It changes the course of life, it
announces a nation's doom. Men see and shudder, or they see
and exult. Sometimes they ask to see more, sometimes they
cover their eyes.

Alan Ecclestone, *Yes to God*

The few months after she left Oxford was a momentous
time for Cicely. Between June and September she had got
her degree and her diploma, her parents had separated
and she was converted to Christianity.

One may well wonder why Gordon and Chrissie stayed
together as long as they did. They were complete opposites, not complementing each other as opposite tempera-
ments can do, but grating almost audibly. Everyone who
came to the house was aware of their difficulties, the
atmosphere was darkened by unvoiced anger and resent-
ment, yet for twenty-eight years they endured it. This was
partly because separation and divorce were not as
commonplace then as now, partly because of the persistence of what Cicely feels was a kind of love, but most
significant of all was Chrissie's dependence. She needed
her status as Gordon's wife and the mistress of Hadley
Hurst; she wasn't able to manage on her own, she had
nowhere to go, none of her children was prepared to live
with her and she had few friends. Left to herself, she would
have tolerated anything rather than what she saw as the
shame of separation, though she must have known in her
bones that the breaking-point would come for Gordon. It
was only a question of when.

One can have nothing but sympathy for them both.

Gordon, his enthusiasm, vitality and zest continually meeting apparent indifference; Chrissie, never a confident person, squeezed out of the running of the house by the warmth and competence of Lilian and her successors, and worse, unable to give or receive the love she craved. Christopher feels that this was probably because she tried too hard. 'She was always seeking something from us and she couldn't give us the affection and love that we wanted. She had so much money and she was so unsure of herself, every minute of the day. She couldn't express affection.' Even the children's friends, without any emotional involvement, realised how difficult it must be to live with her. A friend of Cicely's says harshly, 'She was a whining, failed wife' and another thought she was 'a pathetic thing who needed support'. Cicely was by now all too aware of how irritating she found her mother, and felt guilty about being irritated – a complex spiral aggravated by Chrissie's continuing misery.

By the summer of 1945 Cicely began to feel that her father was being driven to the edge of a breakdown. He did not want to leave Hadley Hurst, in any case Chrissie could not have managed the place without him. What could they do? Cicely was firmly on Gordon's side and while admitting that it was he, in the end, who initiated the separation, says 'it was my mother's fault in the long term that they separated, she'd have gone on for ever like that. Somehow she couldn't manage to give, she found it very difficult.' As Chrissie retired to her room more and more frequently with migraines, Gordon, worn out by a feeling of failure, found his irritation reaching the point when he could hardly sit in the same room with her. Something clearly had to be done. John was married and abroad at the time, Christopher was only nineteen and at Oxford, Gordon and Chrissie seemed to be beyond communicating, so the emotional burden fell on Cicely. After a long talk with her father and one or two close family friends, she took her mother out to pick raspberries. There she told her that her father had had enough and that she'd 'really got to pack up her pride and leave'. The storm that followed can be imagined. Scenes like that are etched on the mind with needles of fire.

Later John and his wife Barbara were to befriend and support Chrissie – it was Barbara who realised that 'her loving needed to be turned into doing' – but for the moment it was Cicely who, having persuaded her to leave, had to keep her away, cope with the emotional scenes and make practical arrangements. She helped Chrissie move to share a house near Bedford, then, when that failed to work out, to a friend's in St. Alban's, but Chrissie could not settle and threats of suicide became part of the currency of her conversation. With a monotonous regularity that would have been boring were it not frightening, she would go out of Cicely's flat saying she was going to walk under the nearest bus. Though these threats probably were not genuine, they could not be taken lightly; the atmosphere was charged with worry and guilt. Eventually Lilian, who had left the household when she married in 1937, came to the rescue. Gordon bought her and her growing family a large house on condition she would care for Chrissie. Even Lilian's good nature was sorely tried, but she seemed to be the only person able to cope; though the suicide threats continued and Chrissie would never agree to a divorce, the arrangement worked tolerably well. Gordon stayed on at Hadley Hurst for some years, where he was looked after by Mrs. Diamant, a family friend, and his sister Daisy, by then retired and able to help her brother. There was one attempt at a reconciliation, a disastrous weekend during which Gordon spent most of the time escaping with Christopher, and Chrissie clung pathetically to Cicely. After that Gordon and Chrissie never saw each other again.

The effect of Gordon and Chrissie on each other and their family was to reverberate for many years. The children helped Lilian with the burden their father had shed; John and Barbara often had Chrissie to stay and Cicely took her on holiday. Though for many years Chrissie was lonely and ashamed of her separated state, her final years, especially after Gordon's death left her an honourable widow, were more settled. She died peacefully in 1968, at St. Christopher's Hospice. Cicely, deeply happy to have been able to look after her put 'In Him is our Peace' on the tombstone of the family grave and never worried about either of them again.

While her parents' problems were occupying much of Cicely's emotional energy, another voice was making itself heard – the insistent need for a religious faith.

Apart from Aunt Daisy, who was a devout Christian and whom Cicely used to call her 'Holy Godmother', the Saunders were not religious and never went to church as a family. John can only remember one occasion when his father went to church voluntarily and it was not until Cicely was confirmed at school that Chrissie decided to follow her example. Even then there was a suspicion that she did it largely in order not to be left out. When she went to Roedean Cicely at first attended Chapel as a matter of course, but reading Bernard Shaw in the Sixth Form caused her to declare, with characteristic resolution, that she was an atheist; she refused to go except to sing in the choir. During her first year at Oxford her spiritual life was non-existent, but while she was waiting for a vacancy to start nursing she read a book called *Good God* by a man using the pseudonym of John Hadham, and this 'began to flip the switch'. Cicely does not do things by halves and soon the search was on. She thought, she talked, she argued, she went to church again, and she read, most of all she read. She read C. S. Lewis and found herself caught up in his inescapable logic; she read William Temple, whose ideas on the equality of man and emphasis on the social aspects of Christianity appealed to her emerging liberalism; and she was captivated and tremendously moved by the ring of truth she found in Dorothy Sayers' *The Man Born to be King* – she would arrange her nights off so that she could listen to the plays when they were broadcast on the radio. When she went back to Oxford she went to the services at Balliol College, where she sang in the choir. She also joined the Socratic Society, a group run by C. S. Lewis for atheists and Christians. It was intended pri-

marily for people unwilling to go to any of the other
Christian groups, like the Christian Union or the Church
of England Society, and at the time, Cicely was such a
person. The university chaplains used to take part. She
once met Charles Williams and C. S. Lewis would read
papers that later appeared in his books.

All this, however, was in the head, her heart was not yet
touched. It was as if she knew how electricity worked but
lived in the dark. She longed for the light to be turned on,
for the real conversion she had read about and heard of
from her friends, but it eluded her. She began to wonder
whether her prayers would ever be answered. As so often,
it was to happen in a way that was both unexpected and
closely bound up with the pain and darkness of the pre-
ceding few months.

Some friends of Cicely's, six or seven of them, had taken
a bungalow in Cornwall, in a village called Trevone. They
were all evangelical Christians, the leader of the group
being Meg Foote, who later became Vice-President of the
All Nations Bible College. They were having a fortnight's
holiday, but it was to be a holiday in which Bible Study,
worship, discussion and prayer were to play an integral
part. They had not invited Cicely. They realised she was
interested in Christianity and had been praying for her
conversion, but they felt she would find them all 'very
earnest and sedate'. They knew what a powerful personality she had, how independent and rebellious she could be;
they were frightened she would be sceptical and be a spoke
in the wheels of their new commitment. They also felt that
none of them, except perhaps Meg Foote, was up to her
intellectually. So when she invited herself to join the
group they were 'utterly devastated'. However, they felt
they could hardly refuse and they knew she was lonely and
unhappy after her parents' separation, so they said yes, of
course she could come.

Their fears were justified. At first she seemed out to
shock and she didn't fit in at all; she was cynical and mocking, deliberately challenging what she saw as their puri-
tanical ways. For instance, they didn't approve of sport

on Sunday, so she pointedly went swimming. By degrees, however, she realised that even if she did find them earnest and sedate, there was a real commitment among them which she must take seriously. One of their central ideas also began to draw her – the idea of letting go to God. They were saying 'Come to God with nothing, because that's all you've got to bring' at a time when the Japanese unconditional surrender to the British was in everyone's mind. The two powerful themes came together. After one of the services Cicely went upstairs and prayed. '"Oh God, I must have been emotional or not really meaning it when I said I wanted to try and believe and serve you before, but *please* can it be all right this time?" And the Lord as it were said to me, "It's not you who has to do anything, I have done it all." At that moment I felt that God had turned me round and that it was all right. It was for all the world like suddenly finding the wind at your back instead of battling against it all the time.'

At last it had happened, and the joy surpassed all her wildest hopes. She was elated, radiant and all the world could see how she had changed. One of her friends kept a poem that she wrote at the time; Cicely would not claim it was great poetry, but let two verses serve as a testimony to her experience and the happiness it brought.

Trevone, July 1945

We saw Him in the foam of curving waves
That broke in thunder on the sunny shore,
The whiteness of the wind-whipped crests at sea
The surf that rolled in with majestic roar
And touch of water, smooth and cool and clean,
The swiftness of the dive down breakers slope,
The fight back out again in tumbling foam,
Were all His gift to us, His call of hope.

We knelt before Him, our Redeeming Lord
We gave ourselves to Him, who in His Love
Had come to seek us who were all His own
That He might send his spirit from above

And in the hush of evening's purple clouds
The truth came flooding through our minds so dim
That He so loved us that He sought our hearts
And peace and joy came in to dwell with Him.

Cicely Saunders

Cicely had searched and she had found. But why were
her prayers answered then, in the summer of 1945, and
there, at a seaside village in Cornwall? She had prayed so
often, 'Lord, let it be *this* time, today', and her prayer had
not been answered. What had changed in her, so that, as
she puts it, 'the switch was flipped'? And why did it happen
in the context of evangelicalism, a branch of Protestant-
ism that had not, until then, attracted her?

The timing must owe something to the increasing tension at home and her parents' final separation. Monica
Furlong has written of conversion experiences, 'He may
choose fulfilment or heartbreak, but so often it's heartbreak', and this idea of God making himself known in
extreme situations is one that holds real meaning for
Cicely. She had been working very hard for her exams and
was tired, she had had the stimulus and gratification
of gaining two distinctions, she had then gone through
the painful ordeal of not only witnessing, but participat-
ing in, her parents' parting. She was vulnerable, open and
tired; 'softened up' as she says. Pain and exhaustion had
made her receptive. For the first time in her life – there
were to be many more – she was able to let go, to surrender
to the moment, and to receive.

Why she was drawn into the evangelical stream of
Christianity is complex but understandable. It was the
context of her conversion, and that alone would have
encouraged her to look kindly on it, but once she had
encountered evangelicalism there was much in it that
fitted her needs at the time. She was dissatisfied and
insecure and it gave her an assurance, a security, that she
craved; even more to the point, the emphasis of this
particular group on surrender, so different from her pre-

vious questioning and probing, proved to be just the
catalyst she needed. All sorts of things began to fall into
place, and as one of her friends in the Trevone group said,
'There's a lot to fall into place with Cicely.' Rosetta Burch,
who was to become a life-long friend and who Cicely met
soon after her conversion, understood the appeal of
evangelicalism very well. 'It is a natural beginning for
someone starting out on a Christian life because things
are explained very clearly and made quite simple. You
know what it is about – that a response is required from
you, and if you mean business you make that response and
get on with it and there's a lot of help.'

The basis of that help is, of course, the Bible, the first
pillar of the evangelicals and regarded as the supreme and
infallible authority in matters of belief and conduct. The
absence of critical scholarship becomes a problem for some
people once they start questioning, but Cicely's religious
journey had started with the intellect; now it was her
heart that was calling out for sustenance, not her head.
Since evangelical Christianity *tells* you what is true and
what is not true (or rather what is 'sound' and 'not sound'
in evangelical phraseology), there was no need for theological wrangling any more. For Cicely, that was a welcome change.

The second pillar of evangelicalism is the individual's
relationship to God, which is through Christ and must be
by faith alone (we cannot be saved by good works, only by
the Grace of God) and this of course was the basis of her
conversion. For evangelicals Jesus is a personal friend and
worship is homely, simple, almost domestic. And Christ is
proclaimed overtly; if the middle-class, English part of
Cicely was at all uneasy about this, the enthusiast in her
responded with relief.

Beyond all this, the assurance and the security, the
straightforward authority and the personal relationship
with Jesus, surpassing everything else, Cicely felt forgiven. Forgiven for what? 'I needed to be forgiven for being
unkind, for snapping at my mother, for not understanding
my father, for being stroppy to my brother when he got

married. I had a strong sense of sin.' If these seem pecca-
dillos from the outside, they can be overwhelming to the
perpetrator; more specifically, there was her crucial role
in her parents' separation. However right she may have
been, however essential it was for somebody to do what she
had done, to be the one who wields the axe that cleaves a
twenty-eight-year-old relationship, and your parents' at
that, is not an easy thing to accommodate. And underlying
the tangled weeds in the muddy waters of her conscience,
there was a sense of guilt, simply 'for being'. She had never
known a world of innocent acceptance. As a tiny baby she
had been greeted by a mother whose ability to love, even to
cope, was so limited that someone else, Aunt Daisy, had to
look after her. When she responded naturally to this warm
and loving woman, preferring the mother substitute to the
mother, her mother was jealous, and Aunt Daisy too was
taken away. In less than a year she had experienced two
separations. Then her adolescent years were spent with a
mother who was unable to express her love for her husband or her children, and whom they in their turn, could
not love. Society expects us to love our parents, and if we
do not, we feel guilty, though we may not quite know why.
Small wonder that by the time she was twenty-seven
Cicely was weighed down by a crushing burden of guilt
and a need for forgiveness and reconciliation. The intellectual Christianity of her years of searching had not been
able to deal with this, but evangelical Christianity could.
It says, 'If you really admit your guilt it is wiped off. You
should have paid the penalty, because you are so guilty,
but Jesus has taken your place. His death has saved you.'
So Cicely was free of her load, and so light that she 'was
walking a foot above the ground'. And she knew it – 'Quite
a good old burden, like Christian, to roll off on seeing the
Cross for the first time, which is what I felt I did.'

Cicely returned from Cornwall with all the enthusiasm of
any new convert and more besides. She was bubbling with
joy, wanting to tell everybody, convert everybody. Her
family were predictably cool; even Aunt Daisy, whom she

might have expected to rejoice with her (and who certainly did), just said 'Yes, yes dear' indulgently. She knew her Cicely, and realised she needed solid common sense rather than exhortation. Cicely's need for a public proclamation was met when she went to a meeting given at the Central Hall, Westminster, by the evangelist Tom Rees. He asked people who had decided to commit their lives to Christ to come forward, adding that if anyone had made that commitment in the last few months and had not yet had the chance to give public witness, would they come forward too. This, of course, she did.

Cicely's life was now filled with Christian activity; it took on an inner momentum she had not known before. Her friendship with Rosetta Burch ripened and they took a flat together with Rosetta's sister and two other friends. Three of them were Christians, who prayed together regularly and studied the Bible every morning after breakfast, working systematically through *Search the Scriptures*, the evangelical's friend and handbook. Cicely carried her Christian life into her work too, quite undaunted by the disapproval she met. (In some circles it was far tougher to be a Christian in the agnostic forties than it is now.) Even Betty Read, herself a Christian, was slightly doubtful about it. 'She had an evangelical, almost emotional attitude. We had an extremely healthy minded staff who used to take it out of her like mad. She used to have prayer meetings before work and this didn't go down awfully well with some of them.' Cicely says now that she felt she was 'too enthusiastic about being a Christian' and realises the danger of pressurising people, but during those 'very pious years' as she later called them, nothing could stop her. The switch had been turned on and she rejoiced in the light.

But behind all the activity, the meetings, the prayer groups, the Bible readings and church-going (she became a diligent member of John Stott's evangelical congregation at All Souls, Langham Place) was a question. 'What have I got to do to say thank you and serve?' She was impatient to know the answer to this question, but since her conversion she had learnt to be attentive, receptive, to wait for her future to be disclosed. For the moment she was content to do all that she felt she could do at the time, which was to carry on with what she was doing. So for the remaining two years of her training as an almoner she worked, prayed and waited.

4

DAVID

And think not that you can direct the course of love, for love, if
it finds you worthy, directs your course.

Kahlil Gibran, *The Prophet*

By the autumn of 1947 Cicely was a qualified nurse, a
qualified almoner and a devout evangelical Christian. She
longed to be married and she longed to know what to do
with her life in response to her dramatic conversion. She
was about to meet the man who would give her her first
experience of reciprocated love and of parting and who,
more than any other single person, was to be the catalyst
and inspiration of her work.

David Tasma was a patient in the first ward she took
over once she was a fully-fledged almoner. He was a Polish
Jew, an agnostic, who came from the Warsaw ghetto and
had come over to England before the uprising. He was not
very educated, he referred to himself as 'only a rough old
fellow', he worked as a waiter and he had no relations in
this country and very few friends. He was only forty, felt
his whole life had been wasted, and now he had inoperable
cancer. Cicely knew very little else about him. She knew
he was one of four sons and that his mother had died when
he was young, that his grandfather was a rabbi, who loved
to argue with his grandson, that he went out to work when
he was very young, that he had fallen in love with a
friend's wife and that he had spent the war in France. She
knew also that he was dying. She kept a special eye on him
because she knew 'he'd be in trouble quite soon' and when,
after a brief spell back at work, he was taken ill again, it
was she, as his medical social worker, whom his landlady
rang. Cicely told her to get on to David's general practitioner who arranged for him to go to the local hospital.

She then went to see him at home, and it was while they were waiting for the ambulance to arrive that he asked her if he was dying. She told him that he was. He was admitted to the Archway Hospital in Highgate and it was then that the professional relationship developed into a deep friendship. This soon ripened into love.

Inevitably their meetings were few. They saw each other only twenty-five times before he died. The brief entries in Cicely's engagement diary speak volumes; each precious meeting is treasured and encapsulated in a word or phrase. She knew so certainly how little time they had, she was not going to let the smallest memory disappear. To start with they just state 'Tasma' baldly, almost as if she were deluding herself that it was still a professional relationship, but soon it is 'David' followed by some comment on his health, ('ill', 'better', 'weak') or a note about their conversations, which were very largely about religion: 'The Lord', 'The Gospel', 'Judaism', 'Isaiah', 'Peace'. One day she noted that she stayed 'till 8.25', presumably well past the normal visiting hours; in a lifetime of two months every hour is worth recording. Most touchingly of all, she sometimes charts their growing relationship with a cryptic phrase to remind her of the essence of their exchange: 'Beg for forgiveness', 'I knew you wouldn't fail me', 'How we really feel', 'Best ever', and one Saturday, 'A charming afternoon'. It was then that she knew she was in love. She remembers 'walking back from the 27 bus after they had spent all the afternoon laughing and thinking, "well, if I don't ever have anything else, I've had a perfect afternoon."' Finally, on February 25th, there is one word 'Goodbye'. She had been with him till evening and left him sleepy, with his eyes closed. One of the nurses told her later that he didn't open his eyes again. Cicely was the last person he saw on this earth.

The next evening she went to a prayer meeting at St. Peter's, Vere Street. They started to sing the hymn 'How sweet the name of Jesus sounds' and she was feeling very desolate for David and thinking that it never sounded sweet to him, 'when I had one of those very firm state-

ments I get from time to time saying "But he knows Him
far better than you do already." I have never felt I could
worry about him ever again, nor indeed about anyone else
who dies in the world without apparently any knowledge
of Christ.'

Brief and infrequent though their meetings were, like
all really significant emotional events, they are etched
clearly in Cicely's mind and she remembers conversations
in great detail some thirty-five years later. The pathos of
two lonely people finding each other when one of them is
dying does not need to be stressed; it certainly adds a
special dimension to the ordinary exchanges of lovers –
'all my life I've been waiting for a nice girl and now here
you are and look at me.' Despite David being an agnostic
Jew and Cicely a keen evangelical Christian, she was
determined not to pressure him about religion. She remembers saying to him, 'You mustn't believe just because
you like me', and him answering, 'I like you too much to
say I believe just because I like you.' Their contrasting
religious positions do not seem to have divided them in the
spiritual discussion which was at the heart of their shared
experience. One day when he was very sad, he suddenly
said to her, 'Can't you say something to comfort me?' and
she, respecting his Jewish roots, said the twenty-third
Psalm: 'Yea, though I walk through the valley of the
shadow of death, I will fear no evil; for thou art with me;
thy rod and thy staff comfort me.' He asked her to go on, so
she said the *Venite* (Psalm 95) and then, perhaps running
out of suitable things she knew by heart, offered to read to
him, as she had the New Testament and the Psalms in her
handbag. 'No', he said, 'I only want what is in your mind
and in your heart.' So that night she learnt the *De Profun-
dis* – a Psalm pleading for forgiveness – in order to be able
to say it to him by heart the next day; a loving gesture, if
not quite in the spirit of a remark that was to become one
of the corner-stones of hospice philosophy. Just before he
died he told the ward sister that he had made his peace
with God. That he felt able to say this must owe something
to these conversations with Cicely.

Important though David was in Cicely's life, his memory might now be no more significant than any first love, if it were not for another dimension of their meetings – their discussions about how people might be cared for when they were dying. The one persistent theme in Cicely's thirty years had been her desire to help people. But who? And how? She had watched her friends become doctors and nurses, get married and have babies, while she worked and wondered. Nursing had seemed to be the answer, but her back trouble had stood in the way; she was, at that time, working as a medical social worker, but needed to be more extended, to have more opportunities, than this seemed able to provide. Here was someone in real need, a need so great and so poignant that it overshadowed even the tragically sick and lonely patients she had already come across. He was separated from his own country and from his own family, he was in great physical pain, he was desperately lonely (Cicely was virtually his only visitor) and he was dying after an unfulfilled life. Together they talked about what could be done for other people in his situation. As they talked it was overwhelmingly borne in on Cicely how acute the need was, how dreadful the despair of so many people. Gradually an idea began to take shape, that perhaps she, Cicely Saunders, could do something about it. Not only was she learning from the comfort she was able to bring to David Tasma that she had a gift for relieving suffering, but also being so close to someone who was dying showed her the need for a rounded care for the terminally ill that was totally lacking in the hospital care of the 1940s. There was certainly a desperate need for more skilful and more continuous pain relief, but that was not all; there were other needs too, spiritual, emotional and social; if they were met in a context of real concern for the individual person, it might become possible to die peacefully, even happily. The gentle, somehow inevitable, birth of this idea gave sustenance to David too. If his illness and death were to plant the seeds of a new, creative possibility, then perhaps his life had not been pointless. Through this young woman he had met in the last months of his life, his death could bear fruit. And as their discussions became more detailed and they began to consider the practical implications, he realised there was another way in which he could help. He made Cicely his executor and left her five hundred pounds – 'I'll be a window in your home'.

So he died, and Cicely was left with his photograph, his dressing-gown and his watch, a few memories, five hundred pounds (the Hospital gave her permission to receive the money), and a sense of purpose, a feeling that now she knew what to do with her life. Her duties as his executor left her responsible for his funeral, which she organised according to the orthodox rites in the Streatham Jewish Cemetery. She remembers being 'terribly jolted' as the coffin drove up, and his employer and Cicely, the only mourners, followed it to the gloomy little Chapel. They said the ninetieth Psalm, which ends prophetically, 'Let thy work appear unto thy servants, and thy glory unto their children. And let the beauty of the Lord our God be upon us; and establish thou the work of our hands upon us; yea, the work of our hands establish thou it.'

Despite her role as David's executor, their unorthodox, brief and intense relationship left her with the special grief of a bereavement that had to be private and largely unacknowledged; she had not got the small consolations of a shared life with shared friends, possessions and experiences. Nevertheless, her youth and her religion came to her aid and in only just over three months she had an experience which ended her mourning. She was on holiday in Scotland with her father and some friends. 'I was still feeling very sad and as if I was walking through a long tunnel, and the second morning there I got up early because it was a lovely day. We were in a lodge right on the edge of the Loch and there was a lovely little Scottish river running down into it and I sat there and there were blackbirds singing and peaty water running over the glistening stones and I slipped out of time. I remember feeling that I'd stepped into the timeless now, and that David was there somewhere and that it didn't matter whether I was nearer him than that. He was all right and this was all right. It was *so* strong and comforting.'

Cicely is very aware, and was even at the time, that had she had what she wanted and got married in her twenties she would not have met David, and that what they had, short though it was, had been worth the long wait. His loneliness and pain not only echoed something of her own, but epitomised the need of countless others. Now she knew that, somehow or other, she had to do something for these people; she knew the answer to her question 'What do I have to do to say thank you and serve?' She would not have chosen to fall in love with a dying man, but by being receptive and open, she had begun to mark out her future. The whole idea for a hospice crystallised out of these discussions, so that at last she was able to say, 'This is what I have to do.'

5

MORE EDUCATION

He who bends to himself a joy
Does the winged life destroy;
But he who kisses the joy as it flies
Lives in eternity's sunrise.

If you trap the moment before it's ripe,
The tears of repentance you'll certainly wipe;
But, if once you let the ripe moment go,
You can never wipe off the tears of woe.
                                    William Blake, 'Opportunity'

Although she now knew beyond doubt that she wanted to
work with the dying, Cicely had no clear idea what she
should do next. Her unusual ability simultaneously to act
and to wait stood her in good stead. Just as, three years
earlier, she had thrown herself into Christian activity
while waiting for the full meaning of her conversion to
become clear, so now she responded immediately to this
new certainty, letting the seed that had been sown ger-
minate quietly. Within days of David's death she had
telephoned St. Luke's, a home for the dying near her flat in
Bayswater; she asked if she could come and help and she
was soon working there regularly as a volunteer sister for
the evening. She would help with the evening drug round,
take prayers, talk to patients, even sing to them. She
needed, as it were, to test her vocation; the best, in fact the
only, way to do this was to be with dying people. It was
soon obvious to her and to everyone else that she was
indeed in the right place. She loved going there, she felt at
ease with the patients and they with her.

Her choice of St. Luke's, though determined more by
convenience than by anything else, proved to be inspired.
It had been founded in 1893 as 'A Home for the Dying
Poor', and though it no longer exists in that form, both the

place, and its founder, Dr. Howard Barrett, were to be a powerful influence on Cicely, and through her on the modern hospice movement. It was a home rather than a hospital, it was free – patients only contributing if they had the means and wished to do so, it had a strong religious basis and yet was interdenominational; most crucially of all, the staff were intensely interested in the patients as individuals. One of the visiting sisters wrote in 1905, 'Although all the patients are alike in that they are "dying", each has his own separate life, and it is the duty of the visiting sister to regard with absolute sanctity the individuality of each one, and to try and reach that which makes the man *himself*, and does not belong to another.' Dr. Barrett, in his annual report four years later, writes in similar vein. 'We do not think or speak of our inmates as "cases". We realise that each one is a human microcosm, with its own characteristics, its own life history, intensely interesting to itself and some small surrounding circle. Very often it is confided to some of us.'

The sanctity of the individual was not, of course, a new idea to Cicely, though she rejoiced to see theory put into practice. What was new to her was the way the staff of St. Luke's used drugs. As a student nurse and as an almoner, she had seen patients treated aggressively, with continuous operations and treatments in a vain attempt to cure an incurable condition; she had seen them comatose from drugs, or waiting in unrelieved pain. Now, for the first time, she saw patients with both their mental and physical pain relieved so that they were relatively comfortable, yet alert, almost until the end. This was achieved by giving pain-killing drugs at regular intervals, before the pain reasserted itself, instead of waiting until the patient was crying out in such pain that another dose was given. This apparently simple technique was to be the foundation of Cicely's use of analgesics. The system of 'regular giving' had been used at St. Luke's for some time, at least since 1935, when Miss Pipkin, the Salvation Army Matron much admired by Cicely, arrived as a sister, but it had not, for some unaccountable reason, become known to anybody outside St. Luke's. They would also, whenever possible, give drugs orally rather than by injection. This was pleasanter for the patients and had the great advantage of being easier for relatives, when nursing a patient at home.

Cicely's evenings and occasional Sundays at St. Luke's did not, of course, interfere with her work as an almoner. However, she began to find it was not really satisfying her; moreover being so close to dying patients in her spare time brought home to her just how much she missed them. So when an opportunity to change her job turned up, she took it. Norman Barrett, known affectionally as 'Pasty' Barrett (no relation to Dr. Barrett of St. Luke's), because of his high colouring, was one of the surgeons she worked for as an almoner, and when his medical secretary left to get married, she asked him if she could take the job and combine the two roles. Pasty Barrett was a great character, amusing, stimulating and outspoken. *St. Thomas's Gazette* warned its readers 'not to be upset if he addresses you as "You, Stupid . . ."', while one of his students still recalls his insistence that they thank the nurse who tied up their gown before operating. Pasty Barrett is credited with encouraging doctors to 'Publish or perish' and was considered to be among the most inspiring teachers of that period of St. Thomas's history. Cicely admired him greatly and was fascinated by his work – thoracic surgery. He performed the whole range of chest operations which still included the surgical treatment of tuberculosis, and he specialised in a recent surgical development, operating on babies born with structural heart defects – so called 'blue' babies. One of Cicely's jobs was to help the families receive back babies who had had this operation; she would also keep his medical records and accompany him on ward rounds and visits to patients in other hospitals and at home. He was somebody who involved people in his work, and though Cicely felt she was not as efficient as her predecessor, she enjoyed it.

But still she yearned to be with the terminally ill. After about eighteen months, while she was driving to Midhurst with Pasty, she found herself telling him that she had to go back to dying patients and that if she could get a job as a night sister her back wouldn't present too much of a problem. He replied that she would only be frustrated as a nurse, because people wouldn't listen to her; in any case, there was so much to be learnt about pain control and she really ought to do it properly. 'Go and read Medicine,' he said, 'It's the doctors who desert the dying.'

She had not even read science at school. She was thirty-three, she had already done two trainings and got a degree and a diploma. Now here was Mr. Barrett, a man whose opinion she had to take seriously, telling her to go and qualify as a doctor. It was not the first time the idea had cropped up. Her father had wanted her to read medicine after her first spell at Oxford, but she had felt no urge to take his advice; when her back stopped her nursing he suggested it again, but this time she had not felt up to it physically. Now, not only was her back troubling her less after the laminectomy (though the success of the operation was only temporary), she had a compelling reason to make the effort the training would demand. The medical authorities at St. Thomas's told her to get her first MB and they would then consider her, so she enrolled at a crammer. She was the oldest by years and felt very out of place, especially after overhearing two eighteen-year-olds say 'She'll be ninety before she qualifies . . .' Given her tenacity, she would probably have soldiered on, but Pasty Barrett heard of her situation and gave the wheels of bureaucracy another push. This time she got a recommendation from the Matron, who wrote to Dr. Crockford, then secretary to the Medical School, 'Miss Saunders is a gifted person. In practical work she became proficient, although it needed perseverance on her part, for she was a little diffident and too unassuming at first.' She was called for a second interview, at which she was seen by two additional doctors. She didn't admit to the idea of starting a home for the terminally ill – that was to stay tucked away in the back of her mind for many years yet – she simply told them she wanted to do something about pain in patients dying of cancer. They listened with the tolerance of people being indulgent of a good, if impossible, idea, but they were impressed by her record. Two days later, by one of those strokes of synchronicity that seem to accompany people of destiny, she received two letters in the post. One was from St. Thomas's, offering her a place and telling her she'd need soft-soled shoes on the ward, the other was a cheque for five hundred pounds to pay her fees and enable her to stop earning. Her father had sold some shares and told her the money was on its way, but he could not possibly have known when the financial arrangements would be completed or when the money would reach her. The feeling that this new move was 'meant' must have been reinforced by this chance.

So, after only three weeks at the crammer, she arrived at St. Thomas's to do her first MB. She wrote to the Principal of St. Anne's College, Oxford, who had kept abreast of her former pupil's varied career, telling her what she was going to do and why. 'I have become more and more aware of the problems of the dying, particularly of the hopeless advanced cases of cancer, and I do think their feeling that they are deserted by the doctors is to some extent justified. I want very badly to try and find out more about the possibilities of alleviating their physical and mental distress and realise one can only do this by becoming a doctor.' She added that she already realised that it was a problem that had to be tackled from many angles, so none of her training had been wasted; in reply to the Principal's amazed reaction she answered staunchly, 'I know it's the right thing to do, so I don't find it too daunting.'

Reading medicine is tough at any age; for someone of Cicely's age and with virtually no scientific background it must have been a nightmare. 'It was hell,' says Cicely, with characteristic bluntness. In the first physics session they were asked what they had done in this field and she had to say, 'Maths and biology seventeen years ago', but with a little extra coaching in physics and chemistry she passed her first MB in nine months, completed the pre-clinical part of the training well inside the three years allocated to theoretical work and passed her second MB at the first attempt, despite more back trouble, forcing her to spend several weeks in bed while preparing for the exams. Her previous experience in nursing and social work was useful, but it must have needed all her single-mindedness to tackle the formidable array of subjects when it came to the clinical training: Medicine, Surgery, Casualty Dressing, Pathology, Midwifery, Gynaecology, Paediatrics, Post-Mortems, Fevers, Anaesthetics, Bacteriology, Forensic Medicine, Toxicology, Venereal Disease, Vaccination, Mental diseases . . . the training was intended to be comprehensive, but it is significant that there was no training at all in the care of the dying. She put her calling firmly on one side, wondering sometimes if she ought to be making systematic plans, but still not knowing what she should do, she concentrated on being a doctor, and a good doctor at that. Even her tutors were impressed; a single report remaining in St. Thomas's files (the students' medical records for that period have been mostly destroyed) predicts that 'she will be a loyal colleague' and that 'her industry is overpowering'. When it came to preparing for final exams there were no half measures. She moved into a bed-sitting room in Ebury Street where her room was cleaned, her bed made and she was given breakfast. She never gave anyone her telephone number so she did not have to answer the phone, though she could ring out. All her post went to the hospital. 'I acquired a record player and I *absolutely slogged* for that year. I wasn't going to have any nonsense about failing finals.' And she didn't. She qualified in April 1957 (by which time she was nearly thirty-nine) sailing through with honours in Surgery, 'which I certainly never deserved, but I just had a top day'. This must have been modesty, for one of her examining doctors said to a distinguished colleague, Sir Gordon Wolstenholme, that she was the best student he had ever examined in finals. She was also awarded the Beaney Prize for Obstetrics and Gynaecology, 'because I was good at exams' she says. Cicely recalls wryly how she has 'spent such a lot of time turning into a chrysalis and emerging again as something different' – this transformation was the hardest yet, and the most triumphant.

Hard though Cicely worked, she also had a busy and happy social life; she relished being a student again, with no responsibilities except to study and enjoy being with her fellow students. They were all younger than her; she would find herself cutting up a dog-fish next to people fifteen years her junior and would go and see old friends in the main hospital 'desperate for adult conversation'. But St. Thomas's had a policy for taking a few older students – there had recently been a former judge, who was past retiring age by the time he qualified – so gradually Cicely acquired a circle of friends somewhere near her own age. Only fifteen per cent of her intake were women, so she had, to her delight, more men friends than ever before. There was Tony Brown, now a specialist in Community Medicine. He recalls halcyon days, when Cicely and he taught each other physics in the Flower Walk in Kensington Gardens; a little later she met Tom West, now a distinguished colleague in the new field of medicine she was to create. He was a kindred spirit who, like her, had done no physics or chemistry. They were so far behind the others that they were the only two left in the weighing room making up their 'standard solution'. This common weakness was a great bond. Despite the difference in their ages – he is twelve years younger – the shared struggle in what Tom calls 'the pig-sty end of the physics desk and the chemistry lab' was the springboard that launched a lasting friendship. Tom, Tony and Cicely were the nucleus of a typical student circle that Tom describes graphically. 'There was this small group of people who surged into the dining room with Cicely at the prow of the ship. She led the way and Tony and I were very firmly in orbit. Tony was the smart one and I was the farmer's son, – I felt. I didn't mind that particularly. I was the friend who was prepared to remain in orbit and be useful.'

It is hard for her contemporaries not to speak with

hindsight, but they certainly remember Cicely as an outstanding and special person. Her height alone made her
conspicuous and her presence was powerful, though she
never threw her weight about or let people know of her
previous training at St. Thomas's. She had a car, unusual
in those days and she was a great organiser. One of her
talents is to gather people round her and draw on their
skills and enthusiasms, and this she did in her student
days. She would organise groups to study anatomy, physiology, chemistry – whatever was currently preoccupy-
ing them. She led, not because she strove to lead, but
because that was becoming her natural position.

Her powers of leadership spilled over into the life of the
hospital, as much of her spare time was spent with the
Christian Union and the Hospital Musical Society. Medical students of the fifties ranged 'from rugger players to
God-wallopers', and though some held the 'God-wallopers'
in scant regard the Christian Union was strong and Cicely
made it stronger and more lively. They met every day for
prayers at lunchtime in a gloomy Victorian chapel considered by the authorities to be the most suitable place,
and also held weekly meetings, sometimes for Bible study,
sometimes to hear outside speakers. The Union resisted
the idea that the interaction of Christianity and Medicine
was their sole raison d'être and there were talks about
Christianity and Communism, Christianity in different
vocations, Science versus God; they showed films of missionary activities, sent the hospital's discarded instruments to Uganda, received a visit from the Policemen's
Christian Union; Dr. Grady Wilson came to answer
queries on Billy Graham's latest Crusade and one July
day, over a hundred people crowded into the Clinical
Lecture Theatre to hear the evangelical preacher, John
Stott, talk on the problem of suffering. Sometimes members of the Union spent country weekends together, discussing, praying, walking. There was one occasion when
they went to Devon to stay with Cicely's great friend
Madge Drake, and three of them were converted from a
partial to a total Christianity, rather as Cicely herself had

been in 1945. With her greater age and her personality, Cicely could have taken over the Union, but she didn't. Tom West appreciated her ability to 'conduct from behind' and take second place. 'She didn't push herself, but was very good at encouraging people to turn up, to perform, to take office, to talk, to get things going. Then as now, Cicely had more energy than most of us. If she was involved in anything, then it had to be a success.' One of the things she was involved in was the Hospital Christian Union choir, which she started. The men could not read music, so she would thump tenor and bass parts on the piano till they knew them, fetch people from the outskirts of London who could not get to rehearsals, coach them, cajole them, bully them – the group would then help in the routine ward services on Sunday. It *was* a success. She also started the St. Thomas's Carol Parties, which sang so loud and cheerfully that the noise burst through the walls of Riddell House and disturbed the Christmas Show.

She also belonged to the Musical Society, which reached such a high standard in the fifties that Scott Godard, writing in the *News Chronicle*, said 'It has been suggested that this amateur society has reached a standard that deserves the attention of the discerning. It has indeed.' Cicely has sung in choirs since her school days and everybody who has heard her has remarked on her clear, beautiful soprano voice. It says something for the standard she reached that when she sang a solo in Vaughan Williams' 'Serenade to Music' alongside top professionals of the time like Alexander Young and Maurice Bevan, the *St. Thomas's Gazette* reported on 'those exacting bars taken in her stride by Miss Cicely Saunders'.

After qualifying, Cicely left her bed-sitting room and moved to a flat in Connaught Square with a friend. Then she had another of those lucky breaks, those mixtures of good luck and receptivity, that have punctuated her life. Her father ran into an old friend, Professor Harold Stewart, who was the head of Pharmacology at St. Mary's Paddington. His field of interest lay in the mechanisms of pain and the way drugs acted and he had some spare

money for research. At the time no work had been done on
pain in the terminally ill; it was a totally new field and
even he, at the centre of pain research, knew little about it.
However, he was open to the work Cicely wanted to do and
he suggested she come to St. Mary's on a research scholarship. He put the idea to the Halley Stewart Trust and
by the time she had done her two house jobs – at Hydestile
and the Royal Waterloo (which she found even harder
than being a medical student) – she had been given a
research scholarship, working under the aegis of Professor
Stewart at St. Mary's Hospital.

At St. Mary's Cicely was one of twenty research fellows
working on pain, but she was the only one specialising in
pain in the terminally ill. While she was a medical student
she had submitted an entry for a hospital prize; she did not
win it, but the entry was published in *St. Thomas's Gazette*. It was about four patients dying of cancer and while
researching it she had come across St. Joseph's Hospice in
Hackney. She arranged to go there three days a week,
observing the patients, evaluating the use of drugs and,
most important of all, listening. So began a relationship
that was to have incalculable effects on both St. Joseph's
and on Cicely.

St. Joseph's was established in 1905 by the Irish Sisters
of Charity, a Roman Catholic order of nuns especially
concerned with active work such as teaching and nursing.
In 1958, when Cicely started her research work, there
were 150 beds at St. Joseph's, between forty and fifty for
patients with terminal malignant disease, the rest were
kept for the frail and elderly with no homes and those with
long-term illnesses who were not considered suitable for
rehabilitation. It was outside the National Health Service, but contractual arrangements with the Health Service meant that for most patients it was free. Only three of
the nuns were trained nurses, the rest were auxiliaries –
young Irish girls. They all worked prodigiously hard,
seven days a week with just one two-week holiday a year,
nevertheless the nursing care was excellent, the nuns

serene and the atmosphere cheerful. Though the medical care was unsophisticated, the patients felt accepted in their pain and anxiety. The nuns were not trained to cope with acute pain, or some of the distressing symptoms that can accompany terminal cancer, such as intractable vomiting or breathlessness; there were no resident doctors, just two part-time GPs, busy with their own practices. Here at last was a doctor, the first doctor ever to specialise in the care of the dying, dedicated, skilful and tactful. Indeed her tact must have been remarkable, for she effected numerous changes and met only respect, amounting to adoration, from the nuns, who were the first to acknowledge her improvements.

The first and most fundamental change she introduced came straight from St. Luke's – the regular giving of drugs. She was allowed to try four patients on this system and it was so successful that she was encouraged to use it more widely. It soon became, and indeed still is, the normal practice of the Hospice. She started by prescribing the drugs the nuns were already using, mostly Omnopon, but gradually introduced morphine mixture and heroin. The medical profession has always been nervous of giving these drugs frequently, fearful that they would become addictive or that the patient would become tolerant of them and they would cease to be effective. Cicely's detailed studies, admired by Dr. Winner, the Principal Medical Officer in the Ministry of Health responsible for London, proved empirically that this need not be so. Writing in the *Nursing Mirror* Cicely says: 'Constant pain needs constant control, and that means that drugs should be given regularly so that pain is kept in remission all the time. If a patient has his own dose of analgesics given to him as a routine he is not then nearly so dependent, either upon the staff or upon the drugs. If every time you have a pain you have to ask for something to relieve it, you are reminded each time of your dependence upon the drug itself, but if your medicine arrives routinely before the pain takes hold, this does not happen. This is important, for a patient's independence must be maintained in every possible way. We find that under this system we are hardly troubled at all with either tolerance or addiction, and that when we have correctly assessed the patient's need for dosage, he will remain alert. When we do have to increase dosage I am convinced that it is far more often because the patient's pain is getting worse as his lesion extends than because he has become tolerant to the effect of the analgesic.' And in *Current Medicine and Drugs* she writes even more confidently, 'It is our experience that if pain is kept permanently in remission tolerance is remarkably slow in developing and may never appear. We have patients on the same dosage for months and even years, and many who have had drugs on request before they come to us are able to have less analgesic in the twenty-four hours once control has been established.'

The early sixties was a time when many new drugs were becoming available, and by painstaking investigation Cicely learnt more and more ways of using them to control symptoms as well as pain; she also took from St. Luke's the practice of giving medication by mouth whenever possible; unless, that is, the patient could not swallow it or hold it down or was so weak that his body couldn't absorb it. She involved the nurses at every stage, no doubt influenced by her own experience of nursing; for instance she would write the prescriptions in such a way that the nurses administering the drugs had some latitude in the size of dose required. She also reviewed the drugs regularly, the type, the dosage, the frequency of giving. The astonished nuns saw their dearest wish fulfilled – they could now ease their patients' pain without making them comatose. Their delight knew no bounds. Cicely was indeed, as one of them says, 'Manna from Heaven'. News of these changes began to reach the wider world; the invariable comment of visitors being shown round the Hospice was, 'But your patients look so serene, so alert and happy and no one looks as if they have pain.' A nurse from a London hospital said at the end of a complete tour of the Hospice, 'But we haven't been through your terminal wards yet.' She had. In fact she had been talking to some of the patients in them. And Cicely wrote to her former tutor Betty Read, 'I took Dr. Colebrook, energetic member of the Euthanasia Society, round St. Joseph's on Tuesday. He was impressed to the point of bewilderment.' A group of social work students, after Cicely took them round St. Joseph's in 1960, summed up their observations of the patients in six points: they noted, '(1) An absence of pain and drowsiness. (2) Liveliness and peacefulness. (3) An indefinable atmosphere which left one feeling that death was nothing to be worried about – a sort of home-coming. (4) Integration – patients, staff and visitors were all of equal importance, there seemed to be no dividing barriers. We noticed especially how easy it was to talk to patients and how easily they accepted us. (5) Simplicity of approach to the problem of pain. (6) Lack of narrow-mindedness which might so easily be present in a place run by a particular order, e.g. agnostics, atheists or non-thinkers are helped to accept death in the way most suitable to *them* as individuals, besides those who already have strong Christian faith.'

Another important improvement made by Cicely was in the way records were kept. When she arrived there were no patients' notes, no treatment cards, just a drug book. Cicely, working as a researcher as well as a doctor, introduced detailed patients' notes, drug charts and a ward report book. By the time she stopped working at St. Joseph's she had observed and documented over 1,000 cases of patients dying of cancer. Her scrupulous records were the *sine qua non* of this research.

The emotional care of the patients has never been less than loving and concerned at St. Joseph's. Cicely was endlessly impressed by the hospitality of the nuns and loved their phrase 'Oh, he's himself'. The nuns would rather a patient died grumbling to the last, yet fully himself, than drugged into some pseudo-saintly calm. Cicely encouraged them to say 'Feelings are facts in this house'; she also introduced a new dimension by trying to see the patients in the context of their families, not as an isolated human being; the families were involved in the patients' illness, so they would also be involved in the care the Hospice was giving. She also favoured more freedom for patients, encouraging them to get up more if they felt able to, to go to occupational therapy or to join in anything that might be going on. While she was there the specific fixed visiting times became more flexible; it was becoming an open house – visitors could come at virtually any time, just as would happen at home. The whole approach was designed to make the patient feel at home, not in an institution.

Cicely does not consider herself a researcher by temperament, and she never finished her thesis on the use of narcotic drugs. None-the-less, Professor Stewart came to admire her and found her persevering and hard-working. He used sometimes to come to St. Joseph's with her and saw her with patients. He was very impressed. 'She was a very extrovert person and she used to produce quite a remarkable change in people merely by being with them, just talking to them. In other words she was her own therapeutic weapon.'

Cicely was beginning to make her mark. She had entered a totally neglected field, which involved many aspects of medicine and many dimensions of the personality. Now, by a combination of her personal gifts, hard work, and the indefinable workings of destiny, she was formidably qualified to tackle it.

6

PATIENTS AND THEIR NEEDS

The dissatisfied dead cannot noise abroad the negligence they
have suffered.

John Hinton, *Dying*

Cicely's qualifications to pioneer a new field of medicine
did not lie only in her comprehensive medical training,
but also in her response to patients. It was through caring
for them that she came to understand the diversity of their
needs, then to see a pattern in that diversity; it was
through her involvement with them that she found the
stimulus for the work she was to undertake. For over ten
years, before she felt ready to realise her dream, she learnt
from the dying in order to help the dying.

While it was David Tasma who played the lead in this
influence on Cicely, there was a strong supporting cast,
each one contributing something to the unfolding of
Cicely's understanding. This quality – 'her greatest
therapeutic weapon' – was forged, made increasingly delicate and sensitive, by literally hundreds of patients.
Their stories are engraved so deeply into Cicely's mind
that they are part of her, even when the memory is only
the smallest cameo; sometimes just one phrase has been
remembered, treasured and incorporated into her thinking.

Even before she met David there were three patients
who touched her particularly. The first was in 1947, when
she was a shy and still inexperienced social work student.
She was at the Royal Cancer Hospital for two months and
had to see someone called Mrs. Chester Fox. 'I asked
someone who she was and she said, "Oh yes, the one with
the horrid face?" which indeed one might have said (she
had cancer of the face) but this you did not notice. What

you did notice was the wonderful courtesy with which she immediately set me at my ease and put me into the picture of the ward. I remember coming up to the ward again after the weekend. She had had a haemorrhage and died and I had such a feeling of loss and gratefulness.' She was to experience these feelings of loss and gratitude over and over again.

Constantly Cicely was to witness the anguish of patients living, and even dying, alone. This was most poignant in David, with the very special quality of their relationship and his piercing need to find a meaning to his life and death, but earlier, again as an almoner student, she met a retired school teacher who lived on her own in a room in Brixton. Cicely arranged for her to go to a home for her last weeks; she then went back to visit her again and make sure she was all right and was happy with the arrangements. 'The ambulance had already come and taken her away, but the door was ajar and I can still remember going in and the awful smell of loneliness and the emptiness of the room after she had gone.' In contrast there was Mrs. Clifton, whose son Cicely managed to get home from Singapore when it was clear how ill she was. Mrs. Clifton had held her large family together during her life and they were around her bedside during her illness and death. Cicely found this woman's death a tremendous achievement.

If families bring comfort, they also bring problems. Mrs. Elliott, a patient Cicely visited at home, feared dying less than she feared for her policeman husband and their fourteen-year-old son, who would be left to manage on their own. Cicely is still moved by the memory of this young woman's sadness at leaving a growing boy and by the way she said of her husband 'He's big and strong, but he *does* need looking after.' There is unutterable poignancy in having to leave this earth before your job is finished; there is poignancy too, in people struggling to look after sick relations at home. There was a woman distressed beyond tears by her inability to care for her sick husband and relieve his bedsores; and a patient of Mr.

Barrett's, Mr. Sebert, who Cicely used to sit with once a week while his wife went for a walk. 'He was a member of the Rationalist Press and the Secular Society and we used to argue. It was ridiculous just how much this weekly visit meant to his wife, just giving her a chance to get out.'

Physical pain runs through the tapestry of distress like a steel thread. Cicely seemed constantly drawn to people in pain and they to her, not only in her working life but in her private life too. The sister of her friend 'Packie' died slowly and painfully of cancer of the ovary; she used to refer to her pain as 'My child – it's not a child anybody would be proud of and it's walking around in hob-nailed boots today.' Cicely used to go and spend the night there so that Packie could have a good sleep. She tried to ease the pain. 'We went up and up on the morphine and though I did know from St. Luke's about giving it regularly and that I needn't worry about that, I knew this couldn't be right and that one needed to know more about it than just increasing the narcotic – this wasn't enough.' Sometimes she came across cases where even though the physical pain was controlled by large amounts of drugs, there was still intolerable pain of another sort. She wrote to a friend about a boy of seventeen she had met at Hydestile; he had died of cancer 'and had been having 3½ grams of diamorphine three-hourly, and would wake up screaming with fear rather than pain. He had been in a long time and is rather typical of what too often happens in general hospitals where the only thing they think of far too often is to increase the dose of opiate.'

All the time she was deepening her experience, refining her skills. When she heard that her friend Tom West's father was seriously ill, she said to Mrs. West, 'This is important, this is where I'm going to be. Any time you want me I will come.' Cicely was on holiday when it became clear he was near the end, nevertheless she came, so she was with the family for the last three weeks of Captain West's life. She had just qualified as a doctor and the GP, aware of her special knowledge and interest, allowed her to advise on the prescriptions; to his amazement the pain was controlled. The family feel it was Cicely who made it possible for Captain West to die in such peace. Mrs. West remembers with gratitude, 'What she had done was to make it possible for my husband to really live until the end of his life. In this way he strengthened my children's faith and ability to take losing their father. Cicely didn't do that, but she made it possible for him to do it, by keeping things calm and controlling the pain. He didn't have any agonising pain at all, which he might have done.'

This experience was important to Cicely too; it showed her the value of sharing the burden of sickness. 'I have a very good memory of helping friends to care for their father who was dying of carcinoma of the bronchus on a farm in the country. I remember that strong community; the family, the family doctor, the life of the farm, and the interest of the village. The whole thing was a pattern, and everyone had a place in the pattern. The patient had the central place, very conscious of that, and rather enjoying it, in many ways controlling the situation, and even planning ahead, sometimes looking sideways at us to watch our reaction to one of his more Rabelaisian remarks. He was neither uncertain nor fearful, but was typical of himself up to the last, although he well knew what was happening.'

Cicely was continually seeing how little specialised care those in pain, those worried about their families, the lonely, the fearful, received in general hospitals. Sometimes this was revealed in a single remark. She often quotes two patients being admitted to St. Joseph's from other hospitals. 'Will *you* turn me out if I cannot get better?' said one; and another 'It seemed so strange, nobody wanted to look at me.' She realised how often these feelings of guilt, rejection and failure were reflections of the attitude shown to them by other people; Cicely had seen these attitudes for herself. When a doctor said 'Will the lady almoner please cope?' she came to realise that this meant 'Will you please get this patient out of my beds . . . send him somewhere . . . get rid of him . . . I can't do any more.' Medicine was about cure, if they couldn't cure doctors felt they had failed; it was about having answers, they had no answers for the dying. Doctors did not consider it their job to ease the process of dying beyond prescribing pain-killing drugs; as far as possible, they avoided dying patients, embarrassed by what they saw as failure. The prevalence of this attitude is underscored by Cicely's observation that when she was a medical student 'there were one or two, like Mr. Nevin, who always stopped and said "Good Morning" to everyone, dying or not. One noticed it.' A much travelled doctor said that care of the dying was more primitive in Blackpool than in India, Nigeria, New Guinea or Queensland.

While Cicely was at St. Joseph's she was so willing and so constantly available that the nuns would ask her to help with some of the chronically ill patients in the Hospice. In this way Cicely met some people who were to become very special to her and to influence her ideas.

Alice, Terry and Louie were a close-knit trio of friends, all in the same long-stay ward at St. Joseph's. Terry, a rather difficult lady with a strong personality, had multiple sclerosis; Alice, sweet, friendly and attractive, had spent forty of her sixty years in and out of hospital with tuberculous arthritis; Louie's fragile bones had kept her in hospitals and nursing homes for most of her life. Cicely used to visit them regularly, chatting, gossiping, telling them about her dream of one day building a hospice. She involved them so deeply that this ecumenical little group, Catholic, Anglican and Jewish, became the first 'support group', praying regularly for her and her plans and becoming what Cicely was to call 'founding patients'.

Spending so much time in bed, with virtually no lives outside St Joseph's, they drew from Cicely endless pleasure and stimulus; they were fascinated by her and by what she was intending to do. But it would be a mistake to think it was just a case of Cicely being kind to invalids. She is much shyer and, to use her phrase 'soft-centred' than most people realise; these ladies understood this.

They gave their friendship and support unstintingly and Cicely received it with gratitude.

Louie was particularly special to Cicely, their shared Christianity being important to them both. Louie had become a Christian, suddenly and dramatically, when, in her twenties and so crippled that her parents couldn't look after her at home, she prayed that God would reveal himself to her. That night she dreamt that she was walking down a bluebell wood and she saw Christ coming towards her. She woke with the feeling of being with Christ, and that feeling never left her for the rest of her life. She was passionately interested in other people and in Cicely above all. Every time Cicely was doing something especially important Louie would say, 'Tell me what time it is and I'll be there.' After her first trip abroad, Cicely came back to find a card saying 'Welcome, welcome, welcome back'. When Louie died in 1964 Cicely had lost a very real friend.

An even greater friend, an even profounder influence, was Barbara Galton, known to everyone as Mrs. G.

Mrs. G. was thirty-three when she was admitted to St. Thomas's Hospital with symptoms which were diagnosed as Devic's disease, a rare and incurable form of paralysis. Cicely and Mrs. G. met a few months later, in 1954, when Cicely had just done her second MB and was pining to be with patients again after three years of theoretical work. An announcement at Evensong that a blind patient would like someone to read to her, led to a friendship that was to last until Mrs. G.'s death in 1961.

Mrs. G. was a remarkable person. One day she said to a student, 'Some people read their Bible and find help there, others can go to church and find it there, but He deals with me differently, He sends me people.' He certainly did. Cicely was not the only person to be influenced by her; nurses, doctors, consultants all fell under her spell and many people's lives were changed by nursing Mrs. G.

Before she became ill, Mrs. G. had been very shy, but her increasing dependence led not, as one might have expected, to withdrawal, but to a lively independence of spirit and a tremendous interest in other people. She lived more and more intensely as her physical limitations increased; her cubicle became the best clearing house for gossip in the hospital and nurses had to be dissuaded from staying with her too long. The sister would call out 'Don't entertain them, Mrs. G.!' There was something about her which seemed to bring out the best in everyone who met her. Despite blindness, useless jerking limbs and finally total helplessness, she was always fun to be with. Cicely, herself blessed with a good sense of humour, enjoyed her laughter. 'She had a delicious sense of the ridiculous, and especially of the ridiculousness of her own crippled body. She neither pitied it nor hated it; there it was and like everything else in life could be laughed at. From behind the curtains came muffled giggles from the nurses, from the bathroom came quite uncontrollable laughter. It was so hard to remember that she was blind.'

Cicely spent hours with Mrs. G. and feels it was largely her friendship and emotional support that got her through medicine. She would see her almost every day, taking her out in a wheelchair on the rare occasions when she was well enough, reading to her, feeding her, even having her own meals in the hospital with her. And of course she told her about her plans for a hospice – every detail, every practical step was discussed with her over the years. In fact it was Mrs. G. who gave the place its name. Cicely was telling her about the concept of a hospice and Mrs. G. said, 'A place for travellers? Well, it will have to be St. Christopher's, won't it?'

Apart from the very real friendship that Cicely shared with these incurably ill patients, especially Louie and Mrs. G., she learnt from them about another sort of need – the difficulty of finding suitable accommodation for chronically ill people who needed specialised nursing. This realisation was later to become incorporated into her plans.

Cicely did not have to rely on her own observations of dying people or even on those of her contemporaries;

terminal care had not received much consideration, but people were beginning to look at the problem. In 1952 a survey was conducted by the Joint National Cancer Survey Committee of the Marie Curie Memorial Foundation and the Queen's Institute of District Nursing. They visited over 7,000 patients being nursed at home in 1951 and the first of their eight conclusions was the need for residential homes for these patients. 'It is obvious to us that considerable hardship exists in the cases of many families who are taking care of one member with cancer at home. In addition to providing skilled nursing treatment for the patient, the provision of residential homes would save much mental suffering, stress, and strain for the relatives. Beds in the hospitals might also be freed. We found that some old patients were very reluctant to leave their own homes, even though conditions were often deplorable. It is possible that they would be prepared to enter a residential home rather than a public institution. These residential homes would also admit patients for short specific periods in order to give their families a much-needed rest, or during domestic emergencies. These homes should not be regarded as homes for incurables, as they would also admit other groups of patients.'

A few years later the Gulbenkian Foundation commissioned a survey of terminal care in the United Kingdom. It was carried out by Brigadier Glyn Hughes and exposed a serious gap in the National Health Service. The Ministry of Health defined the responsibility of the hospital services as the 'care of the chronic bed-fast who may need little or no medical treatment but do require prolonged nursing care over months and years.' This was followed by the qualification that 'It is not regarded as the responsibility of the hospital authority to give all medical or nursing care needed by an old person, however minor the illness or however short the stay in bed, nor to admit all those who need nursing care because they are entering into the last stage of their lives.' Where then, could the dying patient needing nursing care be looked after? Even the places specifically labelled as 'homes for the dying', mostly run by religious orders or charitable institutions, did not emerge well from the report. 'Like many similar establishments run by religious organisations the patients receive all the love and care possible, but the conditions were far from satisfactory. The staff was inadequate, the accommodation was overcrowded and the investigator wondered whether one would wish one's own mother to die in such surroundings. No patient suffered from lack of nursing care but the beds were almost touching, there were no curtained cubicles, nursing amenities were scanty, and it was obvious that the organisation was strained for money and unable to provide the best facilities.'

John Hinton, in his book *Dying*, published a few years later still, presents perhaps the darkest picture of all. Writing about hospitals and institutions for the chronic sick, which included people with fatal cancer, he says, 'In spite of improvement, however, many of these places are quite unsuited to function as modern hospitals. They are often large, cold, damp buildings with no easy access from one part to another, so that it is difficult to get warm meals to the bedside and any equipment into the ward. The absence of lifts means that some patients, once upstairs, stay there until there is the awkward task of getting their bodies down again.'

J. H. Sheldon in his 1961 Report to the Birmingham Regional Hospital Board, refers to some of its old institutions as 'human warehouses' and 'hospital slums'. 'By and large they do not do more than provide storage space for the patients under conditions of considerable difficulty, and often unpleasantness, for the nursing staff. It was quite an experience to see bed-pans being stored for the night in the bath; to be told of female nurses having to queue up for the same lavatory as the male patients; to find the same room being used for the washing of bed-pans and domestic crockery; and to see nurses having to fill a pint pot with water in order to wash excreta from a bed-pan down an ordinary lavatory.' Sheldon talks of cheerless corridors, passages too narrow for wheel-chairs and bags of dirty linen left at the foot of stairways and spreading their smell throughout the building. Under these appalling conditions the staff did what they could for the patients. Hinton pays them a well-deserved tribute. 'The nurses battled on heroically. They emerged with far greater credit than we, who are still capable of ignoring the conditions which make muted people suffer. The dissatisfied dead cannot noise abroad the negligence they have suffered.'

Cicely's observations had preceded these reports, indeed she had already committed herself to reading medicine in response to them. She realised that her impressions were highly personal and localised, but she also knew that 'if you have a microscope on a very limited area, you may, in fact, get the truth, but you've got to look and see if this is your own bias or whether it is supported by other evidence.' Clearly it was. She had, as it were, seen the answer without seeing the whole of the question.

She had seen for herself the stark contrast between what was manifestly not being done for patients in the various hospitals she had worked in as a student (St. Thomas's, the North Middlesex, the Royal Cancer Hospital, the Bristol General) and the far more effective control of pain and alleviation of symptoms received by the patients at St. Luke's; she had heard patients and relatives talking about the difficulties of being ill at home – one by one the sad stories had made their impact on her; she had heard consultants write off dying patients, unable to cure so unable to care. Now she had objective confirmation that there was a real need, that there was a gap in medical care which needed to be filled. Her response was positive. It was not only that the dying were not cared for adequately, though that was certainly true; she had seen a better way, and the potential of a better way still. In the right setting, with the right care, death could be an achievement; to accept death, when it was inevitable, was not a negative thing to do.

But if she knew this, she knew also that she would meet resistance. Twelve years after the publication of the Marie

Curie Report she wrote with this resistance in mind: 'Some will find it shocking that we should speak of accepting or even preparing for death and will think that both patient and doctor should believe in treatment and fight for life right up to the end. They may question how anyone should be satisfied with what sounds like such a negative role. To talk of accepting death when its approach has become inevitable is not mere resignation on the part of the patient nor defeatism or neglect on the part of the doctor. Certainly they will take no steps to hasten its coming, but for both of them it is the very opposite of doing nothing. The patient may well achieve more in this part of his life than in any other, making of it a real reconciliation and fulfilment. This will do more than anything else to comfort the relatives and help them on to the road to normal living again. Who is to say how far the effects may reach?'

The need was there, of that there could be no question. The person to meet the need was there. Whether Cicely knew it or not, the time to act was approaching.

7

TIME TO ACT

To every thing there is a season, and a time to every purpose
under the heaven.

Eccles. 3:1

On June 24th, 1959, Cicely was reading *Daily Light*. This
selection of Bible readings, known affectionately to
evangelicals as 'Kangaroo exegesis' by reason of its irra-
tional linking of texts, was a constant comfort and source
of spiritual nourishment to Cicely as to many Christians.
She read it every day. But this day was to be special.

The reading was from Psalm 37. 'Commit thy way unto
the Lord; trust also in him; and he shall bring it to pass.'
Suddenly she knew, with complete certainty, that the
years of preparation and waiting were over; at last the
time had come when she must do something practical
towards realising the dream that had for so long motivated her life. It was as if the verse was intended especially for her. 'Somehow these words were the tap on the
shoulder to say "Now you've got to get on with it." It was
quite irrefutable, I couldn't possibly be disobedient to it.'

The call was clear, she must do something. But what?
What was the first step to take? In which direction should
she move? She did what she always did when in doubt, she
waited while this fresh yeast acted on the ideas ferment-
ing in her head. But this time the Lord was not telling her
to wait, as he had done when she was converted fourteen
years before, or after David Tasma died; now she had to
act. First she needed to be on her own to think, so she
arranged to go for a private retreat with the nuns of St.
Mary's, Wantage. She talked to one of the sisters, who had
the insight to say that she shouldn't ask for help from an
existing community. Instead she said, 'This is your own

vision, you've got to do it your way.' So Cicely spent a full day in one of the chapels, sitting in front of a beautiful wooden crucifix carved by a former Reverend Mother, meditating on the fourteenth chapter of St. John's Gospel and asking, 'Lord, what do I have to do?' As she went through it verse by verse she began to find the confidence she needed; by the evening, as she says laconically, 'it seemed to be sorted out'. Her vision had always been as much religious as medical – the retreat consolidated her dependence on the will of God; more than ever she was convinced that the whole venture was in his hands and that she was his instrument. A year later she wrote to the Bishop of Stepney, the Reverend Evered Lunt, 'the verse that I was given when I first began planning was "I am the way, the truth and the life." Nothing that is not his will can be any good at all and all that matters is to find that, isn't it?' That verse is from the chapter of St. John that filled her day's meditation; there was another from the book of Proverbs that was to be as important to her: 'In all thy ways acknowledge him and he shall direct thy paths.'

Cicely returned from Wantage confident about her calling and sure of its foundations, if still uncertain about exactly what the next move should be. She realised that the first priority was to put her thoughts on paper; she would not be in a position to communicate to other people, until her intentions were clear in her own mind. The very next day she wrote the first draft of 'The Need' and 'The Scheme' – two documents which were to be endlessly revised and re-written, but which in essence are all very similar. For the first time her distilled experience was committed to eight pages of closely typed, confident prose.

'The Need' is short and to the point. She quotes the Marie Curie and Gulbenkian reports to prove that the needs of patients dying of cancer were not only great, but, with an ageing population, growing. She continues: 'While it is important that most people should remain at home as long as possible, and true that many families will manage to take charge of the situation adequately, it is evident that many are staying there when they already need skilled institutional care, and that one of the main reasons for this is lack of proper accommodation.' She goes on to tackle, with tactful understatement, the care available at the time. 'Some are admitted to their treatment hospitals as emergencies. Many find this a great solace, but a busy general ward is rarely the right place for them. Others die in Nursing Homes, and while it is impossible to make generalisations, it is safe to say that many do not have anything approaching the care they need. Often their suffering is intensified by isolation and loneliness. There are a number of institutions founded to care for these patients exclusively, and they offer two things above all – love and care, stemming in most cases from the strong sense of vocation of the staff.' Influenced by her friends Alice, Louie and Mrs. G., she also stressed the need for provision for the badly disabled chronic patients, sometimes young, and frequently having nowhere to go but the geriatric ward; nor does she forget the elderly, whose need to be needed is, she claims, as great as their need for physical help. And she deals with the fear of intractable pain with the assurance that was becoming her hallmark. 'It is quite possible to keep the great majority of patients comfortable and free of pain, and there is no need to use large doses of opiates nor to be troubled with the evils of drug addiction. There is a need for more teaching on this subject for students as well as nurses and a new centre for this care should take some responsibility and try to help to fill this gap.'

'The Scheme' is remarkable for its confidence, its detail and for the fact, observable only with hindsight, that it so closely resembles the reality it was to become. The eleven years' gestation period, between the conception of the idea during David Tasma's last weeks of life and the moment she felt impelled to start planning, resulted in an easy birth; the child, like the goddess Athene, was born fully fledged. A visitor going round St. Christopher's today would be forgiven for not spotting many differences, apart from size, between the castle in the air and the hospice on the ground.

In this document Cicely outlines a plan for a 100-bed Home, mainly for patients dying of cancer, but including the possible admission of patients in the last stages of other diseases; there would be a ward for bed-ridden chronic patients and an annexe, with single rooms, for the elderly. She estimates the need for about a dozen nursing staff for each ward, a medical superintendent, some visiting specialists, an administrative assistant, a house mother, an occupational therapist, a part-time physiotherapist and some thirty domestic staff.

This first draft owes much, as Cicely readily admits, to St. Joseph's. She hopes to provide a feeling of belonging and permanence which 'will help both staff and patients to find something of the security that is so noticeable in a Home run by a religious community, and in which the staff may regard the work as a full vocation.' The staff were to be people who had chosen the work and loved it, but while she hoped that they would be as dedicated as the nuns she stipulates that they will be given proper off-duty time, unlike the ludicrously over-worked nuns, and already envisaged a small crèche for the married staff, both nursing and domestic, not only realising the practical advantages for the staff, but also that the elderly residents might profit from the presence of children. The sense of community, while not yet fully articulated, was already latent.

The central hospice idea, a combination of deeply rooted spirituality with the very best care that medicine can provide, while again not explicitly stressed, is implicit throughout the document. The religious basis of the Hospice permeates her whole approach; the central position of the Chapel, with room for wheel-chairs and beds, the inclusion of prayers in the wards 'to be conducted by the staff as part of their daily work', the addition of four theological students acting as male orderlies and porters, who would, she hoped, have plenty of time to talk to patients. Her style of writing is openly religious. She stresses that the Home will be open to people of any religious persuasion or of none, but hopes 'to render higher and more valuable service to our patients in their spiritual and mental than in their physical wants. These will, all the same, go hand in hand, for faith in God is made infinitely easier by the faith in man which is created by the touch of kindness and the relief of pain and discomfort. Our Lord himself sent his disciples out both to heal and to teach; and work which combines both may have something of his own gracious presence. Though we cannot heal, there is a great deal that can be done to relieve the suffering of every dying person.'

She is adamant that religion is not going to be forced on anyone. 'Considering how little used many patients are to paying attention to religion, it is necessary that they be approached with tact and gentleness and that they should suffer from no surfeit of food to which they are unaccustomed.' She is aware too, that some of her readers might find it hard to equate religion and efficiency; 'Although this will be a religious foundation in spirit this does not mean that there will not be a thoroughly businesslike approach to the problem of finance . . . there is no reason that I can see why such an approach should not be to the glory of God and for the welfare of the patients and the best possible use of money must be in the forefront of our minds always.'

The medical side of 'The Scheme' is thinner. This is not a reflection of Cicely's priorities, it was simply that she took it for granted that the medical care would be the most expert and advanced available. The emphasis was not on cure, it is unlikely a patient would be admitted if there was a chance of significant improvement, but on skilled, confident nursing and the experienced use of drugs. Money was to be spent on *time* rather than on elaborate equipment. 'The staff will not have acute emergencies to cope with, nor complicated treatments to prepare or carry out, but can spend their time making their patients comfortable.'

Making patients comfortable is something Cicely planned to do in countless different ways. First and foremost was the control of pain and the alleviation of symptoms, but every detail is imaginatively planned; wards are to be divided into four- or six-bed units and placed 'so that the patients can see the life of the world outside and yet not have the light directly in their eyes or the draught round their necks.' It should be possible to push beds around almost as freely as one might walk – into the garden or the chapel or the dayroom, even nearer another patient for a chat. These dayrooms should have an open fire and the chairs in them must be 'comfortable and rather upright'. Everything must look pleasing and homely. 'Decoration must be imaginative and colourful, as much for the sake of the relatives as the patients. It is good to have something to watch, and for this a fish tank is more suitable and more restful than a budgerigar.'

Cicely is clear that she does not want the hospice to be part of the National Health Service. 'We want to be independent because we need freedom of thought and action; we want to be an inter-denominational but a religious foundation, and we want freedom to develop and expand as we are led to do so.' But she does want arrangements with the Regional Hospital Board, whereby they send patients to the Home and pay for them; she is also anxious to be part of the local community, encouraging liaison with the hospitals and doctors who send patients, so that the patients should not feel deserted.

Finance is dismissed in a few paragraphs. Her estimate in 1959 was £200,000 but this does not seem to alarm her. If the Lord is behind the venture, that will not present her with a problem. 'We do believe that if this is truly planned by Him then the giving of money as well as of service will have his guidance and will be evidence of his blessing.'

Cicely had not written a recipe which simply had to be followed, it was to be an organic structure and would change. There was, for instance, little emphasis on teaching in this original scheme, simply a general encouragement that there should be a warm welcome for anyone interested in the work; there was no reference to

research, which was to become so important; home care
was not mentioned. Few of the staff were to be resident, as
she originally intended; there was uncertainty about
whether it was better for patients to die in the main wards
or in single rooms; the balance between religion and
medicine was not yet confidently struck and she does not
realise that she is, in effect, founding a community. Nevertheless, the bones of the future St. Christopher's are there,
both structurally and ideologically; the changes inevitable
in its fleshing out and growth were surely based. It was the
thoroughness of this scheme, the depth of experience
underpinning it and the loving attention to detail that
were to determine her ability to win support.

Her thoughts on paper, precise enough to communicate
her vision, adaptable enough to allow room for change,
Cicely's batteries were fully charged. From then on, she
says, it was as if God were saying 'I will give you the
opportunities and you've got to wring every last bit out of
them. The people and what they said were the opportunities; it was just being alert and attentive to what was
happening.' She prayed that the right people would come,
they would then 'wait for the leading of the spirit should
he want to draw us together more definitely.' Her prayers
were answered. The early stages of St. Christopher's was
about people. The patients themselves, the source of her
vision, and others, one leading to the other, each contributing something – ideas, contacts, money, prayers, expert knowledge or simply friendly support. The next few
years were to be filled with this interaction, for though
there was never any doubt whose decision it would be in
the end, she sought advice, listened and profited from the
exchange.

As soon as the last page of 'The Need' and 'The Scheme'
was off the typewriter, she sent a copy to Brigadier Glyn
Hughes, the author of the Gulbenkian report *Peace at the
Last*, who she had met briefly two years earlier; another
copy arrived on the desk of Betty Read, then head social
worker at St. Thomas's, with whom Cicely had worked as
an almoner. By the end of the year she had collected what

she calls 'an amorphous body of friends I could ring up
and talk to'. In fact it was not such an amorphous group;
whether consciously or not, she had gathered round her a
balanced collection of people, all focusing on the central
issue with shared Christianity but diverse professionalism. Brigadier Hughes, after his extensive research into
the care of the dying, had a view over the whole situation
unsurpassed by anyone in the country; Betty Read not
only offered her experience as an almoner and her level-
headed Christianity – a sort of consultant service Cicely
called it – but was the source of invaluable introductions,
first to Brigadier Hughes, later to others who would help
in the daunting and essential task of raising money. On
the medical side there was Professor Harold Stewart, the
head of Pharmacology at St. Mary's, invaluable for his
interest in pain control; Peggy Nuttall, a former nurse,
who, as editor of the *Nursing Times*, had commissioned
Cicely's first articles on the care of the dying; and Dr.
Brinton, a neurologist and ex-Dean of St. Mary's and a
member of the Archbishop's Commission on divine healing. Even the people who felt their main contribution was
prayer and support, like Madge Drake and Rosetta Burch,
also had some expertise: Madge, who felt prayer was all
she could bring, ran a convalescent home; Rosetta contributed her skill as an almoner, though she felt her real use
was more personal. 'I knew Cicely so well that I could see
what would suit her style and what wouldn't. For instance
I knew that she must do everything with the highest
professional standards possible. I knew if something
wasn't all right for Cicely.' There was Miss Edwards, also
a former nurse, then working at the King's Fund Nursing
Divison, and Jack Wallace, a solicitor who gave hours of
work to the Home for virtually no financial reward. He
considered it part of his Christian work to help look after
St. Christopher's affairs and was devoted to Cicely. His
widow says, 'He was so *proud* of Cicely, he *purred* in her
presence.'

Though Cicely discussed all aspects of her vision with
everyone, there was some specialisation built into her

choice of people, most crucial at this stage being Dr. Olive
Wyon and the Bishop of Stepney, with whom she discussed
the spiritual foundations of the hospice. Dr. Wyon was in
her seventies at the time. She had been Principal of a
women's theological college in Edinburgh and was a wise
woman with views on ecumenism well beyond her time.
The Bishop of Stepney was the Right Reverend Evered
Lunt, whom Cicely had met at St. Joseph's. She came to
rely on him deeply and he became the first spiritual leader
of St. Christopher's, known as 'The Visitor'.

Cicely has a great gift for attracting people to her vision.
Though the group was to change constantly, some, like Dr.
Brinton, dropping out, many more arriving later, already
there was a strong and loyal nucleus. Given the problems
ahead, she needed them.

It might seem that the first things Cicely would have to
worry about would be medical, organisational and financial. In fact this was not so. What they needed to do
medically had been clear to Cicely for some time. She had,
after all, been studying the care of the dying for over a
decade and was confident that she could relieve all pain
and most discomfort. The organisational side was just a
matter of hard work and she was sure the money would
come once people knew of the venture. Her certainty that
'If it's right it'll happen' runs right through the conception
and growth of the hospice. She also had the conviction of
her own destiny without which an enterprise on this scale
can only be stillborn. There is a delightful mis-type in a
letter to Jack Wallace. She writes 'I do believe that the
Lord means someone of this kind to come to pass.' On
another occasion she quotes and clearly identifies with,
the missionary Gladys Aylward who said, 'I am not like
Moses, but God is the same as the God of Moses and can
work even through me.' And in the margin of her Bible she
wrote, 'Apart from Him I can do nothing. All the fruit that
I ever bear or can bear comes wholly from His life within
me. No particle of it is mine as distinct from His, there is,
no doubt, some part of His whole purpose that He would
accomplish through me. That is my work, my fruit, in the

sense that I and not another am the channel of His life to this end; but in no other sense.' She had a truly God-centred vision, she had abundant medical qualifications, she had drive, energy and commitment. But there was still a good acreage of ground to be cleared before she was ready to start raising money, still less building. Was it to be primarily a medical or religious foundation? Was the religious side to be rooted in a particular denomination or wing of the church, and if so which? Was she in reality founding a community? And if that was the direction in which she was being led, what sort of community? Would it follow the rule of the religious orders or would she have to devise some new sort of community? These were the questions that were to preoccupy Cicely and her group of friends for the next two years.

Her first letter to Brigadier Glyn Hughes kindled a swift and encouraging reaction; he told her that he would show her scheme to the secretary of the Gulbenkian Foundation, that it was just the sort of thing he had suggested in his report and that 'they might fall for yours'. But Cicely was cautious. She wrote to Betty Read, 'All this is very exciting, but I do want to keep my feet on the ground and not be swept into something where I shall not have the amount of control or, more important, the religious foundation which I think is imperative.' Six months later she was 'still going around in circles in my planning of the Home . . . the religious basis and the idea of some sort of community are the most difficult aspects to get sorted out.' She was determined it would be broadly based on the Church of England and not just one wing of it, but she found it easy and natural to work with people of different denominations, as her happy experience with the Roman Catholic nuns of St. Joseph's bore witness. There she had seen medicine and religion work hand in hand, but she was not intending simply to copy St. Joseph's, though it was a prototype of what she had in mind; her medical aspirations were higher and she had not the backing of an established religious order. Help was to come from Dr.

Wyon. Cicely went to see her in the spring of 1960 and wrote gratefully, 'I feel that I have been floundering around in rather a fog for quite a long time, and you showed me one of the first really strong beams of light and I have no doubt as to the real source.'

The light that Dr. Wyon shed was that Cicely was not just doing a medical work as a Christian, nor was she just a Christian who happened to be a doctor; she realised that Cicely had both a medical and a spiritual vision, that the two were inextricably mingled and that it was good that this should be so. This apparently simple statement resolved what was becoming a real dilemma for Cicely. She had been confused by questioning on this. For instance, a meeting with Bruce Reed, a consultant in Christian charitable work she met through Jack Wallace, had worried her by not understanding the dual nature of her vision. She wrote him a long letter in which she repeated back to him what she believed he had been saying. 'You asked me more than once what I thought I was really aiming at. You were not certain whether my vision was a spiritual or a medical one. Whether my interest in the medical side – the control of pain and so on, and my desire to spread my knowledge of how to do that – was really more important to me than my desire that every patient in our Home and in many similar Homes elsewhere in England should come to know the Lord.' Dr. Wyon, by sanctioning her previously unformulated desire to do both, touched a deep chord in Cicely. She believed that she was 'trying to do two things as one so often is. I feel very strongly that there are two poles which are saying quite different things and letting the sparks fly between them rather than trying to put them together.' Dr. Wyon's insight allowed Cicely to be stimulated by any tensions between medicine and religion rather than being torn apart by them.

Rosetta Burch elaborated this important point. She was, says Rosetta, not a spiritual leader with a medical vision but a Christian doctor. 'To the outside world your Home must be first and foremost a medical concern. The patients and relations will look upon it as that; people who are going to give money in large amounts must look on it like that or they won't give you money. You are a doctor (nurse and almoner) with a medical training and experience and with a medical job to do in your Home. That is the medical aspect; then there is the spiritual – that is, in order to do the job properly it must have a spiritual backing and people to work under you who are spiritually equipped to help your patients. In order to be able to do this they will need to be Christians of devotion and maturity, and I have always assumed that there will be some kind of corporate worship and prayer amongst the staff as a regular, necessary part of the Home.'

In a sense Rosetta and Dr. Wyon were telling Cicely something she already knew, but which needed their encouragement to emerge onto a fully conscious level. But it was not hard for Cicely to assimilate and articulate. Perhaps her clearest formulation was to Bruce Reed. 'I long to bring patients to know the Lord and do something towards helping many to hear of Him before they die, but I also long to raise the standards of terminal care throughout the country, even where I can do nothing about the spiritual part of the work.'

Dr. Wyon also encouraged Cicely to go ahead on the medical and administrative side, even if the spiritual foundations were not firm. And on the spiritual side she helped Cicely further by recognising Cicely's changing position within the Church of England. She realised that, while deeply grateful to the evangelical Christianity which had converted her, and to All Souls', that had nourished her for so long, Cicely was 'bursting out of her chrysalis'; that although she did not want to lose what she had been given, she was searching for something wider. Cicely knew well that her whole spiritual Odyssey was involved in the Home, how could she be sure of the Christian foundations of the hospice if she were not sure of her own? Her friends were loyal and patient, their views offering her a bewildering choice, from the broad spectrum she was eventually to embrace to a narrow evangelicalism from which she was struggling to escape. John Stott, the

rector of All Souls', and Jack Wallace, wanted an evangelical committee, feeling that 'so many evangelical
causes have been lost to the Lord, because ultimate control
has been taken out of the hands of the convinced
minority.' They were, however, prepared to welcome non-
evangelicals because, as Jack Wallace wrote, 'evangelicals tend to fly above the rafters and never get down to
earth at all.' On the other hand, the Bishop of Stepney
referred to her work as 'an ecumenical adventure'. No
wonder Cicely anguished for so long.

It was in her conversations and correspondence with
the Bishop of Stepney that this question of the religious
basis of the Home came into even sharper focus. In the first
place she had written to him asking for his advice and
guidance about bringing people of different denominations together. This led, not only to confronting her own
spiritual position but to the hard rock of practicalities,
when she had to consider the Terms of Trust, which had to
be drafted before they could become a registered company
or apply for charitable status and which had to be accept-
able to people who might fund them. 'Of course,' she wrote
to him, 'we would welcome patients of all denominations
or none, and of course we would welcome anyone who
wanted to come and work with us, although they must be
able conscientiously and faithfully to take ward prayers.
But I do want a Church of England chaplain, and I do want
to celebrate Communion regularly in our Chapel,
although I would like to welcome other people to take
services from time to time, and I do not know really
whether I am able, conscientiously, to apply for an undenominational grant.' It was a scrupulously honest struggle. She had no intention of accepting money under false
pretences, and there was a minimum level of formal
Anglican commitment beneath which she could not go. All
the time, she was becoming less exclusive, more ecumenical; in just over a year she had moved from a feeling that
she could not be exclusively evangelical, through a wider
Anglicanism, to a decision that it should be 'an interdenominational foundation'; further, she wanted to be sure

that this was enshrined in the Terms of the Trust. She wrote to the Bishop, 'I have felt increasingly (and here I find that I have rather lagged behind the rest of the committee) that this type of work cannot be exclusive in any way. I was afraid, as I told you, that the work would not remain if we did not have some definite allegiance, yet I could no longer be exclusively evangelical. So I believed that perhaps we should try and found a definite Anglican work. But yet that has not seemed right either as I have thought and prayed about it. I cannot be exclusive at all. It would surely be very wrong if we found ourselves outside any movement for Church Union by virtue of our constitution or regulations?'

Closely entwined with the spiritual basis of the Home was the question of community. Was she founding a new community, a lay order within the Anglican church? Or was it simply a group of people sharing a common aim? She felt it was beyond her capacity to bring people of high and low Church persuasion to pray and work together; indeed she felt more than a little overwhelmed by this new dimension to her work. Her problems here must be seen in the light of the religious climate of the time. Not only was a truly ecumenical attitude the preserve of the few, but Cicely and her scheme for a Home were ahead of the wave of communities, ecumenical, denominational and lay, that were to spring up all over Europe and America during the sixties. Further, the Second Vatican Council, that was to clear the air of so much religious prejudice, had not yet started its sessions.

As with the wrestling over the spiritual foundations of the Home, Cicely's views modified as she prayed, thought and discussed; as before, her views progressed quickly from confusion to some sort of clarity. This initial confusion is seen in some notes she wrote for discussion with Jack Wallace. She wrote, 'I quite agree that what I am in effect being led to do is to establish a dedicated spiritual order, and what I have been trying to find out is whether this does inevitably mean a spiritual discipline and rule with a recognisable basis.' But later in the same paragraph she says, 'I do not believe that I am in the van of a new spiritual movement, I know that is away out of my spiritual capacity. All I know is the way the Spirit has been leading me so far. If it is His way it will be all right if we follow Him slowly. I do not feel that we need hurry over this. It need not hold us up now. We may not know till we begin.' However, despite this apparent contradiction, only weeks later her thoughts were clarifying, as she wrote to her former Oxford tutor, Miss C. V. Butler, 'Now, though I have mentioned a "community" I do not mean that in a sense in which it is used by the religious orders, but as a group of people rather closely held together by their common aims and Christian beliefs.'

Once again Bruce Reed seems to have confused her, but by confusing helped to bring a resolution closer. He felt that the formation of a community should be her first task and suggested three ways in which this might be done. It could be formed in co-operation with an existing order, by the formation of a new community or as a secular work with some degree of Christian background and direction. He even suggested, to Cicely's horror, that a letter to the press could be the first step to finding the right people. Cicely had enough experience of letters from cranks to avoid this and if she was thrown off course it was not for long; her instinct was to rely on God and let things happen organically. She told Jack Wallace that she had enjoyed the meeting with Bruce Reed and found it helpful, though she didn't agree about the formation of a community first and foremost. 'So far the Lord has sent me quite a few people who have seen something of this vision . . . I'm quite sure that if He really wants someone like me to be in some way the founder of something really as important as a new type of work or order, then He will be very definite in sending people with the same feeling and burden. I would much rather leave it to Him, and go on with things which I do see more clearly. I have always been very lucky in having very definite guidance.'

The question of community was always a means to an

end, not an end in itself. What Cicely wanted, passionately, was a setting which would give a real feeling of security, first to the patients and secondly to the staff. Dr. Wyon, who had made a study of communities, again saw her vision most simply and clearly. In a statement she prepared setting out the aims and basis of the Home she wrote, 'It is planned that the staff should form a community, united by a strong sense of vocation with a great diversity of outlook in a spirit of freedom. They all desire to make St. Christopher's a Home to all who come.' Unity of aim, diversity of talents and religious persuasion – this seemed as near as Cicely was going to get to solving the problem of community for the time being. They had to be, as she later expressed it, 'A community of the unlike'. At the end of a year or so wrestling with this problem she simply put it on one side. She wrote to Dr. Wyon, 'It does not seem right to think very much more along the lines of a community for this Home at the moment. I think if we are going to be drawn more closely in this work, that it will happen when we get there. Anyway, there has not been any leading in that direction so far. I do not think this is just because I am lazy (although I am) but one seems to have to cope with one aspect of this whole problem at a time. Probably because one only has energy after usual work to cope with so much.'

It is easy to forget that through this whole period Cicely was doing a more than full-time job at St. Joseph's – it is almost comic that she should refer to herself as lazy. Once she had received the clear call when, as she says, 'The Lord told me to get a move on,' she worked tirelessly: any spare time she had was filled with meetings, letter-writing, visits to St. Joseph's to show interested people the sort of things she had in mind, retreats, prayer groups, supper parties – even so, it was nearly a year before an offer of money for her work made her realise that she had to complete the Terms of Trust and apply to the Inland Revenue for charitable status. She decided that this should be drawn up by a small group of 'Trustees', who would be the legal owners of the Home. This group con-

sisted of Jack Wallace, Rosetta Burch, Madge Drake, Miss
Edwards and her brother Christopher. Christopher had an
important role at this stage. He had just been to Harvard
business school and he applied what he had learnt to his
sister's project. It was he who helped her with the hier-
archical structure of the Home and made her realise fully
what she was already beginning to accept, that just as a
school has a headmaster, a business a managing director,
so a Home such as she was planning had to have some
central person – Christopher's word was 'an autocrat' –
and that person had to be Cicely. She could not escape the
realisation that however much help she got, when it came
to a decision, it had to be hers. She wrote to Jack Wallace,
'In a little while I think I will be getting more dogmatic
and stop asking advice, but I do pray it will be of the Lord
rather than just of me,' and to Miss Butler, 'Our discussions so far seem to lead up to the fact that I've got to
consider being rather an autocrat, I hope a benevolent
despot.'

All these complex and delicate issues – the balance
between medicine and religion, the spiritual foundations
of the hospice, the nature of the community – were not
merely abstractions. The talking and praying which led to
their eventual incarnation in St. Christopher's had to be
articulated in the cold, clear language of a legal document.
The Certificate of Incorporation, making St. Christopher's
a 'Company Limited by a guarantee and not having a
share capital' was registered at the beginning of 1961 and
signed by Jack Wallace and his partner, Madge Drake,
Betty Read, Rosetta Burch, Cicely and her father. The
anguish over the spiritual foundations was resolved, to
everyone's satisfaction, in three short lines saying simply
that there would be a building 'to be used by the Association as a church or chapel available for Christian
worship'; further, there were three other dimensions of
Cicely's vision, hinted at in her first draft, now given
concrete expression. The Association would promote research into the care and treatment of the dying; it would
encourage the teaching and training of doctors and

nurses; it would provide care, not only in the Hospice itself, but also 'in their own homes'. It was this combination of research, training and care, either in the Hospice or at home, that was to make St. Christopher's unique.

8

ANTONI

> He shall be as the light of the morning, when the sun riseth,
> even a morning without clouds; as the tender grass springing
> out of the earth by clear shining after rain.
>
> 2 Sam. 23:4

In the midst of all this activity – working at St. Joseph's,
planning St. Christopher's, meeting countless people interested in her vision – Cicely, at another level, was living
through a relationship of piercing intensity. She called it
'the hardest, the most peaceful, the most inhibited and the
most liberating experience I have ever had'.

Antoni Michniewicz was a patient in St. Joseph's. He
was Polish and had left Poland as a prisoner during the
war, eventually serving in the army in the Middle East;
his wife had died four years earlier and though he had
friends, his only close relative was his daughter Anna. He
was a devout catholic and everyone who met him was
impressed by him; by his faith, his gentleness, his dignity,
his courtesy. He was rather special to all the staff of St.
Joseph's, including Cicely, but for a long while he was just
that – a patient she liked and admired. For six months he
had fought to live, at least until his daughter passed her
examinations. When at last Anna heard her results Cicely
went to the ward while she was visiting her father to
congratulate her. Antoni's eyes filled with tears and
Cicely took his hand. 'At which he kissed it and Anna said,
"My father has so much fallen in love with you, doctor."
Then he said "I do not know how to express it and please do
not be offended." And I said "Indeed no – I am grateful."
And I left them. But my world was suddenly unmade
without warning.'

That evening she went back to the ward and they talked

103

about his daughter. His English was not very good – it
was after all his eighth best language – and Cicely felt
they were rather at cross purposes. 'Then I sat on his bed
and he asked me if he was going to die. And I said "Yes".
And he said, "Not long?" and I said "No". And he said
"Thank you. Was it hard for you to tell me that?" And I
said, "Well, yes – it was." And he said "Thank you. It is
hard to be told, but it is hard to tell too, thank you." And
then I held his hand and we talked for about a quarter of
an hour.' It was the first time for years that Antoni had
been able to talk so freely, he had almost forgotten how to.
Suddenly they were meeting in a new way.

It was a Friday, and Cicely was going away for the
weekend to stay with the Wests; on the journey she began
to realise what had happened. She was once more falling
in love with a patient, a dying patient; they could meet
only briefly and publicly – Antoni's bed was in the middle
of a six-bed ward – and they would not have long. Knowing how much she would forget, most certainly recalling
David, and how little she had to remember him by when he
died, Cicely kept a diary of her talks with Antoni. For a
long time she had been writing out a prayer each day
based on a morning reading. To these she now added her
conversations with Antoni and how things were for them.
No words can rival her own.

She wished she had known sooner. So often he had asked
her to wake him when she was there and sometimes, if he
was asleep, she had left him sleeping.

And now I cannot do anything about him except pray.
And there are so many things I would like to say and
hear about him. But it's silly really, for if he has gone
when I go back tomorrow he will know all he needs or
wants to know anyway, and will be safe in 'clear shining
after rain'. I wish I had given him more, I wish I had
known sooner, I wish I could help him through the very
last bit but I know it is in Thy hands O Lord and I leave it
there – or try to do so. Please comfort and help him and
his daughter as they part – and may he have abundant

entry into Thy presence and into fullness of joy. And all he needs.

Cicely had not intended to come back from her weekend until Monday, but she couldn't stay away. On Sunday evening she took some flowers for Antoni and for the other five patients in the ward.

He was weaker and could hardly speak. He said good nights and hardly had any pain at all. And he ate a little supper with me feeding him. And I said that I had come back to make sure he was all right. And that it wasn't pity, it was admiration. And that I would be in in the morning. He said 'Monday – a good day – Monday, Wednesday and Fridays are good days!' And he said, and repeated when I didn't catch it, 'For me, the day is easier when you come.' And he looked and smiled. And we said good night, and God bless you. He looked as if he would never be seeing me again and I think I did too. But he was too tired to turn his head when I left the ward.

O Lord, give him joy and peace in Thy presence and Thy full salvation and keep his daughter safe always.

When he was strong enough he told her of his life; how he used to spend the summers in a large estate in Poland, the winters in a flat in Wilno, that he used to sing and loved Schubert and Strauss, about the war, his time in Siberia, hobbies, the countryside, their shared passion for birdwatching. Cicely talked about her days as a medical student, her friends – Tom West, who Antoni had met and admired, and David Tasma. 'He was dear, very dear – but there is room in one's heart for more than one person and no one will take another's place.' And of course she talked about her plans for St. Christopher's. They never had more than an hour together and they knew the days were numbered. Each extra day was a gift.

27.7.60: Went over in the morning – and curtains round as I came in and my heart turned over but he was all

right. Though poor and tried to say something I couldn't
understand. So he said sadly, 'We don't understand each
other,' and then had a fit of coughing and I left him to get
some linctus with a sword in my heart. But at 1.30 he
was more alert and held my hand and said, 'I cannot tell
you how much it means to be visited by you,' and kissed
and kissed my hand and I held to his cheek but I couldn't
stay – we were in the ward.

Antoni had not yet come to terms with death. He would
say sadly to Cicely, 'I do not *want* to die, I do not *want* to
die.' Especially now.

'When I was a child and I saw a toy in a shop I said, "I
want that, I want it *now*," and all my life I am like that
and now I see what I want, and I know it is not for me.'
And I said 'Do you mean that?' and he said, 'Yes, I do.'
And I just said, 'Thank you' and I hope that no-one saw
us looking and smiling. Earlier as he held my hand he
had said, 'There are people looking on every side,' and
did not kiss it. And he noticed my watch and I said it had
belonged to my other Polish friend. And then I had to go
and he thanked me for coming to give him pleasure . . .
but ah, the pleasure was for me too – for he is very
precious.

Always they were inhibited by the awareness of the
people around them – the five other patients and their
visitors, the nurses going about their duties. Sister Antonia, who was in charge of the ward said years later that
she had no idea of the relationship between Cicely and
Antoni, it simply hadn't occurred to her or to anyone else
that such a thing could happen; had she known, she said,
she would have made a point of involving Cicely more in
his care. Perhaps they need not have worried so much. But
a doctor who falls in love with a patient has to be very
careful; Cicely could never escape the discipline of her
profession.

30.7.60: I did tell him that I loved him – rather – but that the Lord loved him much more and that was what mattered, not me. He made me repeat it to be sure. And just smiled. And then I said good night and kissed him swiftly – hoping that the Lord had put up a screen. O sleep well, beloved. I prayed a lot during the night for him, using the blessing from Numbers. O Lord, please may he stay a little longer. The Lord bless him and keep him, make his face to shine upon him and be gracious unto him, and lift up the light of His countenance upon him and give him peace, now and for ever.

Never had Cicely experienced such an outpouring of love and admiration. Unconsummated, unfulfilled, unresolved as it was, his love brought her a depth of peace she had never known before.

And he kissed and kissed my hand and stroked it and held it to him and said 'My love, my love, my only love.' And I held his to me, and we really had peace, alone and quiet, for quite a little while. And he said his breathing was hard and dry and he couldn't cough and I said I had been thinking and would try another pill, but O, I couldn't help really. And then he said that he was dry – and I said that the Lord knew – and had to explain that a bit. And he talked quite a lot about me with such love and admiration as made me feel very humble and ashamed, and he couldn't understand why I loved him, 'I can do nothing for you.' So I answered that being himself was enough. Then he said that when I went away everyone suffered – and I said I wouldn't again – (nor will I while he is there) and we were quiet and happy and just loving each other – till nurses came and lights on, etc. So I gave him his Chloromycetin and Ephedrine and said 'Good night and God bless you' and 'Be here tomorrow' and he said 'Be happy.' And, O I am, as long as he is here.

There were moments when Antoni seemed better; at one point he thought that Cicely had performed a miracle and that perhaps he wouldn't die. They longed for more time, though they knew they could not have it. 'Could we have one million years of eternity please – and we *would* be there – and that it didn't matter how long or short a time together.' And all through the short three weeks their love for each other mingled with love for their Lord.

4.8.60: Agony to wait till midday – and then I had an excuse to ring and so did just about know when I drove in – but it gets worse and worse. Short sessions and left photographs and books. Then busy until five when I just *took* an hour, I couldn't, couldn't help it. He felt breathless and looked most awfully frail but talked and talked – and looked and looked his love. I tried several times but couldn't leave. And at the end when I said, 'I love you, I love you, I love you,' very softly, he said 'I know, I too, but for you hard.' And I said, 'We are one in Christ Jesus,' and his face lit up and he looked at the crucifix in the next bay and said, 'I can see my Saviour.' I looked at the one above him, for that is what reminds me of where and only where we meet and love. So I said, 'He is my Saviour too, so that wherever we are, we are together.' And we loved and looked and were held for one brief moment of communion with our Lord and with each other.

The end was drawing remorselessly nearer.

I can tell him anything now, I think I have perhaps had my last long session – and this once again is how the world ends or rather, how my world ends – by screwing myself up to be controlled when by nature I am the reverse. O Holy Spirit, direct and hold me.

7.8.60: Had to make an excuse to ring this a.m. so at least I knew he was alive, but O the day was long till I got there at four forty. Nothing happening elsewhere so

I went along to him soon after five and had nearly a whole blessed hour . . . He was rather low and said 'Why short breathing?' and I said 'Lumps there' and he said 'Anything to do?' and I just closed my eyes in misery. But he is calm and quiet. He said he was sorry for me. 'For me it is all right, for you it is hard.' I said, 'Well you can see the crucifix over my shoulder and I over yours and when you are not here, He will still be there, and you will be with Him and it will be all right' . . . they lit the candles on the little table and he turned and looked at them so wistfully and they reflected in his eyes. Such a loving and longing person, and such perfect manners in all things and it is hard for a man to be so dependent.

10.8.60: He said, 'I am waiting till you come.' I said, I had a quiet heart. That if I could have a long time it was lovely and if I could have only a short time – it was enough. And he said, 'I want you beside me all day long,' and I agreed. He said, 'I can only hurt you. I can give you nothing but sorrow' and I said, 'The only way you could hurt me would be if you didn't love me anymore.' And I remembered E. M. Prescott, 'Love drinks up sorrow rejoicing,' and said so. And we talked of sharing and suffering for each other, and of the Lord. And we had such peace and quietness and confidence together . . . Later. We really just wanted to be quiet together, but that looks more suspicious than talking – so we did. Many things. 'I am not worth that you should care about me.' 'You are, you are, just because you are you.' 'Thank you.' And he hated suddenly finding pyjama buttons undone – and coughing – and having to spit into a mug – and felt so unworthy and yet we could forget it all (so much easier for me) and just love one another's company. And he brought out his fear of 'a very hard death-bed.' And I promised and I promised that I would somehow be there – but that the real thing was the Lord being there. He said, 'Will you give me injection?' with a sort of glint in his eye. And we talked of Him, and he said it helped him so, that he could see the crucifix. And he does truly love and trust Him. I remember how once long ago I had said something to him about all hard things being allowed to come to us in God's love – and how he said, 'But, of course,' as if he would say, 'But who would bother even to say so – of *course* that is so.' Now it is deeper for him, I believe. And I finally had to go, but still my heart is quiet – and I think his was too – and we could not touch at all but only look in love and caress with our eyes. And said good night and God bless and lighten your darkness. And he could wave.

And all the time Cicely was also Dr. Saunders, responsible for his care and his drugs as she was for so many others.

12.8.60: Rather poor when I came in – O_2 – bronchospasm. Settled with Ephedrine and Reassurance – and slept all morning and until three p.m. I did listen to his chest which meant that we held hands briefly. Then at five he had a lot of bronchospasm and looked very ill and frightened. 'Do please help me.' Isoprenaline, O_2, and Am. Supps between them dealt, and I hung around till six, when he was better. Then I stayed and talked a bit. Earlier had had Brigadier Glyn Hughes. 'I am glad your plans go well,' he said when I told him briefly. When he felt ill, he just automatically prayed. Nothing tremendous in talking – just quiet and loving and prayerful. And he could wave.

He went to prepare a place for us – by the Cross. He comes to fetch my dear love – by the Cross. And I watch and wait – by the Cross. We are together in Him, by Him, through Him.

Eventually Cicely stopped praying for him to live; he was so very ill, so tired. Sometimes love has to allow the loved one to die.

O Lord he is weary and I couldn't ask him to stay for me. Please take him home in Thy perfect time – and I don't ask for more; but take my hands off.

He too, came to accept, saying 'I only want what is right.' And their last days were filled with a strange peace. Cicely was with him on August 14th, a sunny summer afternoon, when he said 'It is getting dark.'

So I knew he was getting near. I told Sister and she said he should have his Viaticum, and so she set the table. He lay watching the crucifix and I went in for a moment to see he was all right. His eyes were wandering a little but he was there. When I said, 'Do you really want me to stay?' he said, 'Of course I want you . . . you are my . . . love or angel' he called me both and I didn't catch it then. And then he just looked at me with such quiet love and trust. And when I said, 'Please believe me, it isn't just I who have given, but you who have given to me, and I am grateful,' he said 'I believe you.' And we just stayed and looked at each other. And his eyes went down my face and over to the crucifix and back again. He was at peace. I think that was our best moment of all and really timeless. I do not know how long.

The next day he was distressed and asked for Cicely and for the first time for a while, as she helped the nurses, she saw his body.

He was so incredibly emaciated, I had not realised. Quieter, indeed almost semi-conscious till two p.m. Then more conscious and I was in and out (as I had been all morning), but now I lifted him up several times to see the crucifix (the only time I have ever held him in my arms) . . . and once could just rest my head against his for a second. Several times I gave him a drink and adjusted the mask. I began once to say 'The Lord is my Shepherd', but that puzzled him so I stopped. After that I didn't say anything. There was no need of words any more and there weren't really any thoughts in my mind either. He could see the crucifix I think — once he tried to make the sign of the Cross. And then, suddenly, he gave me a really heavenly smile. And as I think of it I am not certain of all that was in it. Not sorry at all. It looked so happy and there was certainly a gleam of amusement and strong somehow. And then that look of pure love, I have so often had from him. Then his eyes went down my face and wandered in weariness – but it was peaceful – and my feelings were quiet. I was just there to keep him as comfortable as I could. No time to think, no thoughts to come.'

Cicely was with him as he had his last injection and slipped into unconsciousness. He died an hour later. And the diary ends.

O Lord, I do not deserve so wonderful a gift in any way ever, but just accept it with open hands and heart. A quiet heart at last. And now he is comforted, and now he can see his Saviour, he is in His presence now and for evermore. And there I shall find him again. O Thank Thee, Lord Jesus. Amen.
And then so far to go . . .

Cicely was so happy with Antoni that she did not anticipate her grief while he was alive – but once he had died she was absolutely broken. She could hardly bear to go into the ward that had been their only home, the pain was so great; she thought and talked about him incessantly and exclusively; she cried herself to sleep for months. It was a long, she now feels a pathological, grieving.

It was through going on working and through the support of her friends that Cicely managed to keep going and eventually to integrate the experience into her life, but it was a bleak process. The first week she spent mostly with Betty West and Madge Drake, who both listened and supported her in their different ways. Betty, only just steady after her own widowhood and deeply grateful to the way Cicely had helped her husband to die peacefully and without pain, was able to understand her and comfort her more than anyone else. Her letters, full of insight and affection, treated the short relationship as seriously as if it had been a long marriage. Cicely was feeling 'so silly to be so completely lost after such a short time' and Betty's acceptance of it as a profound meeting between two people, irrespective of time or social convention, helped Cicely herself to realise its true significance. While Antoni was still alive Betty had written, 'All my thoughts of you are two-sided. I believe you are blessed beyond thoughts and yet my heart aches for you . . . you have been chosen to cherish Antoni M. *now* and help him – body, mind and spirit and he has been chosen to teach you more than you already know of what it means to love in the Lord – it's Heaven – and when he is safely there it will not seem quite so empty here as you expect.' Betty had not met Antoni, but she had listened long and well, and she writes with an understanding of his nature which must have been a special comfort to Cicely; she certainly appreciated the extent to which their love of each other was connected with their love of God. 'I am quite sure you are right when you say A.M. is ahead of you – I have thought so all along – he is not ahead because he is in heaven – that is a different thing – but because he had here on earth learned to love our Lord in a deeper way and this showed inevitably in all he was and in every word he spoke. I do not think this made any difference to your love for each other. You *both* love the Lord. The fact that he has gone further extended you very much – and continues to do so – love tends – brings about growth – it is not easy but neither will it strain.'

Cicely's relationship with Antoni was more important, more profound, more mature, than with David Tasma; but in one respect they are alike. After both deaths she was left to mourn with no past, no context, no shared life to remember. Her union with Antoni had not been blessed by Church or State or Society – once again she was without a role. How much easier it would have been had she been a widow. So she had to try to create a context, an environment for their love. She went to Polish films and read books about Poland; she found a sixteenth-century portrait in the Courtauld Gallery which was so like Antoni that it drew her back again and again; she listened to the Schubert and Richard Strauss songs that he had loved; later she went to Poland. She needed to be where he had been, to share something of his life.

The time may have been short, the circumstances unconventional, but there was a fiercer fire burning in those three weeks than many people experience in a lifetime. She had seen God and death and love in one face. No wonder it took her so long to assimilate. Plunged, as she was, into the heart of experience, she was surrounded by contradiction, caught in the play of opposites in a drama of almost cosmic proportions. In the midst of death she had been in life; at the bedside of a dying man, surrounded by the dying, she had lived more intensely than ever before; in the face of eternity, she had loved for three weeks, never sure which day, which hour, would be their last; she had found human love and she had lost it. The Lord had given and the Lord had taken away. Could she, like Job, say 'Blessed be the name of the Lord'? She had met Antoni at the borders of life and death; she had also met him in that seldom frequented place where human and divine love meet, overlap and exist together. The image of Cicely, sitting beside Antoni, seeing his face and the crucifix over his bed, while he saw her and the crucifix on the opposite wall, captures the essence of this extraordinary relationship. 'My real goodbye was this afternoon,' she wrote in her diary, 'when I had such a look of pure love and it was mingled with looks at his Saviour.' It was almost as if God and Man had become one in a new incarnation. 'And I had that last afternoon giving him his drink ("I thirst"), lifting him up and just being there in silence.' When Antoni died, was it almost as if God had died too? Yet she also had the human love, the admiration, the tender concern, that belongs to the relationship of a man and a woman. 'The supper came and he was wondering what to eat, decided on sausages and to be fed (his hands cannot hold things). I said I would feed him and he said "No," and when I said, "Please let me" he said "You mustn't. People will be looking. I am looking after you too."'

Desolate as she was, 'in such cold cloud and darkness', Cicely's mourning was filled with gratitude. Gratitude that she had loved and been loved after the long years of waiting and hoping, and by such a man; gratitude that he was now, as she was quite certain, at peace; gratitude that her heart had been quiet while he was alive, and in a strange way still was, through the agonising pain. She did not feel worthy of Antoni, but through him she felt 'lifted up to be so much better than myself'; she also had a constant sense of his presence. 'Just as I read of Poland, see a picture, hear that song – and think he has been here before – so I find he has been along the valley of weeping. That sense of his presence wasn't sought, can scarcely be held, shouldn't be grasped. But O Lord I am grateful.'

She began to realise how much she had grown through this relationship. She seemed to love God more because they had loved each other and one love had dissolved into the other; she related in a new way to all who suffer 'through war, persecution, prison, famine, nakedness, sword, refugees and the desolate and the oppressed'; and of course she identified especially with the bereaved. 'Because I belonged to him as never to anyone before so I belong to others – and to life itself more deeply. He gave me a way to others – to those who walk through bereavement and to others too – but I have to learn to use it and be ready to be involved and to try and understand them.'

David Tasma had helped her to find her calling; for twelve years his memory had motivated and sustained her work. Now Antoni lit up her vision of St. Christopher's in a new way. He gave her and her vision that special charge that only first-hand intense experience can bring and set the seal on her long preparation.

Through this 'glimpse of love in eternity in one golden moment of union with our Lord' she learnt, at the deepest and most subtle level, things that were to permeate St. Christopher's. She learnt that it is possible to live a lifetime in a few weeks; that time is a matter of depth, not length; that in the right atmosphere and with pain controlled so that that patient is free to be himself, the last

days can be the richest; that they can be a time of reconciliation that makes the dying peaceful and the mourning
bearable.

She learnt, with her whole being, that in work with
people the giving is two-way, the caring mutual. The
patient gives to the relative as much as the relative to the
patient; he gives as much to those who care for him as he
receives from them.

She knew that however great the pain, there was comfort. 'I have shared this grief and know that there is
something stronger behind it all – not an answer, no
explanation but a presence. We believe, many of us here,
that this is the presence of God who has shared our
suffering with no more than the equipment of a man and
who, having come through, shares the sorrows of all men
and will transform them.'

9

BUILDING

Creation is only the projection into form of that which already exists.

Srimad Bhagavatam, *The Wisdom of God*, III 2

The early 1960s, crucial in the planning and building of St. Christopher's, were deeply lonely and painful years for Cicely. On the one hand she knew what she had to do with her life and she was eager to press on with it, on the other her grief for Antoni was so great that she frequently reached the point where, without him, she simply didn't want to live.

It was to get worse. Early in 1961 her beloved Mrs. G. died and in June, while she was in Switzerland, she heard of her father's death. In under a year she had lost lover, friend and parent.

Cicely's grief for Mrs. G. though profound, was uncomplicated – the sadness of the loss of a close friend. The death of her father aroused emotions so painful, so complex, that she simply couldn't face them at all. Twenty years later she broke down, in a staff group on bereavement, still weeping the tears that she had not fully shed at the time.

Her father had not been well for some time. Cicely had spent a weekend with him to give Mrs. Diamant, a family friend, a rest; then, at his insistence, she went to stay at the community of Grandchamps in Switzerland, a visit Dr. Wyon had been urging her to make and which she had put off the previous year, realising that Antoni would die while she was away. As soon as she had settled in she went to see one of the priests and made her confession. It was the first confession of her life and her problems with her father loomed large; devoted though they were to each other,

117

their relationship was seldom free of the tensions that so often bedevil close relationships. The next morning she had one of those profound but elusive mystical experiences that words can never quite capture. 'I went into their beautiful big chapel and I spent ages going through Psalm 95, the *Venite*. Then I went out alongside the river and was sitting by the river bank with a great big tree behind me and the tree sort of changed into a huge cross which was for the world, and I had the feeling of "Come, for all things are now ready" which is one of the things they say before you go forward to Communion at Grandchamps.' She returned to the convent to find that she was wanted on the phone. Her father had died while she was sitting by the river bank.

Her grief was further complicated by the terms of her father's will. He had divided his considerable estate into fifths and left two-fifths each to Christopher and John and one-fifth to Cicely. Worse, she was only to get the income, the capital was to be under the control of her brothers.

Not surprisingly, Cicely saw this as a rejection and was furious. Though it can only be surmise, it seems that he had his reasons, which did not reflect his love for her. Other conditions of the will make it seem probable that he had a Victorian attitude to the division of money between men and women; it has been suggested that he felt Cicely could succumb to an unsuitable man, attracted by the prospect of her money; but the most likely explanation is that he was protecting her from her own generosity – she had a tendency to give money away with an open-handedness that made him nervous. She was by then forty-three and unmarried; he did not want to risk her coming to an impoverished old age.

While Cicely could express the anger she felt on this score all too easily, she could not acknowledge the deeper anger that surged within her at her triple bereavement. 'I was not able to be cross with God, maybe I should have been.' Her spiritual diaries speak of gratitude rather than complaint, 'We will rejoice in Thy Salvation O Lord, whenever we rejoice and we rejoice in Thee then we are together. A.M., my father, Mrs. G., all my patients. O Lord here is home and safety, here is strength and redemption, here is love. All in Thee and from Thee.'

She found some comfort in the Psalms ('and after all, they complain enough') and in a little book by Dr. H. C. G. Moule, published during the First World War as a manual of consolation for those who had lost relations or friends. The well-thumbed pages and marked passages indicate the way in which she struggled to make sense of her suffering. These passages concern not only the role of Christ as Healer, the 'Sufferer-in-Chief' who knows all about it, but the mystery of the joy at the heart of sorrow and the understanding that can be learnt through becoming a member of the community of suffering. 'Your loss, your pain, brings you into a sacred fellowship, a large yet intimate companionship . . . there is a fine and beautiful freemasonry in the shared experience of affliction . . . You are a privileged person; you have title and qualification for entrance into the fraternity . . .' This was where her consolation lay.

None-the-less she reached a pitch where, despite her dislike of introspection and self-analysis, she went twice to a psychiatrist. He encouraged her to recognise her anger, but although she saw the sense in this advice, it did not suit her nature or her Christianity. She told a friend – a nun in an enclosed Anglican order – about the psychiatrist's suggestion and her own instincts were reinforced by the letter she received in reply. 'I cannot think, though, that a Christian of your intelligence and with your faith can be helped by the cathartic of anger. Anger is a sin for a Christian and to indulge in it deliberately is only, surely, to lay up more sense of guilt in store. God has shown us a better way, and in this particular matter it would be better to follow your redeemer than your psychiatrist I would think.' Later Cicely discovered that anger and Christianity need not be mutually exclusive, but at the time her needs were met more by religion than psychology; by the wise counsel of Evered Lunt, Bishop of Stepney, and in talking to Metropolitan Anthony Bloom, who she had recently come to know and admire. His words rang true. 'The pilgrimage is plodding along and if you fall in the mud, don't sit and make a fuss about it, just sit up, brush it off and get going. When you get to Paradise they'll take off your clothes and deal with the mud and you'll be all right.'

So she plodded along, showing a smiling face to her patients while she went through her own private purgatory. Her father had said to her the weekend before he died, 'You have been prepared in some rather strange ways for what you are going to do' and this intense suffering was a vital part of her preparation. There is no substitute for experience. 'At least I know from inside what it's like. I won't ever cry it down. It *does* feel like the end of the world. I had to do this work and though I wanted to do it, I could hardly bear to go on living. I often thought how nice it would be to die.' Her pain took her to rich depths – depths that were to be the source of her ability to comfort the dying and bereaved and to understand their needs. She was coming, painfully, to a rare understanding of crucifixion, of suffering and of wholeness. Her spiritual diary of the time speaks much of this. 'August 1961: Thou shalt break them in pieces like a potters vessel. O Lord Jesus I am, we are – (Lord forgive my selfishness even in prayer) only safe with Thee. O Lord we will only be whole when Thou has broken us in pieces. O Lord please do not let me go back into enclosed and selfish indulgence. O Lord please help me to see Thy way and serve Thee to-day. In Thy name, Amen.' It was this understanding for which she was grateful. '25.8.61 I know their sorrows. Always that is the wonder of it. O Lord Jesus, who meets all of us in all our griefs – I am so grateful to you. Thou hast wounded and Thy hands are making whole. O Lord I pray for guidance and strength as I cope with all this. Rather I pray for true abandonment to Thee. And I commit all those who are so wounded to Thy hands. In Thy name, Amen.'

The suffering of this period of Cicely's life, the confusion – 'I got my bereavements muddled up' – and the intense spiritual activity, were the throbbing background to an outer life of endless industry. By 1961 St. Christopher's was a charity ready and eager to receive money, and as such it had to have a Council of Management. Jack Wallace, who had worked so hard on the legal problems, became the first chairman;* Cicely's father, who had been vice-chairman for the last months of his life, was succeeded by Professor Stewart; Captain Lonsdale, a man much involved in charitable work, took on the job of honorary treasurer (their funds at the time of his appointment consisted of David Tasma's five hundred pounds) and Miss Muriel Edwards, who had just retired from King Edward's Hospital Fund, became the first secretary. They were supported by people like Betty Read, Peggy Nuttall, Madge Drake and Rosetta Burch. The 'amorphous body of friends' had hardened into an official committee.

Cicely's father, who had once wished that his daughter would work with the living rather than the dying, ended his life with a deep appreciation of what she was doing. She remembers him saying, 'I thought all my children were good, I did not know I had a world beater.' He was grateful that he had been able to help her realise her dream – one way in which he had helped was by impressing on her the need for credibility in the eyes of the world. He insisted that when it came to finding a firm of accountants, they should be well-known; it was his idea that she should have a group of people, who came to be known as 'Vice-Presidents', who would not be expected to give much in the way of time, but who could provide something the embryonic Hospice needed just as much – their names and support. Cicely has always been able to mix enlightened liberals with strict evangelicals, businessmen and doctors, friends and acquaintances, and this presented no problem to her. First to fall victim to her powers of persuasion was Lord Amulree, the Liberal Whip and geriatrician, who she persuaded to be their first Vice-

---

* Cicely was told that she must have a better known chairman if she was to impress charitable trusts and he was succeeded two years later by Lord Thurlow. Jack Wallace's 'unique humility' in stepping down and continuing to help St. Christopher's impressed Cicely deeply.

President. Soon she had an impressive list of people prepared to back her in this way, introduce her to others and allow their names to be quoted. Sir Donald Allen of the City Parochial Foundation was the spider in the middle of the web – he knew everybody in the world of fund-raising; Sir Kenneth Grubb, Vice-President of the British Council of Churches, soon joined him; as did Lord Taylor of Harlow, prominent in both medicine and politics. He gave her both practical and moral support. After a long interview at the House of Lords he said, 'I wish I could help – this is such a jolly good thing, but it's going to happen, isn't it?' When Cicely said 'Yes' he assured her again. 'You know it will, don't you? I am sure that this will come about, it is just that you have got to find the right way to do it.'

At about the same time, as a result of a paper she read in the Blackpool Health Conference, she met someone who not only supported her inside the Ministry of Health and with the Regional Hospital Boards, but who eventually came to work as her Deputy Medical Director, Dame Albertine Winner (then Dr. Winner). 'Cicely came to see me in the Ministry of Health and described everything, practically as it is now. I thought, "This woman's mad." I, who am a civil servant, had kittens about the way she approached the questions of budgets, but her vision was both detailed and practical. She is a visionary.' Dr. Winner introduced her to Dr. Fairlie, the Senior Administrative Medical Officer of the South-East Metropolitan Regional Hospital Board, 'and of course she bowled him over too'. She had the same success with Dr. Godber (later Sir George), the Chief Medical Officer at the Ministry of Health.

There was always the possibility that the Ministry of Health would take Cicely's vision as a criticism of the existing services, in fact Cicely anticipated this when she asked Dr. Winner if she felt her scheme was something the National Health Service should be doing itself. Dr. Winner, a clear-sighted and wise person, knew that there was a gap that needed filling. She said, 'No, we can give them comfort, you can give them hope.' There were inevitably some doctors who felt the projected Hospice was unnecessary, but with Cicely's tact and Dr. Winner's and Dr. Fairlie's bureaucratic skills to oil the wheels, they got backing from the Regional Boards without much difficulty. The officials in the Health Service recognised that they did not know a great deal about the care of the dying, that it would be expensive and that if, in the strong tradition of English medico-social work, the voluntary side would pioneer it, they would do all they could to help. The help could have come in various ways, either by giving a research and development project grant or by contracting to fill a certain number of beds. In the end they did both, though it was some time before the actual number of beds was confirmed.

However eminent, however enthusiastic, her supporters, nothing could move any further without money. In any fund-raising venture it is always the first promise of money which is the hardest to get; the charitable trusts then take confidence from each other. Cicely's first promise came in 1961, the month after her father died. Sir Donald Allen telephoned her to say that the City Parochial Foundation would give her £50,000 but that she couldn't tell anybody until it was announced in October. 'I was very taken aback and didn't say anything and he said, "Did you hope it was going to be more?" I've got used to being told we've got £50,000 now, I can immediately pick up my jaw and say thank you more quickly. I remember going away from the phone and thinking I couldn't tell my father and then thinking he would know anyway as he was safely in Paradise.' But there was a catch – they could only have the £50,000 once there were 'satisfactory assurances' that the Hospice really would be established, they couldn't use the money to buy the land. So they were still caught in a vicious circle – until they had the land they couldn't estimate exactly how much money they needed and couldn't put in a formal request to another Trust for further money. So Cicely applied to the King Edward's Hospital Fund for enough money to acquire the site.

The nature of the site had always been clear in Cicely's mind. She had resisted pressure to adapt an existing building, to run it as part of one of the large hospitals or to take over somewhere like Hydestile. She was adamant that it should be purpose built and that it should be in the city, within easy reach of the London teaching hospitals. 'We want to be somewhere where there are stations at each end of the road and buses going up and down. Patients want to see that, not lovely green fields.' She was also determined that it should be south of the river, so that they would not be competing with St. Joseph's for funds from the same hospital authority – or indeed for patients.

Soon after her application for money was lodged with the King's Fund, her brother John, like their father also an estate agent, rang to say he thought he had found a suitable site in Lawrie Park Road in Sydenham; the asking price was £27,000. Cicely immediately went down and walked timorously around, not sure if she was trespassing. It seemed perfect. One and a third acres where two houses had been demolished, in south London, buses running past the door, a tennis court opposite, Penge and Sydenham stations near at hand and not too far from St. Thomas's. There were even some mature trees in the garden – something she had always wanted. She rang the King's Fund and the secretary Mr. Peers encouraged her to bid for it. So with just five hundred pounds in the bank she bid £27,000 and applied for planning permission.

The tension was to increase. The King's Fund, while in no way retracting their hope that they would come up with the money, realised her application had to go on to another committee – the original committee didn't deal with grants of that size. But Cicely's bid was in, negotiations for planning permission continued, the architect began drawing the plans and Cicely was grilled endlessly about what she would do if she was given the money and acquired the site.

She had several weeks to wait. The fateful day was February 7th, 1963. The town planners and the King's Fund were to meet; the decision was to be made. If the money was not available, Cicely and her Council of Management were legally responsible.

On that day the patients of St. Joseph's were 'praying like beavers'. So, of course, was Cicely. As usual she read her *Daily Light* that morning, to find the text was 'Thou shalt bless the Lord Thy God for the Good Land which He hath given Thee.' So, as she instantly knew, God was on her side. At five o'clock that evening Mr. Halton from the King's Fund rang her at St. Joseph's telling her that she could have up to £30,000 to include the cost of purchase. The patients had been asking her all day if she'd heard anything. 'Mr. Pettit was the first person I could tell – he was the nearest to the phone. I remember saying "We've got it, we've got it," and he died only five days later and I remember saying to him on that last afternoon when he looked at me shaking his head, "I'll never, never forget you." There was something so special about that moment.' Then she went over to the chronic ward to tell Alice and Louie. 'I knew we'd get it' was Louie's excited response. Notice the 'we'. Cicely might be alone in the sense that any leader is alone, but people were beginning to share her vision and her involvement. Mr. Peers said wryly to Cicely 'Your supporters are on every side. I began to be quite nervous because wherever I went they would come up and attack me, I knew that you couldn't have put them on to me because there were just too many of them.'

There were set-backs. The town planners deferred them twice, an insurance had to be raised against a restrictive covenant – in fact at one point there was talk of putting the site back on the market. Cicely had spent these tense weeks in the States, but she returned in time to sign the contract on June 7th. A few days later she and the Bishop of Stepney went to bless and dedicate the site. The Bishop committed to God all those who would ever come to St. Christopher's – the patients, the relatives, those who would work, those who would come to be taught. 'Like all land, this is Our Lord's but we did need to say it right from the beginning.'

Cicely's ability to find large sums of money might make most professional fund-raisers envious. Over the years she has raised thousands of pounds for St. Christopher's. What is her secret? Her own answer is, 'Never miss an opportunity to tell the tale, never stop saying thank you.' But there is more to it than that. In the first place her letters to the secretaries of trusts are models of clarity and civility; she would ask for, and usually get, a personal interview and she would then 'tell the tale'. This would involve showing photographs of patients in different stages of their last weeks of life; on admission to St. Joseph's, clearly in pain, depressed and listless; then, with their pain controlled and spirits eased, looking alert, peaceful, sometimes even happy. 'This patient died three days later' she would then say. Her message was dramatic and full of hope and they listened attentively as she explained that this way of caring for the dying must be researched and taught so that it could spread more widely. Whenever possible she would take potential donors round St. Joseph's, using it as the closest there was to a prototype of what she wanted to do; and there would be much gleeful plotting as she briefed chosen patients about the visitors – 'He's from a very rich trust – you charm him.' And they did.

Behind Cicely's ability to put up a case for financial backing, lay her own attitude to money and what she wanted to do with it. Mrs. Diamant, a family friend, who has known her since her teens, says 'She's always been able to collect money because she has such contempt for it. She always had it and never had to earn it. It was like something that came out of a tap when she wanted it.' 'You think that money comes out of the air,' said her father, the source of her attitude to money through his own generosity. She was not in awe of large sums of money, and this attitude undoubtedly made the keys to the vaults of the charitable companies more accessible. The secretaries of the big trusts came to see St. Christopher's as something that was most certainly going to happen, it was just a question of whether or not they were going to be involved.

Deeper still is her faith in a destiny beyond herself. She

knew, as she wrote to her first sponsor Sir Donald Allen, that 'if we find the pattern we are meant to have, the other things will follow. I really do know that without doubting.' This concentration of 'rightness', part practical, part mystical, was echoed in her attitude to money. Money was valued as much for the spirit in which it was given as for what it could purchase. So the little gifts, the widows' mites, had especial value. Like thirteen shillings and eightpence, sent by the men's ward of St. Joseph's in a tin box, with 'Good luck' written on sticky plaster; or one pound sent by Jack Wallace's wife's cleaner in memory of her mother-in-law; and, in a very special way, the few pounds sent by a Miss Curle whenever she could afford it. She first gave five pounds when her sister died and from then on Cicely is convinced that two pounds from Miss Curle heralded a large gift from a trust. Ever since, small gifts have brought in the larger donations.

Soon the big money began to come in. The acquisition of the site released the £50,000 promised by the City Parochial Foundation and at the meeting of the Council in March 1964 Cicely was able to announce a generous grant of £50,000 in five yearly instalments from the Drapers' Trust. This was destined either for the Chapel or for the wing for the frail and elderly, then known as 'Grasshoppers' but eventually becoming simply the 'Drapers' Wing.' 'By this time,' said Cicely at the St. Christopher's Day meeting in November, 'I was much better at accepting £50,000 on the telephone and was busy saying "Thank you" before the first sentence was finished.' They received over £5,000 from a BBC Appeal and a legacy for £2,000 brought the total to nearly £138,000 (never forgetting the original five hundred pounds from David Tasma). This was nearly a third of the amount they needed. Should they start building? She told the St. Christopher's Day meeting how they resolved this question. 'Dame Dorothy Vaisey, with all the authority of a Dame Commander of the Victorian Order, twenty-five years as General Secretary of the Friends of the Poor, some seventeen Homes to her credit and a purple taffeta hat, gave us a very splendid go-ahead. "This is a good and right thing; you have many people praying for it. You should go straight ahead. I wouldn't wait five minutes." And so that is exactly what we did.'

In fact by the time the plans had been drawn up and approved by the Ministry of Health and the King's Fund, builders found and tenders accepted, a further £60,000 had come from the Nuffield Foundation and £22,680 (the cost of a ward bay) from the Sembal Trust. This grant was the source of considerable anguish – should they accept money that came from gambling? After much discussion they decided that it would be arrogant not to accept if it was offered; in any case the Bible was full of instances where God had gladly used gifts of money made in strange ways. In fact the secretary of the trustees invited Cicely to lunch, put the application forward and gained the grant for St. Christopher's. At about the same time a legacy from the USA enabled them to acquire a second site, at 57, Lawrie Park Road. This was a far-sighted and brave decision, as there was no possibility of developing it in the immediate future.

The man who now became crucially important to Cicely was the architect, Justin Smith (usually known as Peter Smith) of Stewart Hendry and Smith. Cicely had met him in 1958 when he was working on a ward extension at St. Joseph's; with his expertise in hospice design and her debt to St. Joseph's he was the natural person for her to consult. Peter Smith has a maxim, 'Make, your architect your friend, never your friend your architect,' and this is exactly what happened. It was a fruitful and happy relationship, their ideas so intertwined that they were soon barely able to separate their contributions. 'At first I thought I was just being useful,' says Peter Smith, 'later I realised I was highly privileged.' He was delighted by her insistence that it should be a welcoming, spacious, airy building with the needs of the patients and their relatives always put first; he was stimulated by her attention to detail and her wish to incorporate pictures and sculptures into the initial design; he welcomed – and who wouldn't? – working directly to her without having to go through formal structures and committees. Cicely – as almoner, nurse, doctor and driving force – was a complete planning team in herself.

He had done some designs for her, showing the size, shape and approximate division into wards, rooms and offices, as early as 1960, before they had money or a site, so that she would have something on paper to show people. It was based on her brief, and just as the theory was so clear in her mind that the original documents 'The Need' and 'The Scheme' hardly needed changing, so in her brief on the building she had envisaged with amazing accuracy the building that was eventually to grow on the site in Lawrie Park Road. The years of thought had given her vision such clarity that it was just a question of giving it outward form.

She wanted three wards for patients with terminal illness, divided into bays of six and four beds, with three single rooms in each; the beds were to be sideways to the windows and there should be 'a feeling of space on entering the ward'. The bathrooms were to be roomy enough to bring in the beds, there was to be a treatment room with steriliser and trolleys, a sluice at each end of the ward, a nursing station with a good view, separate sisters' sitting-room and a cupboard and toilet for the nurses. She suggested a balcony, and one of the ideas of which Peter Smith is justly proud is that rather than a small balcony at one end, he incorporated the balcony into the whole length of the ward, giving it a much more spacious feeling and enabling patients to sit at the window in all weathers, just apart from the ward but still in its warmth and security.

The wing for the elderly was to have two general sitting-rooms and twenty bed-sitting rooms with kitchenettes for light meals. Here too, Cicely was aware of the practical details. 'It must be possible to move patients about in wheel-chairs, so we shall need wide doors, ramps not stairs and lifts.' There was to be a nurses' home with facilities for entertaining, a flat for the medical superintendent, four guest-rooms, kitchens and a dining-room with movable doors so that the room could be divided into two if necessary. She wanted a small physiotherapy and occupational therapy department but the latter should have plenty of storage space 'as the things will mainly be taken round the wards or sitting-rooms.' The Chapel was to be large enough to accommodate beds and wheel-chairs and about 150 people seated.

The pews disappeared, the superintendents' flat turned into an Out-patient Clinic and there were similar changes inherent in growth and expansion, but the only major difference was that the chronic ward was never built. In practice it turned out to be better to have long-stay patients intermingled with the terminally ill.

So on March 22nd, 1965, a small group gathered together in Lawrie Park Road to dig the first spit. There were Verena Galton and Joan Steel, who were to become the first Matron and ward sister, Jack Wallace, Mrs. G.'s mother, Peter Smith, the Bishop of Stepney, the sculptor and several other Poles, the treasurer, a dog, a few children and plenty of birds. Cicely and Lord Thurlow, the new chairman, together took a gleaming new spade and, after a few prayers from the Bishop, the first spit was ceremoniously dug. It was the end of the beginning.

Cicely and her Council were now the proud possessors of two sites, an enormous hole in the ground, something over £220,000 and endless determination. The next two years were to be filled with excitement, apprehension and setbacks, steadily punctuated by ceremonies marking off the progress towards the realisation of Cicely's dream.

The next milestone was a larger and more formal affair – the Laying of the Foundation Stone. Cicely and those closest to her vision are all very conscious of the symbolic value of such ceremonies; it is typical of the spirit of St. Christopher's that when the huge stone was found to have been laid in a position slightly inconvenient to the builders, Peter Smith would not let it be moved – the workmen just had to build round it. They felt too, that it was symbolic that in a wet summer, with rain the day before and rain the day after, with rain in Camberwell and rain in Penge, it did *not* rain at St. Christopher's. The sun shone bravely as about 150 people, including the Reverend Mother and staff of St. Joseph's, the former staff of St. Luke's, Cicely's mother, the Mayor and Mayoress of Bromley, an American Vice-President of the Council and many of the faithful band of people who had been working for so long, gathered in prayer with no less a figure than Lord Fisher, the former Archbishop of Canterbury. The service was short, simple and to the point: the theme – 'Except the Lord build the house, they labour in vain that build it.'

A board went up, a crane moved in and work began. They were putting up a floor every six weeks and Cicely went down with her camera regularly to record progress, and sometimes to put up a fight for a fence or intercede for the life of a mulberry tree. In a little over six months the building had grown to its full height and there was a 'topping-out' ceremony. Again the weather was fine – it came to be called 'St. Christopher's weather' – and Cicely and a few friends climbed up on the roof, ran up a flag, said a prayer and gave the traditional beer to the men working on the site.

The builders, Fairweather and Sons, were working very fast. The foreman was exceptionally skilled and assumed that the Council of St. Christopher's, like everyone else, was anxious that the work should be done as quickly as possible and that the money was guaranteed. In fact by the summer of 1966 there was nothing left in the bank and the money they had been expecting had not materialised: they had trusted in God, had he let them down? A grant they had hoped for had gone to another project, a confidently expected bridging loan had not materialised, a loan could not be arranged. Reporting this at the Annual General Meeting Cicely said, 'It felt as though one was trying to push a very large mountain into the sea with a very small wheelbarrow and an equally small amount of faith. The words, "Faith is the substance of things hoped for, the evidence of things not seen" never seemed more appropriate, nor indeed, more real.' Cicely had to do the unbelievable and totally uncharacteristic thing, she had to ask the builders to slow down, possibly be prepared to stop altogether for the time being.

She had to find over £100,000. '£1,000 every day except Sunday from now until the end of the year,' (it was July) she reflected to her friend Gill Ford, 'It doesn't sound too bad put like that.' Even so, she didn't know what to do. She felt a real sense of doom hanging over her. 'The vultures are on the balcony outside the window, the vultures are on the piano. The contractor was a vulture as well as someone in trouble as he had subcontractors and so on . . .' She had tapped every source she could think of, in any case it is difficult to approach a new trust when an application is already lodged with another. She rang the Drapers', intending to ask once more if they would release more of the money, and was greeted by a cheerful Hugh Farmar. 'Oh, it's you! We've just been talking about you. We are releasing the rest of the grant, some straight away and the rest as a very low interest loan.' Her faith had not been misplaced. She rang Mr. Fairweather to say that she had got £30,000 more than she had half an hour before and the work could continue. From then on the money arrived as it was needed. Just.

So the building continued, the symbol of St. Christopher, lovingly designed by the Polish artist Witold Kawalec, was put up above the main entrance and it was time to commission the Hospice.

Commissioning a hospital is nowadays a specialised procedure, but it was not so in 1967; nobody at St. Christopher's had done it before or even knew much about it. However, with a great deal of help from the Bromley Hospital Management Committee the Hospice began to fill up with beds, chairs, equipment, bed-pans, sterilisers, pillows, blankets, bedcovers; the kitchens were stocked, drugs laid in. A fish tank, given by someone who had been later in the same ward as David Tasma, was filled with the fire-hose, nurses stitched hessian to put on the beds, gangs of children weeded the garden and the fire-brigade, for some unaccountable reason, hung the curtains. It was, according to Dr. Winner, who was very much involved at this stage, 'pretty average chaos'. But they struggled through, Cicely keeping her head and managing not to panic.

In June 1967 the first inhabitants of the old people's wing began to arrive. This must have seemed miraculous enough, but Cicely had always had a special feeling about the first patient to come into the wards; this person would, she felt, be the inheritor of Mrs. G., Louie and Alice. Her instinct was affirmed when, on July 13th, 1967, Mrs. Medhurst, the first long-term patient to come to St. Christopher's, arrived by car, with her personal bits and pieces coming after her in a little van. She was to live in St. Christopher's for a year and a half, a constant source of gaiety and encouragement to the first members of staff. It is not hard to share Cicely's emotion. 'I almost sat down and burst into tears, though that would have been rather silly.' But it was a long time since February 1948.

Significant though Mrs. Medhurst's arrival was, there had to be an official opening. The Chapel was dedicated on June 15th and on July 24th Princess Alexandra, who later agreed to be St. Christopher's Patron, came to perform the opening ceremony.

The Drapers' Wing was almost finished and four people had already made it their home; twelve patients were installed; two more wards were almost ready. Again it was a brilliantly sunny day as key people – members of Council, the architect and contractor, the Matron, the sculptor, the bursar and the head porter – were presented to the Princess. After the dedication by the Bishop of Stepney, the Princess unveiled the statue of St. Christopher trudging indomitably through the stream with the Christ-child on his back.

They still needed £65,000 for furniture, equipment, transport and settling outstanding accounts; running the Hospice was estimated at £12,000 a year; they had not even begun to develop the second site; but it was built, it was open, it had a skeleton staff and patients were arriving daily. And already it was a happy place. A visitor said, 'Everyone here is always smiling, I have never seen so many smiling people.'

It was nearly twenty years since David Tasma had given Cicely five hundred pounds 'To be a window in your home'. Now a home had been built round that window, and it was a home that was already fulfilling the ideals that Cicely had set at a St. Christopher's Day meeting when she was speaking of the need for the staff to understand at all levels. 'It means every kind of detail – the right outlook for a bed, the right kind of day-room, a general feeling of ease and beauty, not too solemn at all, something that you can feel homely in. It means trying to understand how to make patients comfortable, what it is like to be so ill, to be parting. It means learning how to be quiet and how to help them to be quiet and safe so that they may find their true safety in God.'

10

THE COMMUNITY

I am convinced that communal life can flourish only if it exists
for an aim outside itself. Community is viable only if it is the
outcome of a deep involvement in the purpose which is other
than, or above, that of being a community.
Bruno Bettelheim, *Home For the Heart*

Cicely planned St. Christopher's as a medical and a
Christian foundation and, more loosely, as a community.
It is all three. In sixteen years, like any healthy organism,
it has grown and changed, but it has, with some difficulty,
kept its ideological basis and the spirit in which it was
founded. Cicely's personality permeates everything about
St. Christopher's, for it is her child and has grown up in
her care. Though it owes much to others who work there,
inevitably it owes most to her, and still depends on her.

Given the tension that permeated the Saunders family
home and her unhappy experience of school life, one would
not expect Cicely to find it easy to live in a community,
which is after all an extended family. While living in a
community is invariably a challenge, it becomes even
harder for those who are not at ease with themselves.
'Comfortable people tend not to achieve great things,' says
Christopher Saunders. His sister is not a comfortable
person.

One manifestation of this is her shyness. Many people
cope with shyness by not exposing themselves to situations where it would be revealed, but Cicely's determination to fulfil what she sees so clearly as her role in life
inevitably involves public attention and the exposed,
vulnerable position of leadership. The pioneering qualities of a founder do not necessarily include the gentle,
reconciling qualities that make for an easy life as a leader.

Like so many leaders Cicely has problems in relating to her peers. This leads her into awkward personal relationships in which fear and inner insecurity tend to oust the affection which is undoubtedly there. She finds it easier to relate to people who are content to play second fiddle to her; then she brings out the best in them and rejoices in their success. It is another matter if they challenge her. While she can enjoy anonymity and while she fits quietly into professional groups like the Medical Research Council, at St. Christopher's she needs to be the leader not the led.

How then, does this community work under its charismatic but sometimes difficult leader? To what extent, in practice, is St. Christopher's a community?

Cicely's concern over this had led her to read widely on the subject; visiting places like St. Mary's Wantage, Grandchamps in Switzerland and St. Julian's in Sussex; talking to anyone who might help her formulate her ideas. As early as 1960 she had come to the conclusion, as she wrote to Dr. Wyon, that she 'was not really thinking of anything nearly so definite as a real new community, I think I was using the term in a much less technical way. I asked Sister Penelope (of St. Mary's Wantage) whether I was attempting the impossible to hope that a secular group of people without any rule, would be able to hold together and give the feeling of security which I want so much to help our patients.' Two years after the Hospice had opened, she wrote 'We hesitate to call ourselves a community.' Strictly speaking she was right. The word is generally understood to imply a group of people with a shared interest, usually organised in some way, often sharing their possessions. St. Christopher's has no formal structure as a community, no religious rule, no vows to be taken or commitment made, they do not share their possessions. But though Cicely had not set out to form a community, there is a very real sense in which St. Christopher's *is* a community, and a successful one at that.

St. Christopher's is a microcosm of the wider community around it. This owes much to the inspired idea of including the Drapers' Wing, sixteen bed-sitting rooms for retired members of staff or volunteers and their relatives, and the Playgroup, where up to twenty children of the staff, from eighteen months upwards, are happily surrounded by paint, sand, clay, books, a guinea pig, two budgerigars, two terrapins and numerous fish.

So it is a place where life begins as well as ends, where people are by turns the teachers and the taught, the carers and the cared for, the workers and those who can no longer work, the sick and the healthy. The inclusion of the Drapers' Wing and the playgroup was both pragmatic and ideological. The Drapers' gives the reassuring, fairly constant presence of the frail elderly; the playgroup enables working mothers to relax, knowing their children are close by and in good hands. In practice they add a dimension missing in many communities; granny and grandchild – a constant reminder that being is more important than doing – belonging to the Hospice as much as patient and nurse. St. Christopher's is about living as well as dying.

St. Christopher's is the people there. 'We're a village' says Cicely. 'You don't necessarily know everybody's name in the house, but you know their faces. We are a reaction against the impersonal medical city.' As St. Christopher's grows, it now has over 200 people on the payroll, it struggles very hard and not always successfully to remain a village rather than a city, a family rather than an institution. Where it succeeds in retaining the 'village' atmosphere it is in their acceptance of the fact that they are many communities – the patients, the ward teams, the doctors, the study centre, the research department, the workmen, the laundry, the administration, the senior staff – each contributing in their own fashion. Sometimes they may seem small ways. For instance, the kitchen, providing birthday cakes for patients and meals for relatives and able to say 'We try to make them all feel at home and part of the family of St. Christopher's'; the reception desk, receiving calls from relatives 'just to talk', even from a complete stranger, advised to ask them how to get to St.

Thomas's Hospital from Hayes, 'because they're so helpful'.

St. Christopher's is a community because of the way people feel about it, because of the way people who have known it for some time show new visitors round proudly, as if it belonged to them. Dr. Gillian Ford, a close friend of Cicely's who works at the Hospice as a volunteer doctor at the weekends, calls it 'A healing community and a super club'. In a study carried out by Dr. Colin Murray Parkes comparing the families of patients who died at the Hospice with families of patients who died elsewhere, eighty-seven per cent of the St. Christopher's families found that the statement which best characterised St. Christopher's was 'The Hospital is a family.' (The figure for relatives of patients who died elsewhere was a mere eight per cent.)

St. Christopher's truly deserves the label 'community' because it has a common aim on which everything is centred – the patient and his family. This is of course true of any hospital, but it is true of St. Christopher's in a very special way.

One of Cicely's original drafts about St. Christopher's was called 'A plan for a hospital and a home' and that is what she has achieved. The patient is not taken away from his home or out of the wider community, so much as welcomed into another community, specially designed for him. The Bishop of Stepney saw this clearly before the Hospice opened. 'The idea of a community that will take over smoothly and without interruption the dying patient from the security of his home background into the security of a community built around his needs.' The patients' needs are so varied and sometimes so great, that only a mixed community – Cicely's 'community of the unlike' – are able to meet them. She had learnt the full significance of this at St. Joseph's and applied it to St. Christopher's. A patient once said, 'When I tell my troubles to the family I still have them just the same at the end. When I tell you I leave some of them behind.' Like so many whose mental pain outweighs their physical distress, this patient needed someone who could hold the balance between caring and detachment, someone whose experience of such problems gave them confidence. Above all, she needed to be supported by some kind of community. Cicely concludes 'We cannot come helpfully if we are filled with self-consciousness concerning the problem and our own reactions and responsibilities. We can come if we can say, "This is the whole community that is helping this patient, I just happen to be the one here at the moment."'

Looking after the dying is a corporate act, everyone is involved; the nurses who make him comfortable, the doctors who prescribe him drugs and answer his questions, the priest who visits him, the physiotherapist who eases his movement, the occupational therapist who interests his mind, the kitchen who tempt his appetite, the study centre who teach others of his needs. One of the secretarial staff remarked, 'It didn't feel like this when I worked in business, even though everyone there was involved in the same thing too. The presence of death is a unifying thing.'

St. Christopher's is designed to make the patient feel at home. The whole family are encouraged to visit at any time (except Monday; relatives need to have a day off without feeling guilty, so Mondays are set aside for the hairdresser and entertainments). You can drop in to St. Christopher's as casually as you would drop into somebody's house, the restrictions are only the obvious ones of courtesy and consideration, not bureaucracy. Family pets are welcome too. A circus owner once brought a baby elephant to see his father. No one objected, but the elephant couldn't fit into the lift, so the sick man came down to the reception hall to see the animal. That may be exceptional, but there is nothing unusual about finding husband, son, daughter-in-law, grandchildren, friend and friend's mother sitting around the bed, drinking tea and eating cakes – probably provided by St. Christopher's. Birthdays and wedding anniversaries are celebrated. In like vein, the patients have the same freedom they would have at home. If they feel well enough, they can walk round the gardens, have a drink at the pub, go to Wimbledon or of course, go home for a few days, a few weeks or a few months. Their happiness and comfort is all that matters.

This easy-going atmosphere is well illustrated by Tom West, who became Deputy Medical Director of St. Christopher's in 1973. 'Mrs. B., aged thirty-six years, with three children, was admitted on a Friday. She was very ill and had severe physical pain. While admitting her it became clear that something other than pain was worrying her. She and her husband finally confessed that they had not expected a bed to be available so soon and Mrs. B. was deeply distressed at missing her best friend's birthday party the next evening. Hoping that the nursing staff would support me, I told Mrs. B. that there was no reason at all why she should not go to the party and then asked when she expected it to finish. "About three a.m." was the reply. Trying not to express any surprise I proposed that she should go out to the party and that her husband should ring the ward around nine p.m. to let them know how things were going. He could then say whether he would bring her back or whether she felt able to stay out on the tiles for the rest of the night. Needless to say she was the last to leave and was re-admitted to her bed in St. Christopher's late the following morning. Then the important but secondary matter of her physical pain could be successfully tackled.'

This flexibility on the part of the Ward team in their support of their doctor's assessment of what would really help the patient most, illustrates the way the whole community tries to let the patient know he is still part of the world around him, both welcome and important.

The most valuable thing the community give to the patient is time. Cicely learnt, in her brief but intense relationships with David and with Antoni, just how much can be lived in a short time and how the last days can be the richest and the most fulfilled. She was once talking about this giving of time and attention to an audience at Whipp's Cross Hospital, when a rather pompous consultant said it was all very well for her, she was a doctor with time to spare. (He had ninety beds with the help of registrars and housemen, she was responsible for 120 beds, virtually on her own.) To this Cicely crisply replied, 'Oh no, Doctor, time isn't a question of length, it's a question of depth, isn't it?'

Cicely has an almost uncanny capacity for really listening and enabling people to speak of their deep inner pain. Helen Willans, who was Matron from 1971 to 1983 and whose contribution to St. Christopher's is immense, greatly admires the way Cicely blends professionalism with spiritual insight. 'In encountering a newly admitted terminally ill patient and teasing out their problems and arriving at the immediate way to help their symptoms, giving the assurance and comfort and peace to their families in the shortest possible time – and I don't mean rushed – she can knock spots off us all. It's absolutely marvellous to see. She's got the ability just somehow to perceive what the person is experiencing, brushing aside all the frills. In a very simple but utterly true way, she's able to bring in the whole spiritual aspect of God's love and presence without offending or embarrassing.' Though some of her colleagues find the presence of other members of staff helpful, Cicely does not like other people with her when she is seeing patients, and Dr. Richard Lamerton, her first houseman at St. Christopher's, feels he was unutterably privileged to be 'allowed to tag along' while Cicely was doing her clinical work. 'She has this capacity to sit down with a person she has never met before and instantly be an old friend. She has that quality of listening and makes a person open up immediately and in a very short time, maybe a ten minute interview, they would have told her their deepest fears, their family secrets and all sorts of things – the instant trust that Cicely inspired, withholding nothing, the completely committed way that she will accept anything, any problem, no limits. It doesn't matter how long it's going to take, it doesn't matter how much effort it's going to involve from her, the commitment is there, open and willing. That was an example, a model for my life.'

Perhaps part of Cicely's secret lies in a Hasidic question

and answer she often recalls. 'Why do you say you should listen to someone as if you were looking on water rather than as if you were looking on a mirror? Because you have to be very still if you are going to see in water, you can so easily disturb it.' Often she will listen by being very still, but she seems to know intuitively how to respond to patients, leaving openings for them to speak freely and never flinching from the direct question. Sometimes the most superficial chat is the right approach. A friend was visiting a patient at St. Christopher's once when Cicely dropped in on her way to some celebration. She was chatting away, 'Which hood shall I wear, my Oxford one or my London one?' (The patient was a professional woman, still intellectually alert, who would have been interested in such things.) Gradually the mood changed and the following conversation took place. The patient said, 'What will it be like when I die?' and Cicely said, 'Well, one morning you'll wake up and you perhaps won't feel so well. You'll feel a bit sick, but you certainly won't feel so well. And then perhaps you'll go on feeling not quite so well and then one day you'll just go to sleep and that will be it.' And the patient said, 'And there won't be any pain?' 'Absolutely none.' 'And will I be alone?' 'No, you won't be alone.' This exchange calmed the patient and remained an extraordinary experience for her friend.

Giving is seldom all one way. People at St. Christopher's feel that they learn and receive just as much as they give. Cicely has written, 'The dying need the community, its help and fellowship and the care and attention which will quieten their distress and fears and enable them to go peacefully. The community needs the dying to make it think of eternal issues and to make it listen and give to others.' Cicely also needs the dying; they bring out the best in her.

Just as the community and the patients need each other, so do the community and the friends and relatives of the patients. St. Christopher's welcomes the whole family. On the one hand, they are grateful for the relatives' special knowledge of the patient and immediately include them as part of the treatment team; on the other hand, they lift from the families some of the load of responsibility that is such a frightening part of illness, reassure those who feel guilty that they are unable to keep the patient at home until the end and share, as far as they can, the emotional strain and the pain of impending loss. It is the whole family that is being cared for, not just the patient.

The welcome might begin at home, if the patient has been visited there, at out-patients, on the telephone, or on arrival at St. Christopher's. A former admissions secretary tells how two sisters came to see her about the possibility of their mother being admitted to their care. As she was explaining the application procedure to them, one of the sisters said quietly, 'It's all right, we're safe. I'm totally blind, but when we came through the door I could sense a feeling of safety and kindness.'

The peace and welcome of the building strikes everyone immediately; the profusion of plants and flowers, sculptures and paintings; the dedications to some of those who have helped St. Christopher's – the window in memory of David Tasma, the kneeling woman inscribed to Cicely's Aunt Daisy, the plaque in gratitude for all the small gifts, the various wings and wards named after their sponsors.

When a new patient is due to arrive, the bed is brought, already warmed, down to the entrance, and Matron waits to greet him and his family, take them up to the ward and introduce them to the other patients and any relatives who might be there at the time. The part played by the reception desk is seen in Dr. Parkes's survey. He found that eighty-five per cent of the families of patients who had died at St. Christopher's know the Hospice receptionist, compared with three per cent of families elsewhere. Everything about St. Christopher's is part of the welcome, from the bricks of which it is built to the Medical Director.

Responsible for the family in a very particular way is the social work department. They see their work as an attempt to bring together families whose divisions have been highlighted by illness; the community of St. Chris-topher's plays a major part in this therapy, not only by caring for the sick member but also by helping the rela-tives to feel part of the team. Despite Cicely's training as an almoner, for a long time she did not fully recognise the part that social workers could play, feeling that most of it could be encompassed by the doctors and nurses. It is typical of her openness to new ideas that when Elizabeth Earnshaw-Smith, a highly qualified member of the pro-fession, applied for a job advertised as a senior social worker, she was prepared to listen to her ideas.

Elizabeth Earnshaw-Smith was very concerned that the world's leading Hospice was undervaluing social work and felt that the department should be headed by a Prin-cipal Social Worker, not just by a Senior. Only thus, she argued, could it have the prestige it needed to relate to the skilled professionals in St. Christopher's and in the out-side world. It says much for Cicely and her senior staff that not only were they flexible enough to appoint Elizabeth Earnshaw-Smith as Principal, but that they gave her the freedom that she needed to develop the department as she saw fit. It now consists of a Senior, with experience in family and group therapy and psychiatric work, a social work assistant and a Bereavement Service Co-ordinator.

This team is theoretically responsible for the social needs of up to 120 families at any one time; sixty-two with members in St. Christopher's and about sixty at home, under the care of the Domiciliary Service. In practice not every family needs their help and the social workers are very aware that to press unwanted help can diminish people. They know too, how much the rest of the staff contribute.

When the social work department do become involved with a family they are looking for strengths rather than weaknesses, for instance how a family has coped with crises in the past, and the emphasis is on what they can do together, using those strengths. The team will listen and work with rather than for a family, always encouraging independence and maintaining self-respect. They start with a full and leisurely discussion; as many of the family as wish to come are joined by a doctor, a nurse, a social worker from St. Christopher's and possibly the local social worker and district nurse if they have been involved. They will deal with practical problems – finance, housing, arranging to install a telephone, advising on grants for special needs or co-ordinating community services for those living alone, even arranging holidays for patients and their families. Together with the ward teams they will also be alert to identify particular emotional problems or people likely to be at risk. For instance the elderly, whose last surviving relation is dying, people with chronic anxiety or psychiatric problems, teenagers who have been engaged in a healthy struggle for freedom and are likely to feel guilty if the parent, from whom they have been trying to escape, dies in the middle of it. Hospice care is aimed at improving the quality of the life remaining to the patient; that the family should make the most of that time together is a crucial part of it. 'Fantasy can then be replaced by a more manageable reality, symptoms recognised, understood and better controlled, anxieties shared, questions answered and plans made.' If there have been tensions, they can be resolved. Reconciliation before death makes parting more bearable.

The work of the Hospice does not end with the death of the patient, indeed death and bereavement are not considered as two separate things. Both involve loss. The patient has to face the loss of his life, the surviving relative has to face life without him. The bereaved family is supported after the patient dies. On the first Monday of every month there are the informal meetings of the Pilgrim Club, to which patients, family and staff automatically belong; here relatives have the opportunity to meet members of the staff and perhaps even more important, to meet each other and share their griefs, confusion and hopefully, their progress.

More structured help is also available. The family service was started ten years ago by the distinguished psychiatrist Dr. Colin Murray Parkes, a world specialist in bereavement. Cicely had been impressed by an article he had written, got in touch with him, found they shared the same ideas about the family, not just the patient, being the unit of care and Dr. Parkes joined the staff as soon as the Hospice opened. He spends one day a week there, an important support to the home care team, helping in the training of students and nurses on courses and doing research.

Sometimes he joins ward groups, helping the staff with patients who have particularly acute psychological problems. It was he who introduced the idea, considered revolutionary in 1973, of using volunteers in bereavement counselling. At first they trained specially chosen volunteers from among those already working at St. Christopher's but recently, encouraged by other hospices, they have done extensive research on the recruiting of volunteers from the general community. They now have fourteen specialised volunteers, helping the nurses, social workers and chaplains, and are training more. It is fitting that St. Christopher's, the creative outcome of Cicely's pain and loss, should give so much of its collective energy to the support of the bereaved.

Many other skills and countless hours of help are provided voluntarily, something less available to the National Health Service because of the trade unions, but enjoyed by St. Christopher's because of their charitable status. The Volunteer Service was started by Mrs. Sheila Hanna as the Hospice opened and now consists of more than 200 people who contribute some 34,000 hours of work a year. They act as drivers, help in the Pilgrim Room tea bar, on the wards – in fact they work in every department of the Hospice. Many of them enjoy it so much they feel it is *they* who benefit.

Cicely believes that people involved in Hospice work tend to take their own bereavements terribly hard. 'After all, I made the most monumental fuss about Antoni.' Indeed the staff often feel bereaved themselves by the death of a patient. This is particularly true when someone, like the

first patient, Mrs. Medhurst, has been in St. Christopher's
for a long time and has become a part of the community in
a very real sense; it is also true when there have been a lot
of deaths in a short time. It is hard to cope with continual
loss.

Who cares for the care-givers? The short answer is that,
as in any community worthy of the name, they care for
each other. A nurse who had worked for a short time in St.
Christopher's wrote, 'How can one express in words the
quiet, endless learning here? I expected to see patients
being cared for, the surprise was to find myself automatically included in people's perceptive loving and caring.' A
member of the administrative staff even said that at first
she found the constant concern for her well-being made
her feel slightly claustrophobic and irritable. She has now
come to appreciate it.

People who work continually with the dying and the
chronically ill *do* get exhausted, drained, helpless in the
face of so much suffering, unable to cope any longer. That
the majority have such a remarkable capacity to manage
is partly because they are well-recruited, partly because
they work alongside people who understand their problems. There are some who feel the staff do not get enough
support, but Cicely's attitude is tough – 'If you can't stand
the heat get out of the kitchen and leave us to get on with
the cooking.'

Support comes from the patients themselves – in fact
Tom West says they, by their courage and concern for
others, provide the best support of all. Dr. Parkes feels
that in a caring community the question of who is caring
for who is always open. 'There are times when patients are
caring for families, patients are caring for doctors, doctors
are caring for families. We're a network of people who
through our care for each other are growing and enriching
each other. The only difference between the dying patient
and me is that he's going over the top before I do.' Cicely
has always received great comfort from patients. A special
one was Ted Holden, who died recently of motor neurone
disease. During the four and a half years he was in the

Hospice she would constantly take problems and anxieties to him and come back refreshed.

What kind of people choose to dedicate their lives to the dying? What are the qualities that give them the strength to do it? One of the yardsticks used in recruitment is that those who have easy answers to the questions of life and death with which they will be confronted are not suitable, nor are those who won't face them. The ones most likely to fit in are those who do not pretend to know, but are searching and try not to dodge the questions. Dr. Winner says that they soon learnt to avoid people who were trying to sort themselves out emotionally, it always ended in disaster. 'You must have people who are reasonably stable, who have a faith of some sort even if it's humanistic, but who aren't afraid of death or dying and who are prepared to face the very real trauma of people one gets fond of dying.'

There are as many reasons for people working at St. Christopher's as there are people there, but one which crops up time and time again is Cicely herself. 'She's a pied piper, isn't she?' said Professor Stewart. In the early days, particularly, people had a way of arriving. Cicely felt that it was almost as though they were 'meant' to participate in the working out of this project. They were drawn in the first place to what she was trying to do, but they wanted to do it with her, feeling she had the drive and vision to make it happen. She has a quality which pulls people to her and inspires them.

It is easy to forget that in the early years Cicely was the only person who knew anything about terminal care. Barbara McNulty, one of the first ward sisters, says, 'Learning from her was not just on one level. One absorbed from her a whole attitude to life, a whole religious ethos, a whole medical expertise, a whole attitude to death and dying, which in many ways was novel and was certainly enlarging, expanding. It was a very growing sort of experience with her, because her knowledge of people, her sensitivity and her love of people was so profound.'

Cicely is a charismatic figure and her leadership pervades St. Christopher's and all it stands for. Dr. Klagsbrun understands this side of her well. He is Assistant Clinical Professor of Psychiatry at Columbia University College of Physicians and Surgeons and Cicely met him when she first went to America in 1963. He feels that Cicely's personality is one of the foundation stones of St. Christopher's. 'Dr. Saunders is strong, courageous and persistent – some might even consider her stubborn. She is articulate and has a basic faith and trust in her message. She is relentless in pursuing her goals and is quite unconcerned with the opinion of others, if these opinions jeopardise her work. She evinces humour, and a sharp wit when it is needed. These characteristics have been crucial in the establishment of St. Christopher's Hospice; yet Dr. Saunders has never acknowledged the importance of her personality, or the impact of her leadership, in the field of medical care for patients facing death.'

If she does not acknowledge the importance of her personality it is probably because, for someone with her record of success, she is curiously modest. She refuses to become a cult figure, as two stories amusingly show. Dr. William Lamers, one of the first Americans to develop hospice care in the States, was in San Francisco when a group of people trying to start a hospice had a reception in honour of Cicely on a cliff overlooking the Golden Gate Bridge – a fantastic setting. 'The Mayor made a flattering speech, named it Saunders Day, presented Cicely with an illuminated scroll and invited her to speak. "You've all been very nice to me and now I'm going to be very nasty to you," she began – and proceeded to remind them that in all their glorious rhetoric no one had mentioned the patient. She froze them in their tracks and she was right.' On another occasion, in England, an American woman approached her in awe, saying, 'Are you really Dr. Saunders? May I touch you?' Pathetic though the request was, the poor woman can hardly have anticipated the explosion that followed. 'No, you *can't*. I *bite*. I am *not* a cult figure.'

Self-effacing though she is, she is also, as Dr. Klagsbrun indicates, capable of being ruthless. This should not come as a surprise. Anyone who has the courage and the persistence to pioneer a new dimension in medicine is likely to put ends before means, likely also to cause some distress in the process. She expects a great deal from people, herself included. Only the best is good enough for St. Christopher's.

What is surprising is that she does not always handle such situations with the kindness and understanding that she certainly possesses. 'She does not seem to realise quite what a devastating effect she can have on people,' one friend says. Dr. Richard Lamerton admits she calls out of him 'nothing short of obedience and reverence'. He is a blunt person himself and appreciates honesty. But it can go too far, even for him. As when, a few months after his appointment, having said he was just the person they'd been praying for, she said, 'I don't know what we did pray for, but it certainly wasn't you.' Or, on a later occasion, when she looked down at him from her fairly formidable height saying, 'I'd forgotten the full horror of you.'

In overcoming her natural shyness and diffidence Cicely can become awkward and sometimes hurts people quite cruelly. She does not intend to wound, it is as if she cannot help herself. A former chaplain remembers her saying that she will spend the first 100,000 years of the next life apologising.

Many people are in awe of Cicely, her ability to go straight to the heart of a problem, her tendency to humiliate people, sometimes even in public. Some will admit that they could help by giving her more abrasive support, more directly truthful responses. It is a vicious circle, with unconscious collusion between Cicely and those she hurts. She is at her best dealing with the dying, the bereaved, the suffering; she is always there, supportive and comforting, when needed by friends or staff. In those situations she knows exactly how to relate and what to give. She is less at ease with ordinary healthy human beings who have in some way crossed or disappointed her: they in turn do not always appreciate her vulnerability.

She is aware of this herself, and it saddens and rather

puzzles her. When she was discussing her early ideas with
Madge Drake, she asked Madge what she thought she
would find most difficult in carrying out her plans. 'Personal relationships' was the answer. Madge, who knows
her well, wishes that she could deal with people in a kinder
way. 'Where her patients are concerned she's got complete
understanding of other people but she hasn't always got
understanding of other people apart from that. She can
be quite ruthless. Her work and the fulfilment of it is so
important to her that she has to clear out of the way
anything that isn't fitting in.'

Cicely is full of contradictions; the play and tensions of
the opposites are the source of much of her creativity and
much of what makes her an inspiring, if at times a difficult, leader. Just as she is both concerned about people's
feelings and yet ruthless, bold and afraid simultaneously,
so she is a woman of vision passionately concerned with
detail, open to new ideas and yet wanting to be in control,
attracted by both the technological and the spiritual,
practical and intellectual, autocratic and democratic. She
says of herself, 'If I have a talent with staff it is to enable
them to be strong.' Certainly it is true to say that those
who survive grow. Her ability to let people develop in their
own individual ways and develop their special areas of
work is the source of some of the most fruitful developments at St. Christopher's. Elizabeth Earnshaw-Smith
had reason to be grateful to her for this; so had Barbara
McNulty, when she started the Domiciliary Care Service.
Barbara, herself a powerful woman, has a special insight
into the way Cicely's drive to get things done works in
counterpoint with her ability to allow things to happen.
'She was autocratic, she is autocratic, and she used occasionally to throw tantrums if something wasn't done exactly as she felt it ought to be. But there is another aspect
of her which is very humble, very tentative, very much
aware that the Lord would see to it if it was right, and that
if it wasn't it wouldn't work anyway. It was the little
things that upset her – unexpected things. I understand
that very well as I'm like that myself. A pot plant in the

wrong place – that sort of thing. The big things are handed over to the Holy Spirit to deal with. He hasn't time for pot plants, so she does it! For all her autocratic behaviour, which must have been very difficult for her immediate administrative staff, she does have this sense in which she lets things happen, or puts forward an idea, then sees how it jells.'

When St. Christopher's opened Cicely had had no experience of administration, but one of her great gifts is her ability to change and grow. So, over the years, she has developed as a leader as in so much else. But it is one of the miracles of St. Christopher's that even when there are tensions, they are absorbed into an almost tangible serenity. In the early days Miss C. V. Butler wished St. Christopher's 'not continuous peace but essential peace.' This is what Cicely has achieved.

St. Christopher's is not only Cicely's child, it is also her home and her family. Cicely is a deeply feminine and home-loving person and she has filled the Hospice with the atmosphere she might have brought to a house full of children and friends. Every Christmas sees a nativity play and the staff go round the wards singing carols by candlelight. To see the expression of pure joy on the face of a determinedly agnostic and gravely ill patient gives some idea of what this can mean. Parties are encouraged, a glass of whisky by the bed is commonplace, there is a bar once a week.

And always the attention to detail. Lucie Wallace has a vivid memory of Cicely, deeply involved in finding thousands of pounds to build the Hospice, coming to dinner and shooting a mass of material patterns onto the coffee table. 'Now you're in bed, you're not well – what would you like for curtains?' Joan Steel, the first ward sister, remembers an occasion when they were short of nurses and particularly busy. She found a note on her desk from Cicely saying, 'Betty would like her toe-nails painted.' Kitty Cole, Cicely's devoted secretary for many years, says that she always wore beads when she was going round the wards, 'They are so much nicer for the patient than a stethoscope.'

This love of detail is translated into traditions. Families always receive a card a year after their relative's death; all the staff, all the volunteers and all the residents are sent 'Coming Day' cards for the anniversary of their arrival – much treasured notes, hand-written in a charmingly appreciative way by Cicely herself – and after a certain length of time at St. Christopher's staff, residents and volunteers are given 'Verena Galton Badges'. (Verena Galton was the first Matron, who had nursed Mrs. G. for years and who married her widower, Jack Galton, the chief steward, in 1969; after her tragic death some of the £2,000 collected for her memorial fund was spent on the little silver and enamel badges.)

As in any family there are tensions. Nobody can hurt, irritate or annoy like relatives. But as in any family, if there is an attack from outside, if someone is rude or critical, then the group stands firmly together. Once or twice a year Dr. Klagsbrun comes over from America to give the staff a chance to talk out the problems inherent in working so closely together with someone from outside the community. He is regarded as a thermometer of what is going on, such is his perception in picking up tensions.

Cicely had been impressed by hearing him challenge the values of a group of American clergy and felt St. Christopher's needed his irreverent approach. He encourages the staff to air their grievances, to throw darts at the senior staff, even to take the part of the Medical Director in psycho-dramas. Despite Cicely's encouragement, the combination of British reserve with a real fear of what might happen if they went too far proved at first almost totally inhibiting – they simply couldn't do it. Nevertheless, they persisted and Dr. Klagsbrun's admiration for Cicely increased, 'Because dragging her heels and wishing it weren't so and setting up barriers, she still nevertheless was able to overcome her own reluctance to have egalitarian systems grow. So she does it, though she hates doing it.'

Let the last words on St. Christopher's as a community come from the ever-wise Bishop of Stepney. 'St. Christopher's Community must be of such quality that the members of the community will learn how to pass through time to eternity and will be teaching each other to fit themselves and each other to make the journey. Staff will give and receive service of the community; everyone will begin by coming to an understanding and appreciation of the contribution made by another . . . it will be a teaching community in which Church and medical professions together will make provisions in all aspects for the care of the family and the patient can learn afresh how the mysteries of life and death may be met with triumph and peace.'

11

ST. CHRISTOPHER'S AS A CHRISTIAN FOUNDATION

> We can die gladly if God will live and work in us . . . we die, 'tis
> true, but 'tis a gentle death.
>
> Frank Zfeiffer, *Meister Eckhardt*

St. Christopher's is the incarnation of a religious ideal –
Cicely's religious ideal. Her spiritual journey is expressed
in St. Christopher's; St. Christopher's reflects the spirit of
its founder. They cannot be separated.

Cicely's deeply held faith and firm ideas as to how it
should be expressed, lead to a tension between opposing
values which is sometimes fruitful, occasionally destruc-
tive. The overwhelming effect of her dynamic spiritual life
is beneficial to the Hospice, though it can lead to the kind
of problems from which no religious community is entirely
free.

It is one of the ironies of saints and visionaries that they
often have a petty and unworthy side. It should not surprise us as much as it does. What the Swiss psychologist
C. G. Jung calls 'the shadow' – the unconscious area of
unlived potential which contains much that is repressed
and inferior – is, like any shadow, stronger where the
light is bright. Cicely's religious attitudes are hard to live
up to, and if she is hard on herself, she can be hard on
others too, particularly those who take an active part in
the religious life of the Hospice. Beware whoever wishes to
change the shape of the Chapel, the order of a service,
without consulting Cicely; he would do well to move
cautiously. Though she espouses religious tolerance she
has her own views as to how it should be practised.

One of her most admirable qualities is the extent to

which she is still, in her sixties, growing, changing and developing. Before the Hospice opened she had moved from a rigid evangelicalism to a position where she could say, 'No one can think of imposing their own faith upon another person, least of all when they are helpless, but those who have a belief that there is love, meaning and purpose hidden in these mysteries see many of their patients finding relief and peace in their own way.' What are the milestones on this journey?

For well over a decade after her conversion in 1945 Cicely found spiritual nourishment in the evangelical church of All Souls, Langham Place. She was enthusiastic, diligent and zealous – even for a while counselling for Billy Graham. But her loyalty became increasingly strained during the fifties and finally snapped after Antoni's death. 'I went back to All Souls after Antoni died when I was absolutely numb and needed the Communion of Saints and the Church as a whole to carry me and it couldn't do it. It was very much your own individual relationship to God and although I wasn't saying "Why?" to God particularly, I went to All Souls trying to feel I had some communion with Antoni and that the Communion Service would be the closest place. I remember going on All Souls Day and of the two prayers in the 1662 Prayer Book one of them does talk about the whole communion and they used the other one and I felt so bitter about that. I couldn't understand how they didn't realise how much we needed the whole Church. It isn't just a one to one relationship with God – it's all the rest as well.'

She then went for a while to Christchurch at Lancaster Gate, where Tony Bridge (who later became Dean of Guildford) was drawing an enthusiastic congregation. Cicely was not yet ready to stray too far from her evangelical roots and when, at a discussion at the Rectory, Tony Bridge began 'de-mythologising' elements in the Bible, she remembers saying rather pathetically, 'But there *was* a star.' Her father had just died, she was still coping with the loss of Antoni and Mrs. G. – 'I simply couldn't take having everything unpicked on me like that.' So she climbed another step higher on the liturgical ladder and, at the suggestion of a priest she had met at Grandchamps, she went to a high Anglo-Catholic church near her flat in Connaught Square. She was fairly happy there for a couple of years, though she felt she was 'still floundering around rather', when a new priest arrived, keen to know his congregation; he would stand at the door after services shaking hands, asking people how they were, who they were. This apparently innocuous action was too much for Cicely. She fled into the anonymity of Westminster Abbey.

Cicely's delight in being able to disappear into Westminster Abbey comes from something deep inside her, beyond shyness or modesty. She is not an analytical person and does not dwell on the meaning of her dreams, or even recall them very often. But she does remember a long and vivid dream about a journey – significantly most of her dreams are about journeys – in which she had got out of some kind of prison and was walking along a road saying to herself, 'I'm too visible, I must make myself more invisible,' and covering herself with dust from the road. She really *does* believe that St. Christopher's and the care of the dying is more important than she is, that God is infinitely more important than both. (This may sound obvious, but of how many pioneers can one truly say it?) She tries to do what she honestly believes to be the will of God, she does not wish to promote herself. This is rather charmingly proved by a recent exchange with someone from the National Hospice Organization in America. He wanted to dedicate a book he was writing to Elisabeth Kübler-Ross, Mother Teresa and Cicely and would she please send a photograph of herself? She wrote back, 'The whole community's done this, not me,' and enclosed a photo of St. Christopher's.

This deep-seated and genuine humility before the face of God has led her to what Elizabeth Earnshaw-Smith calls 'a religious position independent of the institutional church from which she can soak up what she needs from other faiths.' Despite some theological problems (Hell –

'it's there but it's empty. Hell means separation from God, so God could not want people to be there unless they wanted to be – and how could they once they'd seen Him.' Mary – 'Difficult. The epitome of mourning, watching people suffer') she calls herself 'a basic Christian', and while she describes herself as an Anglican, she is both grateful for her evangelical years and attracted to Roman Catholicism, though she 'could never take anything that said there was only one way.'

For Cicely, as her dreams reflect, the spiritual life is an endless journey; now, in her sixties, she can embrace all faiths in the conviction that they lead to the same God. She is delighted that St. Christopher's has a Jewish founding patient (David Tasma) and a Jewish chairman (Dame Albertine Winner); her anthology on suffering includes Chinese, Jewish and agnostic writers as well as Christian and shows the breadth of her reading as well as her sympathies. She does not seek to impose her faith, rather to set people free to find their own.

Yet at the heart is a profound Christianity which can say that St. Christopher's is 'fully committed to the belief that, in Jesus of Nazareth, God knew a human life and the ultimate weakness of death as we know them, and this for all men, whether or not they believe.' In a book primarily for the medical profession, she quoted Isaiah: 'In all their afflictions he was afflicted, and the angel of his presence saved them,' and continued, 'Only a God whose love shares all pain from within can still our doubts and questions, not because we understand but because we can trust. There is a sense in which we say, "This is my body" of each dying person and in which the small transformations that we witness continually speak of a Resurrection which will finally redeem and encompass all creation. This is the edge of that unsearchable abyss of deity which we meet in our daily experience, the beyond in our midst.'

Cicely's Christianity is practical. She has had experiences which must be called mystical: when she was converted, after David's death, in her relationship with Antoni and in Switzerland before her father's death. Im-

portant though these experiences were, Christianity for
Cicely is above all in responding to God's call in a very
down to earth way; if that includes seven years training to
be a doctor and several more battling with bureaucracy
and trusts to build a hospice, then that is what she does.
She knows that the Church has a special responsibility to
the dying, she knows that she is called to work for them,
believing that 'If God calls, He also enables.' The maxim
'God helps those who help themselves' appeals to her – she
believes we are independent of God as well as dependent
on him. Having this freedom brings a responsibility to
respond to a vocation; she does respond – with that unusual combination of being able to act when action is
called for, to wait and listen when the next move is
unclear. Though she has something of 'the faith that
moves mountains', she does not sit back and wait for it to
happen. A sermon on this in Westminster Abbey impressed her. 'He described the faith that would move a
mountain in what was for me a new way. One person,
looking at a mountain above a cliff, became convinced that
it should be moved into the sea. So he took a wheelbarrow
and a spade and began, load by load, to push it over the
cliff. For a while he kept on alone, then one or two others,
instead of mocking him, thought that this was something
that needed doing, and joined him. Later others saw it as a
possibility and joined also. Eventually the mountain was
no more.' The preacher could have been describing the
planning and building of St. Christopher's.

The tension between the inner and outer in the spiritual
life is something that Cicely seems to have resolved. 'We
know ourselves so little and we know God still less.
Sometimes the way of finding Him is by a readiness to
plumb our own inner depths. If we can find our own well
spring of being we may have found something of our link
with the maker of all things. But another, and for many a
less hazardous way, is in knowing others. We are more
likely to find our Incarnate God in others than in words or
concepts. I believe that the response to His call through
patients, in their need and their achievement, has been a

place of safety for us.' (A sometimes confusing indication
of Cicely's modesty is her use of 'us' and 'we' when she
means 'me' and 'I'. She often disclaims her own importance
in a conversation with a patient by saying 'He said to
us . . .')

Legally St. Christopher's is both a religious and medical
foundation, there has never been any doubt about that.
The Articles of Association undertake to promote the
relief of suffering 'By providing or assisting or encouraging the provision of spiritual help and guidance for any
persons resident (either as patients or otherwise) or working in any such home or homes as aforesaid.' To this end
they promise 'To provide or arrange for a building or
premises to be used by the Association as a church or
chapel available for Christian worship.'

These few lines, which result from so much thought
in the very early sixties, hardly reflect the place religion
has at St. Christopher's. They hardly could. A religious
approach to life has permeated every aspect of the Hospice
since before its conception. An agnostic St. Christopher's
would be like bread without salt.

The first breath of religious inspiration was, in a sense,
in 1945, when Cicely asked what she should do with her
life in gratitude for her conversion to Christianity. During
the three years she had to wait for the answer and the
nineteen years working to create a context for its expression, this wind was always behind her back, inspiring her
and those she gathered round her. Before the first spit was
dug the Bishop of Stepney articulated their aim, 'so to
minister to the whole personality that those whom we
shall serve may be able to lose their fear of death and to
find in it, not primarily an end of life in this world, but the
beginning of a fuller life in the world to come.' A bare two
days after the Hospice had been officially opened, Cicely
wrote to the Bishop, 'Today we are having our first Communion Service, with two patients down from the wards in
their beds, so we have really gone straight on with the
important things.'

The infusion of a religious attitude is symbolised by the central position of the Chapel. After considerable extension in 1973, it is now a long room, occupying almost half the width of the building. At the front and slightly below ground level, it is immediately visible to anyone coming into the Hospice or even passing by it. It is a simple room, though not austere. The only picture is a glowing triptych, in which the incarnation, the crucifixion and the resurrection are united. There is an altar, a cross, plenty of chairs and room for wheel-chairs and beds. It is, as it were, a *tabula rasa*, reflecting the essence of faith but leaving each individual free to interpret it in his own way, uncluttered by symbols which, while helpful to some, might be confusing to others. It is essentially an ecumenical chapel, as was the intention when it was dedicated at a service conducted by the Bishop of Stepney, a Methodist minister and Father Larn, who is still the Roman Catholic chaplain, a few weeks before the Hospice was officially opened by Princess Alexandra. The order of service, drawn up by the Hospitals' Chaplains Council, was approved by the Anglican, Roman Catholic and Free Church Authorities. St. Christopher's was making official its declared intention of being open to people of any religious persuasion or of none – it is not merely ecumenical by default. 'We must remember,' wrote Cicely, 'that we belong to a much wider community of the whole Church, to the whole Communion of Saints and, indeed, to the whole community of all men. It is because of this that St. Christopher's is ecumenical and undenominational. We are not emphasising that there is just one way but rather that there is one Person coming in many ways.'

So St. Christopher's was conceived, planned and built as an ecumenical Christian foundation. How does it work in practice?

There is not much structured religious life, probably not much more than in many hospitals. There are short services in the Chapel every morning and evening, Holy Communion two or three times a week, a Roman Catholic

Mass on Tuesdays and prayers in the wards at the beginning and end of every day. This is a moving occasion. The ward is very quiet and everyone working there – nurses, auxiliaries, volunteers – stands by the bed of a patient and together they say a few prayers from a card. The patient may be taking part, vaguely aware or asleep; he may be a believer or not. Somehow everyone is taken up into a stillness, a peace. Death is very close for someone, but the air is full of gentleness, not fear.

There is a Roman Catholic priest who comes in regularly, the tradition of a 'Visitor' started by the Bishop of Stepney continues – the current occupant is the former Chaplain Philip Edwards – there are ordinands, usually six at a time, who stay for a year, assisting the Chaplain and working as auxiliary nurses, and a full-time Anglican Chaplain.

Cicely's relationship with the Chaplain has never been an easy one. The Chapel is the one place where she has no professional role. It is also her parish church, for she has attended no other church regularly since St. Christopher's opened. Her concern for detail, her strong feelings as to how the place should be run, her views on how the Chaplain should do his job, and the fact that he is the official spokesman for her religious vision, all make for strains and tensions. To be Chaplain at St. Christopher's is no sinecure.

But what distinguishes the religious climate of St. Christopher's is neither Cicely nor the Chaplain, but the extent to which all the staff, at least potentially, are involved in the spiritual care of the patient.

Dr. Gillian Ford has spent long hours discussing this with Cicely. They argued that Christ's sacrifice was for all humanity, not just those who happen to hear about it. 'It follows that all may need to minister and all may need to be ministered unto, and that help for those in spiritual pain may be required from any member of staff, not just the hospice Chaplain . . . the Hospice is a religious foundation in the sense that all – staff, patients, families – are perceived as fellow travellers with something important to share about the pilgrimage ... the assumption of a pastoral role by any and everybody might look like religious arrogance, but it is part of this attitude of respect accorded to all – not just patients. The ward orderly or the volunteer may be the person who wittingly or not plays a crucial role. If help is asked for, staff are expected to don a pastoral mantle and give it.'

And they do. First and most important they give *time*. Nobody is going to feel able to discuss questions of life and death and the existence of God, still less their own life and death, if they feel an invisible meter is clocking up the minutes. At St. Christopher's the relaxed atmosphere provides a climate in which patients have the freedom to talk or not, as they wish. It is quite usual to see two or three nurses chatting round a patient's bed. This is not a formal session focusing – perhaps embarrassingly and at the wrong moment – on the patient and his needs, but a natural exchange of news and views between people. Ted Holden, who had motor neurone disease and could hardly speak, experienced this from a special and rather extreme position. 'I rarely feel lonely because, although I am alone for many hours I always have the feeling of belonging. So one way or another I do pretty well for companionship. What is so good is that it is all free and easy. People just drop in for a chat or to give me the latest ward news and, dare I say it, even the occasional moan. Unless they are very good actors I have the feeling that they come because they want to, which is good for my ego . . . You can find out what makes people tick through normal relaxed conversation, not by inquisition on an obviously limited timescale.' Ted Holden, one of Cicely's favourite patients, remained an agnostic until he died.

The way in which the staff of St. Christopher's respond to the spiritual needs of the dying is summed up in Christ's words to his disciples in the Garden of Gethsemane. 'Tarry ye here and watch with me.' Cicely used this as her theme in an article in the *Nursing Times*. '"Watch with me" means, still more than all our learning and skills, our attempts to understand mental suffering and loneliness and to pass on what we have learnt. It means also a great deal that cannot be understood. Those words did not mean "understand what is happening" when they were first spoken. Still less did they mean "explain" or "take away". However much we can ease distress, however much we can help the patients to find a new meaning in what is happening, there will always be a place where we will have to stop and know that we are really helpless. It would be wrong if, at that point, we tried to forget that this was so and to pass by. It would be wrong if we tried to cover it up, to deny it and to delude ourselves that we were always successful. Even when we can do absolutely nothing, we still have to be prepared to stay. "Watch with me" means, above all, just "Be there".'

There is always someone at St. Christopher's to 'be there'. Tom West is continually moved by the change in a patient's face when they are assured they will not die alone. If there is no friend or relative present during the last hours, then someone from the ward will sit by the bed, just waiting, watching, perhaps reading a book. The patient wants a friendly presence, not necessarily undivided attention. If someone dies unexpectedly, alone, it is a source of real pain to the nurses, who will agonise over what they see as something which should never happen at the Hospice. It rarely does.

Cicely often remembers that when she asked Antoni what he needed above all in those caring for him, he said, 'For someone to look as if they are trying to understand me.' It is a meeting of people that is needed. To look them in the eye, to try to understand; Antoni did not ask for success, only that someone should care enough to try. 'We should face honestly the thought of the anxiety and depression of a long illness or the loss of faculties, all the humiliation and deprivations, the guilt aroused by dependence, weakness and incontinence and the sometimes desperate feelings of isolation from life and living.'

People at St. Christopher's aren't afraid of being involved, they're not afraid of having a real affection for a patient, though they recognise the dangers. The help they try to give is not learnt by a special therapeutic or pastoral technique, it is harder than that. David Tasma said 'I want what is in your mind and in your heart'. Did he realise just how much he was asking for? The dying usually shed the masks of everyday living, let the barriers down. This demands that the person with them must come as themselves, no defences, attentive, vulnerable. That is very demanding.

This attitude of loving respect may or may not be linked with a religious faith. The majority of people working at St. Christopher's are committed believers, for some it is simply an extension of being a caring human being. But there is no doubt that the attitude comes from Cicely in the first instance, nor from where Cicely's compassion is derived.

We rightly give emphasis to the truth that it is our hands that are used for His work of healing; but we tend to forget that it is also to Him that we minister. As we remember this we learn more of the respect and attention we owe our patients. They respond more to our thoughts about them than to our words to them, and it is honour and not pity that we owe them. The former will lift them with its expectations of achievement and the latter can be so corrosive to their morale. Suffering was – and is – the place where Christ is glorified. He is there whether He is recognised or not. The simple truths that He knows so much better than we ever can, that He knew such dependence that He even had to have His own cross carried for Him, seems to have meaning for the most unaccustomed ears and to need little explanation. I believe that this is because such sufferers are in the place of his deepest identification with us all.

If the involvement of the staff in the spiritual care of the patients is one distinguishing feature of St. Christopher's approach to religion, the other is the sensitivity with

which religion is always available but never pushed.
Philip Edwards used to say 'We don't talk about religion
here, it just happens.'

One way in which it happens is, of course, in prayer.
Prayers are continually offered for patients and their
families both collectively and individually. A board outside the Chapel lists the names of everybody who died at
St. Christopher's a year ago; Cicely's correspondence with
people like the Bishop of Stepney and Sister Mary Eleanor
is full of matter of fact requests for people who need their
prayers. 'We have some splendid patients. Would you
please take on Mrs. Elliott, aged thirty-five with four
young children under eleven, who has been told lies all
along the line and has no idea, so far as I can see that she is
so ill. She has a delightful husband. I know little more
than this at the moment. Thank you for remembering
Miss Hooker. She died yesterday morning in complete
quietness having reached a peace which showed through
her semi-consciousness of the last ten days, till on Monday
she suddenly opened her eyes and gave a most wonderful
farewell smile to her devoted friend. This has completely
altered the friend's acceptance of the situation and the end
has been more peaceful and positive than we could ever
have imagined.'

While it is Cicely's faith which has built St. Christopher's it is her refusal to put pressure on anybody to
think as she does that has kept the Hospice spiritually
alive. Though she does not always find it easy, she tries
hard to balance the certainty of faith with the flexibility of
tolerance. Dr. Gillian Ford, a Deputy Chief Medical
Officer at the Department of Health, is impressed by the
way Cicely's work and attitudes are appreciated by people
in her department and in the National Health Service,
many of whom may have little or no share in her beliefs.
'Perhaps it is an instance of faith and works being so fused
together that willy-nilly both are perceived even when
love of God is instantly transmuted to love of man by the
individual who accepts no God. There are I believe instances where a deep and professed faith such as Cicely's

provokes hostile and even fearful reactions in those who do not share it. That this does not happen is not because of compromise or trimming on Cicely's part. Why? How? No precise answers save that I suspect that her faith is not felt as a condemnation by those who do not aspire to it. Nor is it a threat; perhaps at the very least its valuation of each individual (not necessarily a patient) causes the individual to recognise within themselves their own capability to love and to give.'

'He's himself', the phrase that Cicely learnt to value at St. Joseph's, lives again at St. Christopher's. There is great joy when someone discovers meaning in their situation, finds their own way of handling it, perhaps even accepting it peacefully. St. Christopher's does not seek 'death-bed conversions'; but they rejoice at small transformations in the context of the individual's own personality and spiritual background; transformations which come from *within* the person.

Like Paula – young, blonde and beautiful, facing her death in the tough, realistic way in which she had lived her life. However ill she felt, she was always immaculate and demanding, so determined to assert her atheism that she put a horny little red devil in the wall niche by her bed where the cross had been, looking sideways at the nurses to make sure they had noticed and taken the point. The night before she died she questioned the night sister about her beliefs – what was the meaning of life? Was there anything beyond it? At the end she said, 'I can't say I believe like that, would it be all right if I just said that I hoped?' A very small transformation, but it enabled her to take off her false eyelashes saying, 'I don't need these any more' and die peacefully.

Living with dying means facing reality. One of the realities which has to be faced daily is whether a patient knows that he is dying, and if he apparently does not, should he be told?

This is something which has touched Cicely's life since she was in her early twenties, training to be a nurse. She wrote from Botley's Park War Hospital to her friend Bridget Gibb, 'What I was going to say last night was – do you think people should be told they're going to die? We are given classes on Ethics and so on but we are never told anything about that. It is the sister's responsibility of course – but when one is asked outright it's very hard to know what to say. When I know Sister hasn't told them – which is nearly always – and they bring the subject up – usually indirectly but not always – I just promise them that by the same time next year they'll have forgotten what all this pain and misery felt like. But when they are prepared to face up to it I think we should let them.' She went on to tell her friend of a woman dying of cancer of the neck, depressed, irritable, unhappy. The patient asked the sister what was wrong with her and the sister told her. 'She has been a different person ever since. She has faced and accepted it. She has confidence that they won't let her suffer more than they can help and she has been a new person – much happier. There is no limit to what human beings can stand.'

In this awareness that people can be happier knowing the truth, Cicely and that ward sister were years ahead of their time. Over twenty years later, in an article about the opening of St. Christopher's, the *Lancet* commented that many doctors 'hold sincerely that their patients (and the patients' relatives) must not be told their illness may be mortal.'

During the years between, Cicely had been wrestling with this problem; it had cost her deeply both professionally and personally. When she was working briefly at St. Luke's as a research doctor, after much thought and prayer she told a woman patient she was dying. Those in charge felt that this should not be done by a visiting person, and despite the nurses rising to her defence, Cicely was asked to leave. Not surprisingly this hurt her, badly, though she found some comfort later in learning that several people working with the dying in those days were thrown out at some time, for similar reasons.

On a personal level it was she who had to tell both David

Tasma and Antoni that they were dying and in Antoni's response, 'Was it hard to tell me that?' lies the key to her attitude.

It *should* be hard. That patient is hearing the most momentous news of his life; if the one who bears it is entering into the situation with real compassion, it will be an important and taxing experience for him too. It should call out every reserve of sensitivity, for not everyone wants to know the full truth and it is often necessary to wait and listen, possibly over several weeks, to find out just what the patient's needs really are. Perhaps he knows in his heart that he is dying but does not want it confirmed, perhaps he knows with certainty but does not wish to discuss it. The real question, as Cicely constantly repeats, is 'What do you let your patients tell you?'

Though there is no 'technique' for such a situation, nurses and doctors at St. Christopher's are encouraged to return a question with another question. This avoids prevarication or lying, it also gives the patient every chance to handle the situation in his own way, not having the truth thrust upon him before he is ready for it. Dr. West recalls a conversation in which the patient guided him quite clearly as to the answer she wanted.

Patient – 'Am I going to get better?'

Doctor – 'Why do you ask me at our first meeting?'

Patient – 'Because I think you might give me a straight answer.'

Doctor – 'All right – no, you are not.'

Patient – 'I know. I've known for a month. Please tell my husband.'

In fact the husband had known too. Now they were able to share the truth and live fully and openly the time that was left.

Taking the cue from the patient does not give an automatic green light for answering questions he has not asked. There are many ways of telling the truth, it is not simply a choice between silence, denial or stark, brutal honesty. 'We have to try and learn to give the truth the individual needs at that moment in the simplest and kindest way we can offer it, leaving him the choice to take it or leave it as he wishes. One patient may be anxiously preventing us from assaulting him with information he is not able or willing to handle; while another has already come to terms with a hopeless prognosis but needs reassurance to dispel inaccurate and often horrible apprehensions.'

There are people who can bear the continual strain of living so close to death and dying without a religious faith, but for most people at St. Christopher's, and certainly for Cicely, the ability to cope is rooted in the certainty of the love of God and the conviction that death is the gateway to a new and better life. Cicely has no doubt that there is a meaning to human suffering, that dying can be a positive achievement, that God's hand is visible most clearly of all in the meeting place between this world and the next, that the person who sits by the bedside of a dying person is never alone. 'We're not only saying we've got a friendly community attitude to offer, though we have. But over and above that is the knowledge that the God whom a lot of us believe in, even if we express it in different ways, is the God who himself suffered and died. And in no way is one ever the only person on the watch at the bedside with somebody who is going through great anguish of spirit and mind. He's present there, in a way in which we can perhaps never be. But we can perhaps help not to interrupt, by making the other things as efficient and compassionate as we can.'

Cicely was talking once to Louie, one of her friends at St. Joseph's, about death and dying, and she asked her what was the first thing she would say to God. Louie, without hesitation said, 'I know you'. It is this sort of knowing that sustains Cicely – not just knowing *about* God. She too, has her personal experience of God; she knows, as few people know, about loss and parting. Surely she was thinking of Antoni when she wrote of the dying, 'As the complications of life fall away, they meet us with such simplicity and affection and sometimes it seems that they turn back, just for a moment, when they have already seen something of what is to come. It is as if the answer to all their questions is so unbelievably satisfying, as if all suffering were so completely transformed that they could almost laugh at it all. And joy like this cannot help lifting our hearts.'

Anyone who doubts that there can be joy in a Hospice has only to go to St. Christopher's. Whatever the tensions inevitable in a community working so closely together – and they're there all right – whatever the sadness of loss, the pain of parting, the overriding impression is of peace, there's no denying it. Has anyone the right to doubt that this lies in the vision that inspired it? 'God is the centre. But He is also the foundation, the periphery, the ground of our being if you like to call it that. Transcendent as well as immanent and the person who meets the patient. He is everything at St. Christopher's, and our job there will be to get the patients quiet of their physical and mental distress so that they can listen to him who will, most surely, speak to them.'

In founding St. Christopher's as both a religious and a medical foundation, Cicely risked commanding the total respect of neither. In particular she had to contend with the suspicion of members of the medical profession who felt that work inspired by religion could not be scientifically credible. The Bishop of Winchester feels 'she has been motivated by a deep metaphysical concern over the proper definition of what a human being is.' It is this concern that has enabled her to balance religion and medicine – traditionally at odds, united at St. Christopher's.

ST. CHRISTOPHER'S AS A MEDICAL FOUNDATION

Efficiency is comforting.
Christopher Saunders

When Cicely offered to read to David Tasma, thinking to comfort him, he said, 'No – no reading. I only want what is in your mind and in your heart.' She has never forgotten this simple reaction; mind and heart have become twin poles of St. Christopher's philosophy. The dying need the friendship of the heart – its qualities of care, acceptance, vulnerability; but they also need the skills of the mind – the most sophisticated treatment that medicine has to offer. On its own, neither is enough.

If Cicely's heart had not been touched, so deeply and so often, she would not have had the stimulus to use her mind so effectively. St. Christopher's is the creative outcome of her pain. She has had more than her share of pain; she has experienced it, absorbed it, prayed and thought about it; she has used it to ease the suffering of the dying. Entering into their mental and spiritual pain is one side of this coin; the other is the control of physical pain and the relief of distressing symptoms. Unless the body is reasonably comfortable, it is hard for people to be open to the spiritual comfort or to the possibility of the peaceful death that Cicely longs for them to achieve. St. Christopher's set out to establish and maintain the highest medical standards with a firm scientific basis. It has succeeded: the medical excellence of St. Christopher's is recognised throughout the profession.

The aim of a hospice is not to cure; by the time a patient

arrives it has usually been admitted that he is not likely to get better. But that does not mean that medicine has no further part to play. One of the initial battles which Cicely had to fight was against the profession's resistance to accepting that a patient could not be cured. Doctors tend to equate death with failure and all too often when faced with it lose interest, avoid the subject, even avoid the patient. Thus they were not receptive to ideas on how much medicine could still do in the way of treatment. That this attitude has changed so much is one of Cicely's greatest achievements.

To understand the size of this achievement it is necessary to realise how the medical profession reacted to the dying in the fifties, when Cicely was a medical student. Dr. Tony Brown, a friend and contemporary of Cicely's, says, 'We modelled ourselves as students on the Gothic consultants, who did their ward rounds with a retinue, hardly ever spoke to the patient and discussed the patient's illness and symptoms in front of him. The dying patient was hidden away. Doctors were brought up to think of death as a defeat.' So the patient, often shuffled into a side ward, was left alone, as the doctors hurried past them and the nurses talked about everything except the one thing that preoccupied them. They were not allowed to face their own deaths openly and with dignity.

Occasionally someone would try to break through this barrier. Colin Murray Parkes tried to when he was a student in a ward where there was a woman who was very ill, very frightened, dying. 'I was on the ward when she was opening a parcel with a cake in it and she said "Would you like a piece of cake?" I was delighted because it gave me an excuse to sit and chat to her. So I sat down munching my cake and chatting to her, when the senior registrar came into the ward, turned on his heel and walked out again. A moment later a nurse came along and said he would like to see me. Every patient on the ward knew I was going to be reprimanded for being familiar with a patient.'

Cicely had not trained in three branches of medicine

without being aware of this attitude. When she talked to an audience of doctors at a British Medical Association Congress she knew very well that some of them would be shocked that she should talk of preparing for death and would assume that both the patient and the doctor should fight for life right up to the end. 'But to talk of accepting death when its approach has become inevitable is not mere resignation or feeble submission on the part of the patient, nor is it defeatism or neglect on the part of the doctor. For both of them it is the very opposite of doing nothing. Our work then is to alter the character of this inevitable process so that it is not seen as a defeat of living but as a positive achievement in dying; an intensely individual achievement for the patient.'

Her aim was to build a relationship of trust, communication and acceptance between doctor and patient, to make the quality of the life remaining to the patient as comfortable and meaningful as possible, to keep the patient free of pain, yet mentally alert, until almost the end of life.

While Cicely's contribution to pain control is honoured throughout the medical profession, her own attitude is matter-of-fact. 'There aren't too many original ideas in the world, it's only a question of putting several ideas together and giving the kaleidoscope a shake and the pieces come down a bit different.' So she took the regular giving of drugs from St. Luke's, she used the new drugs that were becoming available in the 1950s and early sixties – the tranquillisers, synthetic steroids and antidepressants – and she put these medical skills into the context of what she calls 'total pain'. She had learnt from her own experience with patients that pain is not just physical, it is also emotional, social and spiritual. As early as 1963 a patient at St. Joseph's had unwittingly given her this key. Talking about her pain she said, 'It began in my back, but now it seems as if all of me is wrong. I began to cry for the pills and the injections but I knew that I mustn't. It began to seem as if all the world was against me, nobody seemed to understand. My husband and son were marvellous, but they were having to stay off work and lose their money. It's marvellous to begin to feel safe again.'

In this sad statement lie all the components of total pain. The physical pain, invading her whole body; the emotional pain of feeling isolated and alone; the social pain of worrying about her family and their financial problems; the spiritual pain, already relieved by the welcome she had received at St. Joseph's – the need for meaning and the need for safety.

By treating the whole person rather than just the physical pain Cicely found that the actual pain is often reduced, that if a patient feels that he is heard and understood the lessening of anxiety leads to a lessening of the drug requirements. But her most tangible contribution to pain control, probably her single most important contribution to the medical world, lies in her adoption of the regular giving of drugs that she studied at St. Luke's and developed at St. Joseph's. The pain must be dealt with *before* it recurs, the patient must never have to ask for pills or injections, or wait fearful and ashamed to ask for them. The difference that the regular giving of drugs can make to a patient's state of mind is graphically illustrated by this conversation with a patient. Cicely asked her what the pain was like before she was admitted to St. Joseph's.

Patient – 'Well, it was ever so bad. It used to be just like a vice gripping my spine – going like that and would then let go again. I didn't get my injections regularly – they used to leave me as long as they could and if I asked for them sometimes they used to say, "No, wait a bit longer." They didn't want me to rely on the drugs that were there, you see. They used to try and see how long I could go without an injection . . . I used to be pouring with sweat, you know, because of the pain . . . I couldn't speak to anyone, I was in such pain. And I was having crying fits – I mean I haven't cried, I think I've only cried once since I've been here, that's well over a week. And I was crying every day at the other hospital. I was 'very depressed, ever so depressed. But I'm not at all depressed here, not like I was there.'

Dr. Saunders – 'Since you've been here and I put you on regular injections, what's the difference?'

Patient – 'Well, the biggest difference is, of course, this feeling so calm. I don't get worked up, I don't get upset, I don't cry, I don't get very very depressed – you know. Really black thoughts were going through my mind, and no matter how kind people were, and people were ever so kind – nothing could console me, you see. But since I've been here I feel more hopeful as well.'

But this is not the whole story. Even if physical pain is controlled the dying person can still be troubled by other symptoms, equally distressing – breathlessness and its consequent anxiety, restlessness, depression, nausea, vomiting, guilt and shame over incontinence, bed sores, loss of appetite, a dry and uncomfortable mouth. These symptoms can almost always be alleviated by the proper use of medication, but skilled, careful nursing is essential.

The specialised nursing skills at St. Christopher's are such that nurses increase their reputation in the profession by working there – some come for short periods to do just that. While St. Christopher's has been fortunate in its Matrons, first Verena Galton, then Helen Willans, now Madeleine Duffield, Cicely can take much of the credit herself, especially for the standards set in the early days, when she often stayed the night on the premises and was around the wards all the time. Barbara McNulty, as one of the first ward sisters, feels privileged to have had the close association with her that nurses had in those days. 'One absorbed a whole medical expertise, a whole attitude to death and dying, a whole religious ethos, which in many ways was a novel and certainly an expanding, growing experience. She was there even at eleven o'clock at night if you were on night duty, and she would come down if there was a problem or you could ring her up and talk to her. She was quite extraordinary – she'd be available twenty-four hours a day.'

Her own nursing experience clearly gives Cicely a special insight into the way nurses think. Helen Willans feels that 'her vision of the necessity of being a team, her respect for nurses, the way in which nurses are treated as intelligent colleagues – is something very special to St. Christopher's. It isn't a thing to be taken for granted. There is a school of thought which thinks that the nurses are the doctors' handmaids.'

Far from being the doctors' handmaids, the nurses carry a great responsibility. On the personal level they are more often at the bedside, more often involved in listening and talking to patients and relatives than any doctor. It is often a nurse, for instance, who is asked the crucial question, 'Am I going to get better?' They are almost always present at the moment of death, they say the final prayers for the departed, lay out the body and take it to the mortuary feeling that it is, as one nurse said 'a very great joy to be able to do this very last thing for them'.

They are also more deeply involved in the medical care than the average hospital nurse, and were, even in those early days Barbara McNulty remembers. 'Cicely always taught the nurses to use their own judgement on what the patient's pain was doing, so that the nurse came to know the patient extremely well and learned to listen to what he had to say. The nurses were given the latitude in the giving of drugs – five to ten milligrams of whatever it was – they had freedom to use what they felt the patient needed.' The doctors would then base their prescriptions on the nurses' assessment. Co-operation has increased since those early days, as the Hospice has come to adopt a multi-disciplinary approach to patients and the nurses take their place with colleagues from other professions involved in the total care of the patient.

Cicely's passion for detail, which can be irritating, finds its most creative outlet on the wards, for hospice nursing is above all attention to detail. Patients at St. Christopher's are not likely to benefit from sophisticated technological procedures, the skills the nurses need are not those needed by the nurse in a renal dialysis unit or in intensive care, but they are quite as demanding.

It was a nurse who thought up a solution to the problem of a man with motor neurone disease who was unable to swallow, but who enjoyed his whisky. They froze it into cubes so he could suck it. This concern for the individual wishes of each patient is the key to the very special care given by the nurses at St. Christopher's. They will painstakingly arrange and re-arrange pillows, move the television an inch here, an inch there, to find a comfortable position for someone who cannot move his head; a note on the patient's file might say 'Wind clock daily' or will remind them that a patient likes to sleep with a crucifix in her hand or have the curtains drawn in a particular way. There is also endless, meticulous attention to physical comfort – careful washing out of mouths, bathing sore eyes, putting soothing cream on elbows, placing cushions between sleeping knees.

They are rightly proud of their standard of nursing, but anxious not to seem critical of general hospitals who simply cannot give that sort of attention. Cicely says it is 'just what every nurse would like to give if they had time,' – and time is essential for nursing of this standard. Hospice care demands a high nurse-patient ratio – at present there is more than one nurse on St. Christopher's pay roll for each patient bed, of whom about half are trained. But time is in the mind as well as on the clock, and nurses who return to general hospitals often find they are able to give a little more time than they thought, if only, as one of them said, 'By spending any free moments talking to the patients rather than chatting to each other in the sluice.'

Cicely's nursing training has stood her in good stead with the doctors as well as with the nurses themselves. Until recently she spent every other weekend on the wards. 'On the Monday morning the custom was for the other doctors who had been off for the weekend to as it were line up in front of her desk – that's how it felt anyway – and Cicely, without a note in front of her, would go through fifty-four names and she would tell us about patients we had been caring for the whole of the previous week. She had picked up things we had missed in the course of a mere weekend and she'd been covering three wards.' Dr. West, who recalls this with affectionate envy, had not had Cicely's experience at St. Thomas's – a young nurse having to report, without notes, on half a large ward to an exacting sister.

St. Christopher's have, in a very large majority of cases, succeeded in controlling pain and alleviating symptoms. Twenty years ago Cicely had shown at St. Joseph's that pain could nearly always be controlled. Now detailed evaluation and studies are available as clinical proof. Dr. Parkes' research into the memories of the families of patients who died at St. Christopher's during the years 1977–9 showed that thirty-three per cent had no pain at all during their final phase and none suffered 'extreme or very severe' pain; only seven per cent had pain that was called 'severe' and sixty per cent 'mild to moderate'. (Hospice records of a similar study done ten years earlier show that much of this pain remembered by the families was in fact intermittent and almost always relieved.) There are countless surviving friends and relatives to witness to their experience that death can be peaceful and under hospice conditions nearly always is, that the last weeks of life can be among the most rewarding, that life for those who live on is made more bearable by the use that has been made of the time that precedes separation. How does this effect the proposition that voluntary euthanasia should be legalised?

Given Cicely's religious beliefs, one would hardly expect her to condone the killing of one person by another, whatever their motives, but her objections to euthanasia are not based on her religious convictions or her views on the sanctity of life, but on her knowledge of what medical care can do. She is also very aware of the social pressures that any legislation could bring.

Cicely has been an active and vocal opponent of euthanasia since long before the Hospice opened. Though she does not believe that St. Christopher's should be a pressure group, she has felt that the staff should stand up and be counted. In 1969, when the bill to legalise euthanasia was put before the House of Lords she wrote a long letter to *The Times* in which she listed some of the medical objections to the bill. 'We, as doctors, are concerned to emphasise that there are few forms of physical distress which cannot be dealt with by good medical and nursing care, that the emotional and spiritual distress of incurable disease requires human understanding and compassion and a readiness to listen and help rather than a lethal drug.' She has debated at the Royal Society of Health and the Cambridge Union, written articles, broadcast, been a member of a working party set up by the Church of England Board of Social Responsibility, and, with the Council of St. Christopher's, made a submission to the Criminal Law Revision Committee, who were suggesting that there should be an offence of 'mercy killing' distinguishing it from murder. Her arguments have impressed even the most fervent supporters of euthanasia. In 1961 after she took Dr. Leonard Colebrook, then chairman of the Voluntary Euthanasia Society, round St. Joseph's he wrote to her, 'I still feel that there would be little or no problem of euthanasia if all the terminal disease folk could end their lives in that atmosphere you have done so much to create – but alas that can hardly be for many a long year.' Since then, the proper care of the terminally ill has spread so widely that the arguments against 'mercy killing' have a widespread clinical back-up that they did not have in the early sixties. There is now a track record to support the theory. Let one patient, cited by Dr. West in the *Journal of the Royal Society of Medicine*, speak for all.

I admitted Mrs. M. to St. Christopher's from a local hospital on the 19th May, 1977. She had an inoperable carcinoma of the pancreas with secondary deposits in

the liver. She was in severe pain. The medical student
with me was appalled at her suffering.

On the application form was written 'She does not
know she has carcinoma.' On questioning she said to me
'When you have pain for a year you start to think!' Of
course she knew. She had had a very sad marriage. By
listening to her story and observing her carefully a
correct assessment was made of the physical and mental
components of her pain and the correct drugs were
prescribed. Within a few days she admitted that the
pain was under control for the first time for a year. She
did not remain completely pain-free. But each Monday
she had her hair washed and set, each Thursday she
visited our weekly bar, and each Sunday she came to
chapel. The ward staff soon learned that with meticulous attention to her drugs, and with even more meticulous attention to herself, when pain did break
through, it could almost always be alleviated.

She was with us just under three months. Her last few
days were peaceful and pain-free and she died surrounded by three faithful friends, the ward sister and a
nurse. A few days later one of her friends wrote: 'When I
visited her in a previous hospital she was like a demented animal – consumed with pain ... I was very
frightened, not knowing how to cope ... I saw her in St.
Christopher's restored to the dignity of a calm rational
human being ... from then on I was able to remain with
her for hours, instead of minutes ... discussing things
dear to her heart ... By so doing I, too, have gained in
spiritual strength.'

'Mercy killing' might well have been appropriate for
'a demented animal'. It did not even have to be considered for 'a calm human being'.

The legal arguments for and against 'mercy killing' are
complicated. The Right Hon. Lord Justice Lawton, chairman of the Criminal Law Revision Committee, summa-
rised the fundamental problem in these words. 'Any de-

finition could only be in terms of the motive of the killer. Both English and Scottish law have always eschewed definitions in terms of motive, which is notoriously difficult to establish and cannot, like intent, be inferred from a person's overt acts. How could a jury, for example, decide whether a daughter had killed her invalid father from compassion, from a desire for material gain, from a wish to get rid of a trying burden of care, or from a combination of motives?'

Cicely's arguments against euthanasia have the refreshing simplicity that results from much thought and experience – it is two pronged. First that as pain can nearly always be controlled, as both body and mind can be made comfortable while the patient remains alert and fully himself, euthanasia as an escape from physical pain simply should not be necessary. Secondly that 'human nature being what it is, euthanasia wouldn't be voluntary for very long', as the author Jean Rhys wrote to *The Times*. In Cicely's words, 'Any law permitting voluntary euthanasia pulls the rug from under the vulnerable.' Once euthanasia was legally available it would be bound to put pressure on the sick and elderly, all too conscious of demands they make on their relatives. 'We do not have to seek far to find evidence of the harm such legislation would cause. After a television debate on euthanasia or a bill like Baroness Wootton's Incurable Patients Bill in the Lords, elderly people refuse to go into hospital or to accept medication "because they are going to kill us". Many more become more sure than ever that their lives are useless and that it would be better for everyone if they were out of the way. We know, we hear them. What we do not hear are consistent requests for euthanasia, people asking to be killed.'

If hospice care were available for everyone, the question of euthanasia would be largely irrelevant. Cicely puts it more strongly. 'To make voluntary euthanasia lawful would be an irresponsible act, hindering help, pressuring the vulnerable, abrogating our true respect and responsibility to the frail and old, the disabled and dying. We should resist any effort to bring in such negative, uninformed, and mischievous legislation.'

Cicely is not only a doctor, she is a *good* doctor – Betty Read feels that she could have succeeded in any branch of medicine that she had chosen. She also has the clinical detachment necessary and the judgement to surround herself with other good doctors. She describes Mary Baines, who has been at St. Christopher's since early 1968, as 'an astute physician with a first class analytical brain'. 'She's the doctor I would take my mother or sister to, the doctor I would go to myself if I were dying,' says Tom West. Tom himself, who was awarded an OBE for his work in Africa, balances Mary Baines's skills with his exceptional talent in working with the families of the bereaved, his abilities in the psycho-social field and the indefinable personal qualities which enable him to restore morale – the nurses actively miss him if he is away for a few days.

Cicely has always been determined that St. Christopher's should be unrivalled medically; that in building a hospice as a protest against the shortcomings of modern high technology she would not lose the benefits that modern technology has to offer. To fulfil this aim she needed not only the best clinical physicians, she also needed a research team to establish and develop the scientific foundations on which their teaching is based.

She is not suited to research herself – the fact that she did not finish her own thesis on narcotic drugs substantiates this – but she appreciates its importance and is determined that St. Christopher's should excel in research and teaching as well as in patient care. It was her fierce insistence that ensured the meticulous storage of information that has been achieved by Dr. Joan Haram, a consultant pathologist who has run the Recorder's Department as a volunteer since the Hospice opened. Material culled from nurses' and doctors' notes, hospital records, doctors' letters, is methodically put on punch cards; there could be as many as 250 items of information about each patient. The resulting information is then available for statistical analysis and research.

These invaluable records are amongst the sources used by the doctors working in the department of Clinical Studies. Research has been built into the hospice concept since the very early days and a small but strong team was assembled soon after the Hospice opened. Dr. Robert Twycross, who took up his duties as a full-time research fellow in Clinical Pharmacology at St. Christopher's in 1971, has made a massive contribution to the subject, publishing numerous papers and articles and becoming, when he left St. Christopher's in 1976, the Medical Director of Sir Michael Sobell House in Oxford.

For the last four years the research post has been held by Dr. T. E. Walsh, under whose guidance the department is busier than ever; his recent research is considered to be the most substantial work ever done at St. Christopher's. He has an excellent working relationship with Cicely – the dedicated medical scientist and the pioneer and founder having a real regard for each other and their different talents.

As the respected doyenne of terminal care, it is inevitable that Cicely is sometimes the target of criticism from some of her medical colleagues – she has in fact been accused of not keeping up with pharmacological advances. It must be admitted that, as the hospice movement has grown, it has attracted new young doctors whose research, inspired by Cicely, is beginning to overtake her: but to make this a cause of criticism is to miss the point. Cicely has never claimed to excel in the field of pharmacology, nor has she ever felt that her vocation lay in clinical research. But her passionate commitment to the scientific approach has led her to act as an impresario, an enabler, who has stimulated whole areas of research into pain and symptom control. She has wisely let her talents direct her priorities.

Professor Harold Stewart, who as her professor knows her abilities well, gives a cool assessment of her scientific importance. 'She hasn't made any pharmacological discoveries, she has not discovered a new drug or a new route, it is not that type of thing. What she has done is to get the best out of using a drug and the effect on the patient is enormously different. She came to a neglected field with qualifications and drive and she set the standard. The impact has been enormous.'

Another criticism is that today Cicely does not spend enough time at the bedside. But the critics seem to forget that she did regular ward duties until she was sixty; in any case – how much can one person fit into a lifetime? In her role as Medical Director she handles much of the administration and fund-raising (the need for money is continuous – St. Christopher's still goes from one financial crisis to another) thus freeing others to work at the bedside; she is in continual demand as speaker, writer and broadcaster. It is, none-the-less, a serious loss to hospice care. Dr. West feels that one of the milestones in the development of St. Christopher's was when Cicely stopped doing two weekends a month on the wards, with the consequent loss of her unique expertise. And there are knock-on effects. Dr. Lamerton says 'her lectures recently have less fire and less immediate truth. There is a danger that her teaching will become irrelevant because it is not being fed by constant practice.' Cicely, with her usual disarming honesty, rather agrees.

St. Christopher's earns its place as the mother of the modern hospice movement by its teaching as well as by its patient care and research. It is the unique combination of these three aspects of terminal care that have changed attitudes amongst the medical, nursing and social work professions, among clergy and ordinary people. Its influence stems first from the Hospice itself. Through its doctors, talking regularly to groups in hospitals and health centres; its nurses feeding back what they have learnt into general hospitals; through the many hundreds of professional visitors who will come in a single year; by the help willingly given to all who ask. (Every day several doctors telephone asking for advice; they might have heard of Cicely or one of the other doctors speaking, or visited the Hospice. They want to give the patients the sort of help they have learnt is possible.) Slowly but steadily the ideas practised at St. Christopher's are coming to be practised all over the world.

Gill Ford regards herself as Cicely's first 'hand-reared' student. She was constantly on the phone to Cicely when she was a pre-registration house officer and Cicely was at St. Joseph's and was the first person to whom Cicely passed on her techniques of controlling pain. Gill was allowed to try these ideas in her own hospital and the results were so impressive that, as a very junior doctor, she was allowed a free hand in managing terminal pain.

Now Deputy Chief Medical Officer at the Department of Health and Social Security, Dr. Ford points out that terminal care is still not widely taught in British medical schools as a subject in its own right; she admits that it is not easy to teach. 'The difficulty lies in appreciating that handling the human approach to the patient, after he has ceased to need the exercise of highly technical skills, is just as necessary as any other aspect of his treatment . . . perhaps the most important part of such teaching is that a student should recognise that it does not require a purpose-built environment, or a profound knowledge of pharmacology, nor is it an art to which many can not attain.'

Cicely is an inspiring teacher and she has always taught, by her own example, by writing and broadcasting, by lecturing at conferences all over the world. Until recently she gave as many as two or three talks a week and once went to twelve medical schools in one year. Her first articles on the care of the dying written in 1959 and enthusiastically reviewed in the *Lancet*, are still being re-printed. Peggy Nuttall who, as editor of the *Nursing Times*, commissioned the articles, says 'She writes with extreme difficulty. I can't understand why she finds it so difficult to string two sentences together on paper when she is very articulate, very fluent as a public speaker. I had enormous difficulty getting material out of her and I know she produces it at great personal cost. It's absolute agony for her to write.' Nevertheless she has written well over sixty papers and articles, contributed several chapters to medical publications and edited *The Management of Terminal Disease* – the first substantial book written from clinical, as opposed to psycho-social experience. Most recently she has written, with Mary Baines, the chapter on the management of terminal disease in the new *Oxford Textbook of Medicine*.

On the other hand she actively enjoys public speaking and is very good at it. She has lectured in America, Canada, Australia, Europe and Africa and is very much in demand as a speaker in the United Kingdom, where she is deluged with invitations from schools, universities, hospital and church groups, specialised groups of the medical profession – radiographers, dental surgeons, oncologists.

Soon after the Hospice opened there were lectures and talks for nurses – there could be as many as forty people on Thursday afternoon rounds and the demand was growing. While the staff stress that the real teaching is in the wards, and Cicely has always emphasised that the real teachers are the patients, the need for an outward visible sign of the Hospice's teaching role became apparent. A timely donation from the Wates Foundation and a similar gift from the Wolfson Foundation met the need, and in 1973 the Study Centre, built on the second site that Cicely had far-sightedly acquired ten years earlier, was opened by Princess Alexandra.

Cicely is not a qualified teacher; her ideas on how the Study Centre should be run needed to be fleshed out. This groundwork has largely been done by Dorothy Summers, a sister-tutor who had worked at St. Christopher's as a volunteer and who then joined the staff and ran the Centre for eight years. Though the teaching programme was full, varied and successful, Cicely began to feel the need to upgrade the teaching of senior people, especially doctors, who would be the Medical Directors for the hospices of the future. She invited an American psychiatrist with a particular interest in education, Dr. John Fryer, to restructure the centre with a greater emphasis on the training of doctors and senior teachers. (She had previously said that Dr. Fryer couldn't come to St. Christopher's, feeling that his style was too flashy and that St. Christopher's wouldn't be able to handle him, and though later she had only allowed him to come at a weekend 'when she was on call so that he wouldn't disturb everyone', she was keen to use his talents when she saw the opportunity.)

Re-structuring of this kind does not happen without its casualties, but the extended and enlarged Study Centre is settling down under its new Director of Studies, Dr. Kerry Bluglass. Based on the original groundwork it now provides residential weeks for a variety of doctors. They welcome visitors from Britain and overseas, there are film showings, a library, in-service training for the staff of St. Christopher's and courses run for the Joint Board of Clinical Nursing Studies. Since 1976 over 300 nurses have gained this certificate, a third of them coming from outside St. Christopher's. Thus the skills of terminal care nursing are carried back into general medical care. The Hospice Movement is generous with its knowledge and longs for it to be widespread. In the words of Sir George Young, Parliamentary Under-Secretary of State in the Department of Health and Social Security, 'Like all good movements the impact of the Hospice Movement does not depend on bricks and mortar but on the interest its ideas generate and the changes in practical care which they have brought.'

The dissemination of hospice care is also expressed in the biannual international conferences. The first, in 1980, celebrating the thirteenth anniversary of St. Christopher's, was called a Bar Mitzvah in honour of David Tasma, the Jewish founding patient. In 1982 nearly 200 people collected in the Strand Palace Hotel to explore the psycho-social aspects of terminal care. They came from Canada, Holland, India, Israel, Japan, Luxembourg, New Zealand, Norway, Poland, South Africa, Spain, Sweden, Switzerland, the United States of America, and the United Kingdom. In fifteen years the teaching of St.

Christopher's had spread to cover half the surface of the developed world. Cicely is always looking for imaginative ways to spread the teaching of St. Christopher's – she does not stop thinking creatively. At the moment she is greatly excited by a project for refresher courses and further education for nurses; she even has the promise of financial help.

There is another aspect to the teaching of St. Christopher's – more intimate, more personal – the Home Care Service. While many people prefer to die in the familiar surroundings of their own homes, the responsibility of looking after a very sick person is daunting to many unskilled relatives. Could families be taught how to care for their relatives in a context of professional support from St. Christopher's?

Cicely had anticipated the need for an out-patient clinic and some sort of service for patients at home, well before the Hospice opened. She had indeed put her ideas on paper when she submitted an application for its funding to the Department of Health in 1966. The actual moment when it became a reality shows once again the flexibility and openness which must characterise any creative venture.

It was in 1969. Already the Hospice was succeeding so well in controlling pain and symptoms that they found they were able to let more patients go home than they had thought possible. St. Christopher's cares for two groups of patients – those who will probably die in a week or so and those who, even though they may have been sent there to die, have had their pain controlled and their symptoms alleviated, and can go home again for anything from a day to several years. Cicely was discussing one of this second group with Barbara McNulty, a ward sister and another exceptionally competent, perceptive and powerful person. 'In talking about it the whole concept, for me anyway, just grew and mushroomed and became concrete in about half an hour's conversation between us. Cicely would put an idea, I would put an idea, and it took shape as we talked. At the end she said, "Well, you'd better start hadn't you?"

Within a week or two the office designated as the Clinic
had been unlocked; it had been unused and was full of old
chairs and stacked up wheel-chairs. We opened it up, put
in a telephone and I sat there wondering what on earth I
did next.'

The first thing she had to do was enlist the support of the
local general practitioners and district nurses. The patients would, after all, be returned to their care. This was
an enormous challenge. At that time few general practitioners had heard about the success of the drug regimen
used at St. Christopher's; in any case doctors do not
welcome being told what they should do, especially by
nurses. Barbara, who had been a district nurse, slowly and
tactfully won them round, partly by being able to show
results, partly by hard work and humility. 'I used to tell
my nurses that the best way for a doctor to feel you were on
his side was to make yourself available, even at awkward
times, for instance being prepared to give an injection at
one o'clock in the morning. That was the way to gain their
confidence, to make them feel you were serious in what
you offered and that they could rely on you to do what you
offered.'

It was a success. The responsibility, the suffering, the
pain of separation, can never be taken away, but they can
be shared. As with Ethel, a lady of seventy-five, who had
been ill for two years:

Her devoted husband promised her that she should
remain at home with him. There were times during the
last month when we wondered whether he was really
going to be able to manage but his determination and
love never wavered. There were days when she became
drowsy and difficult to rouse and Mr. M. would phone us
in anxiety. A visit would be made at once to re-assess the
situation and to reassure them both. There were frequent deliberations with their own doctor to discuss and
adjust the analgesics, when she fractured her arm and
later as she began to sink. Throughout her last week the
district nurses were going in twice daily to give nursing

care and Mr. M. would manage his wife's needs in between their visits. The Hospice supplied and monitored the drugs in close association with the general practitioner and during Ethel's last hours injections were given by our nurses. Ethel died early one morning, a few minutes after the Clinic nurse arrived. Though she appeared to be unconscious Mr. M. was sure that 'She waited for you to come'.

With professional help and comfort a telephone call away, and re-admission always available, patients can stay at home for longer and often they can die peacefully at home. They can have both independence and security; the constant presence of their relatives in the constant context of professional skill.

The Home Care Service was in fact such a success that it – and therefore Barbara – acquired great prestige. Barbara is well aware of her own need for power, very aware that though Cicely was delighted at yet another triumph for St. Christopher's she was ambivalent, even slightly jealous, of Barbara's personal success. There was affection and respect between these two powerful women, but Barbara began to feel both that she had done her best work in launching the Clinic and that St. Christopher's was consuming too much of her life; after eight years she left. By then she, with the invaluable help of Dr. Baines, had built up a supporting and consulting service with over 600 general practitioners and nursing teams which had gained widespread professional confidence and respect.

By frequent visits and constant availability, by offering all the services of the Hospice and the reassurance of a bed if it should become necessary, patients and their families can receive the very best care in what is, for many, the very best place – at home. 'Efficiency is comforting,' said Cicely's brother. St. Christopher's has shown that efficiency need not be confined to the hospice wards.

13

RAMSEY'S DIARY

Let us not grow so as to become old after being new, but let the newness itself grow.

St. Augustine

'Speak the truth,' Cicely said to Dr. Richard Lamerton, 'but speak it in parables. Your patients are your parables.'

One reason, perhaps the main reason, for the success of Cicely's work for the dying is that the touchstone is first, last and always the patient. Their stories, their lives and deaths, are the *prima materia* on which St. Christopher's is based; fragments of their conversation, so often quoted by Cicely, are woven into the tapestry of hospice philosophy. 'I only want what is in your heart and in your mind.' 'Was it hard for you to tell me that?' 'It seemed so strange, nobody wanted to look at me.' 'Would it be all right if I just said I hoped?' 'I only want someone to look as if they are trying to understand me.' 'It is good to feel a wanted person.'

So to see St. Christopher's in action, its dimensions as a religious and medical community working together, let one patient speak for all.

Ramsey was in St. Christopher's from June 20th to September 8th, 1978. He was forty-eight when he died. He had been a television producer and just before he became ill he had been very emotionally involved in a series of films he had made about people overcoming great physical disabilities.

He was admitted to St. Christopher's with an inoperable brain tumour, his sight was going, his speech difficult. He was anxious to 'do something useful' with his illness, but how could he think creatively about it when, as he knew, it was his mind that was going to go? At the suggestion of Dr.

Baines and Cicely and with the help of one of the nurses, he dictated a diary.

Ramsey had been in several hospitals before coming to St. Christopher's. A friend who had visited him in one of them said she came away feeling she wanted to cry, but when she left St. Christopher's she 'came away laughing'. The part the Hospice played in such a transformation is clearly visible between the lines of this courageous diary. Ramsey did not have pain, but his distressing symptoms were controlled – his steroid therapy was adjusted, a new tranquilliser made him more alert, he was taken to Charing Cross Hospital for radiotherapy in an attempt to save his sight, or at least arrest its deterioration. The warmth of the community around him, the active and real interest of the nurses, his friendship with another patient, the freedom with which his numerous friends could visit him, all these helped him to find some meaning to his early and tragic death.

Here then are some extracts from Ramsey's diary – the occasionally confused expression is the result of his illness and has been left as he dictated it.

*   *   *

RAMSEY'S DIARY

12.7.78
It's one o'clock in the morning, George died a few hours ago. He is over eighty, his wife and daughter were there and I was at the next bed. I did not expect this to be the first words of the diary I promised to write. The night nurse is writing down the words for me. The ward is very quiet, and I am thinking about George. I cried after he had died.

That the first words I should ask anyone to write down should be about the death of a man, is not an attempt to be dramatic, it just happens to be where I decided to start. I don't know what to say about George, I was not prepared for crying and I don't think there is anything new that I can say to anyone.

13.7.78
It is four o'clock in the morning. I have just woken up. This
is my second attempt at writing how I feel. George, the
eighty-year-old who died last night already seems very
distant. Jill and I had a bad evening when she came back
from the hospital. It takes two hours to get from one side of
London to the other and her motor-bike had broken down.
I was still confused about last night and wanted to get the
words right, and she was angry and impatient because I
didn't know what I wanted.

Jill has looked after me for over a year now. How she has
done it I don't know, she is so much younger than me yet
has somehow taken over the responsibility of keeping me
sane. She has now been a qualified nurse for only a few
months, and I think she is going to see me through until I
die . . . It doesn't worry me but when I finally go it is going
to be the most appalling thing I could think of for her. In
the next month I just hope that she will learn to cope with
me as she has done in the last two years.

14.7.78
I have woken up and it's gone midnight. This is an ordinary night for me. For over a year now, not reading, not
writing, it's strange but I somehow find that I have become
accustomed to apparently doing nothing. It's not nothing,
and after this first year, after three weeks of living at the
Hospice I think I can begin to learn how to live in this
strange life of my head. A year of going to different
hospitals has seemed up to now a practical way of life,
although, of course, it's not, but there was something
about an ordinary hospital which I felt was normal in a
strange kind of way – the Hospice in a short time, such a
short time is growing into something different. Talking at
night with one of the nurses, Staff Nurse Cureton, I feel I
am going to find, if I have the time, another way of life, not
dramatic, perhaps not even very different, but something
that will be the best in my life. It's been a very quiet day,
the night is quiet now, everyone is asleep and I will sleep
for the rest of the night. I am getting confident in this

second year. I am not worried about life or death. In a strange way I am enjoying what is happening in and around my head. The Hospice is somehow looking after me without my knowing quite how it is happening. It's a year, over a year, since I can't read or write. A new year in its fourth week at the Hospice is utterly different from anything else I've known or felt, and I want it while I can to give me something that I think will be the best I've had.

16.7.78
As the weeks go by and if I feel as well as I do now, I hope it will give me more and more insight. Unfortunately not everything is good. My left eyesight is so bad that I have to use the right, I am frightened as everyone always is, that eyes are so important. The left eye only shows a blur as I can see, and is useless and nothing can be done for it. I hope it's early days but it's not likely. Anyway I don't think much about it – the eye will just have to take care of itself.

18.7.78
I'm feeling better – a lot better. I can walk if I'm very careful, on my own. Today is a sunny day and life seems nice. My good luck is spoilt by my eyesight, my left eye is gone and won't tell me anything, and my right eye seems just all right at the moment but frightens me at the thought of getting any worse. It seems that nothing can be done with either eye and all I can do is wait and hope. I suppose that I can really accept anything like other people have had to do. What is nice is that everybody that I like and who are fun are all coming to see me and chat and make life very good indeed. Jill works hard, enjoys it and I love to see her whenever I can. Our big moment of this next week is when she and I are going to have a weekend together. I hope nothing will make this go wrong and it will be lovely to be together again.

20.7.78
Three o'clock in the morning and I am again looking at what is happening to myself. The last three mornings I

have been so good with my head that I have gone almost completely asleep apart from the inevitable, every 4 hours, when I have to put myself awake for a few seconds and get the tablets again.

There is really nothing more I can think about except how this single eye is going to be a good eye. I suppose that everybody is frightened at losing eyes and it seems in my case that there is nothing I can do if both my eyes are permanently done with for ever. Anybody can deal with a disaster if they have to – you must just work out how the disaster occurs and I suppose that I will be no exception and find a way of somehow making the best of a bad job. We'll just have to see if this wretched eye gets any worse.

24.7.78

Last Friday was a really chaotic day. Jill had the problem of getting things organised because this was going to be my first day away. She and I were going to spend the night at home, and it was important that we got it well organised. We all got confused for a time but we all ended up very happy and it was unbelievably nice to have a day and a night and a day to ourselves.

Today at three-thirty p.m. I met again after some time, Anne who like most of the other nurses looks after me in a way that I find quite unique. They all of them are going to have to get more unique because I am definitely losing my sight. All the nurses are going to have to find a slightly different me. Today I am literally on the edge, the very edge of my sight going. There is a faint chance – very faint that it might edge its way back for a while if the treatment of radiotherapy, twice a week can do something for me. But we all know that hope is very thin and I am prepared for the worst and so is Jill. I'm going to need the nurses a lot, Jill knows this and so do I.

25.7.78

It's three forty-five in the sun and I'm amazed that I'm still seeing something of the world outside, though today was definitely going to be the end of the sun as far as I was concerned. Nothing has happened to make me feel very happy but nothing makes me feel that I'm never going to see the sun again because there is still some movement, some things that I can still see that I could see yesterday. It's not much, but it's something – something that resembles sky and people and that means everything to me. What is going to happen in the next few days I just don't know. Today I went to radiotherapy for the second time in Charing Cross Hospital and for a painless six minutes I was hopefully given another lease of my life. There really is a chance that this might help, and in my eyes it has to be there. I see very very little but I can see something and I hope that even if it does no more at least I will not be blind. It really is a gamble, I would not have believed things could have been so much on the edge of life, it certainly makes it exciting – I don't think there is anything I can say any more today – it's too close to the wind.

26.7.78
It's the afternoon and I'm talking to Annie again. Thank God that my sight is still with me – faint, but there, in fact ever so slightly stronger than it was yesterday. It's a very nice feeling still seeing something, albeit parts of it are faint and difficult to see. It makes me nervous to think of how temporary my sight will stay, but every day makes me happy. Of course I would like it to be stronger – I have to strain to look at things, but sometimes it's impossible. Lots of friends came to see me today, one after the other, chatting and talking, it made me feel very happy, almost ironically, too happy. I began to remember another life and that is very confusing. Life is all over the place and I love the thought that there might be a tiny bit of a future somewhere in the talking and shouting that goes on around me. What a life! It can't all be bad can it?

27.7.78
Radiotherapy – I have had my third X six-minute treatment at the hospital today. What I want to do is to get a first meeting tomorrow with Dr. Baines, I'll then make up

my mind with advice from her, what is best for me. I will then have a second 'go' at when I should begin, either next week or wait two weeks.

31.7.78

I have finally lost my sight. It really happened yesterday, and I have discovered that being blind is nothing you can describe until it happens to you. I don't know how to begin it, the new sensation of not knowing what it is I'm looking at. I am going to take this idea as gently as I can. The only thing that has saved me is that I now have a room on my own.

One thing has happened, a few days ago that was a very shaking experience indeed. It nearly shook me down out of where I felt secure, that is, the world of the Hospice. I could hardly believe it that one of the patients here was so utterly impossible, day and night for four nights or more – it seemed like forever, and not only me but six other patients suffered – I was the nearest and I suffered most of all. I couldn't stand this man who dominated everybody with the loudest voice. It didn't seem as if he was going to be moved, and nobody in authority, I thought, was going to move him so I thought I would have to go. It was an amazing experience, but in the end I was moved, in the main because of my blindness I suspect. It is impossible to describe what a terrible effect this man's presence had on me, for days and nights. It taught me a lot. It taught me that in a way I must still make my own decisions, and I will now forget this ugly episode.

I am back almost as I was, and blind but I feel that I have the strength of the Hospice behind me and I am hoping that I'm going to get strength with my blindness and I must admit that already the warmth of the people around me is going to make me feel that I've got a lot to do yet. I hope that I might live for a little while yet and enjoy being a man who can find something new that he's never found before.

1.8.78
It's two o'clock in the afternoon and a few hours ago I had
the most frightening experience of my life. This morning,
just as I was walking with the physiotherapist, although I
couldn't see, I felt I knew that with her help I was gather-
ing strength in my new command of being a blind man.
Suddenly I saw a completely new, bizarre world. I stopped
and saw shapes that made up forty or a hundred or more
buildings that I could make nothing of. It was frightening
to describe strange buildings a hundred years old but
somehow they came right up to my face. I can't describe
what I saw – it was real and unreal. They stayed with me,
these buildings and I was so terrified I couldn't get them
away from me, and at this moment I was out of control and
I wanted to kill myself. The physiotherapist who had
taken me out for a little walk, knew I was in a terrible
state, and took me back to my room. I guess it was obvious
to her and also to three of the nurses, Anne, Gill and
Suzanne. I was so frightened, so knowing that I was totally
in another world and totally out of control and so certain
that I wanted to kill myself. I did everything I could with
their help to stay in command, and with their help,
although I could still see nothing outside my own head,
I did not faint or go mad. The three nurses stayed with
me, they helped me to wash, chatted and talked and
for three hours I tried all I could to stay normal. I've
gone a little calmer now, and to my amazement, something came back for about ten minutes that passed for
normality.

It is now two o'clock in the afternoon and Annie is
taking down how I am. This strange new world has come
back again but at least I haven't gone mad.

2.8.78
This has been a good day. I suppose everything is by
comparison and yesterday was the most frightening of my
life, and so as a blind man who seems to have survived his
own death I am happy. Yesterday morning was so inde-
scribably awful that I felt I had to kill myself. I feel quite

heroic surviving yesterday, and I've told a lot of people about it, or at least as many as I could find. A lot of people came to see me today and I admit to drinking quite a lot of wine. I don't know whether this is a passing phase and neither does the doctor and it's too early to make firm decisions about how total my blindness will be. I don't move very much at the moment, I walk like a crab, slowly, not knowing anything. I'm not frightened but I'm not quite sure what to do, and I know it's going to take me some time to learn how to be a blind man.

I got very excited today, telling everyone how I feel, almost boasting what a survivor I am. I've drunk a lot of wine and beer and laughed a lot. When I do this I feel I have a life, that has a great future, and who knows I could be right. I just don't know what kind of life I am going to lead but it's certainly getting more and more interesting.

3.8.78

I'm amazed at how quickly I can get used to being blind. Getting blind was so appallingly dramatic that to get into the state of mind that I am now in makes me feel that I can in a few weeks' time, become almost at ease with blindness. I can still see the strange buildings that are around me, buildings that make me scared that I'm going to fall down, when I know they haven't moved, buildings that I have to just believe will somehow go away, even though they look so horribly real. The buildings, it's a joke, are either fifteenth-century or nineteenth-century and I walk around them and in them. I think I am now in charge of this strange landscape inside my head and if I am with other people I can somehow suppress them. I had hoped that occasionally a glimmer of real life might come in as it did yesterday and the day before, but today there was no light, be it so ever feeble. I wonder if it has gone – my sight – forever.

The good side has been people coming, drinking together and feeling that life in a very strange way is not bad. I can guess at what my friends think of how I am, but I hope that they won't get frightened, and will help me to get to grips happily with this new life.

4.8.78
The speed with which I have got accustomed to being blind is truly amazing. I thought I would have been at least a week if not more, getting fed up with myself, but it's not true. Of course I've talked to nurses and they have all kept a careful eye on me and it really does help, but I have not been made into a saint. Today, at three o'clock in the afternoon I had the marvellous opportunity of talking to Dr. Cicely Saunders and Dame Albertine Winner. Dr. Saunders talked with me a little and she is an amazing woman. Being here at St. Christopher's is a tremendous education, I only wish I had met them sooner. I am going to try and get them to talk to me again and try and educate myself in this amazing life that they seem to have led. I do hope that I'm not going to have any more changes for a bit in my physical life, and I'm going to try and concentrate on what I want my future to be.

8.8.78
I can see nothing of course, and worse, the one thing I really hate, only the terrible fifteenth-century stone buildings that are inside my head. Less of a problem by a long way is the fact that I eat too much! Also that I find I'm drinking quite a lot. It's a funny old life, one that seems to have all kinds of additions that I wasn't expecting.

11.8.78
I went home with Jill for two days. It was the first time that I was blind at home. I enjoyed being looked after and we discussed my blindness and, very importantly, how she feels about this strange way that my blindness has altered my life. Jill has talked to me strongly and I believe that she is right in trying to push me towards my trying on my own, even if it's going to be painful. Jill really cares a lot and I love her being so firm about me.

I am now back at St. Christopher's and I have just left

Jill four hours ago as she went off to work. St. Christopher's seems just the same as it did when I left three days ago which is very satisfactory. It seems to me as if being at St. Christopher's is becoming very pleasant and I hope that my body will stay on a reasonably even keel for several days at least.

14.8.78
Three days have gone by and I have not done anything about the diary. There is no doubt about it that I am not all that grand, even now, and I know I feel that I'm getting weaker. I will keep an eye on myself and hope that I can get stronger as I was last week but I'm not very happy. For the first time I am beginning to get a strong sense that I don't have long to live.

15.8.78
I have got to try and sort out what the next few days are going to be like. I am still quite energetic and I can still use words quite well, but I don't believe it's going to last for long. I must start to think ahead of time because when my speech gets slower or difficult, as I'm afraid it will, I want to be sure that I will have written as much as possible. I know already, and I think this is rather clever of me, that I am not as good as I was. Obviously, as I see it, I am still reasonably O.K. and yet I know that I'm getting less excited about the work that I'm doing – I'm really on the brink between still being able to be clear in mind and being easy-going and relaxed. If you read this back, you will see that it doesn't make sense – this is the first time I've done this, and I feel my doing it, getting the words wrong, but not worrying about it, almost not really caring either. I can't tell whether I just feel tired or that I'm just slowly becoming easy-going. It's an interesting thought to think that with luck I will feel easy-going, until the end. Really nothing could be better.

16.8.78

I felt very good up to lunch time and just over. I am damn lucky to be looked after so well at the Hospice, so brilliantly well. Jill can only look after me for so long, as her working takes so much time and she's so far away, and to have her knowing Annie is the best I could have got.

21.8.78

It's five days since the diary has been at work. As I read my words I can see, of course, that I am less fluent in the last week – I hadn't thought how I would be as the days pass, but it is obvious now to me that my intelligence is weakening, and what I think about my present is a bit poor. It is interesting that I feel I am caring slightly less that it's an effort to think what I should be caring, but at least I'm still here.

Nobby Harding – a new guy has come into living, at least trying to live. Nobby has something nasty to do with his liver and it may get worse or it may get better. One thing is certain, he's just over seventy. I know that Nobby is as funny and good value as I think he is, because he has become, so I've heard, a great character. If I could I would try to do some filming with Nobby.

22.8.78

This is a strange new addition to my life. Nobby is seventy years old and smashing. He always talks to me every day and he speaks about me with tremendous sympathy. Nobby is about as far removed from me as seems possible and yet I like him a lot and I want to try and do more about him if only because I am hoping that there is no more way of finding other things to write about. One thing that did come today was my seeing quite a number of people who I have not seen before or have not seen for ages. The sight and the sense of people who often have not seen me for years are nice to see again. I am beginning to hope that I can make something out of the bits of my life as they remain. It's worth a try.

25.8.78

I am finding it a bit more difficult to use words but they still make moderately good sense. Today was a good day – I did nothing difficult and there was nothing that made me important or anxious. I would like to try and make the next few days the most important and significant that I can find, but I don't know if I can make it important enough and I will just pray that with help I can do something with of course Martin's help.* It is going to be difficult to use words because I know I am losing words, that I may make mistakes by accident, but I think that I will get help and that the most important thing that is happening to me will be helped by those around me.

26.8.78

Amazingly enough, I believe I'm going to find a God. I don't know how it will happen precisely but the sense that Jesus will find me and make me all that I am and more is not too far away and the fact that He is coming at the time that I need Him most is amazing. To think that in such a short time and in my own way is coming to me Jesus Christ, that is, I hope, going to look after me, seems a most important thing, but I know it's going to be true.

Annie is writing again, Jill is writing, people who know me, love me and will stay with me forever, all will amaze me. Only now am I beginning to realise by thinking of God, what he must know and think of how significant I am. I find it quite exciting to think of my future and to realise that Jesus is going to somehow make my life work and I wish I could have done it before, what does make me excited is the possibility of extending my life in this world or the next in all the ways that I now can.

Living of life and living of death was, I thought, to be a strange thing. I still think it's a strange thing. I want to try and make it a place where I am with everyone else when I am dead or alive, where it becomes a place that's not going to change. I don't know how it's going to happen,

---

* Dr. Martin Lee who had been praying with Ramsey.

but I know it will happen. I don't know whether I'm going to die forever, but I know it doesn't really matter because I'm going to be looked after and everything that God wants me to do I will do to the best of my ability and that is all that matters. I seem to be at the beginning of my life with God and that is amazing.

28.8.78
The afternoon, and I am getting my usual look at the diary. I want to look at the future while I can see it now. I know that I can make very little sense out of anything if it goes on too long – what I mean is that my memory is getting poor. The one part that I am trying to make something of is my relationship with Martin, I am hoping that tomorrow he will tell me more about himself. As he was only with me for three days and that was now two days ago, I hope that Jesus will come into him tomorrow. I am getting so very difficult to remember things, but in a few days I may be quite impossible. Certainly coming to Jesus Christ and to make Him the most important thing in my life must be placed somewhere where I can reach Him. I will need to be helped and thought about in some way understood and this must happen as soon as I can, for the Lord Jesus Christ. Amen.

2.9.78
I have to make the words that we bring together with a most exciting thing of our lives when I bring it all together and covered with words and the words are so simple, and direct, and exciting, I can't believe that it's working so well and yet I know it is.

3.9.78
I keep on thinking that every day is to be my last day, but I guess that God doesn't think quite that way. Of course, why should it be true, when the last day is to come, it comes, and laughing or crying, or anything else will take its due course. Because I think of death (or is it life?) I find whatever the shape of God Almighty, and it is the

Almighty, that I just take it in turn and make the best of whatever I enjoy. What a funny world to take the joy and importance that is going to make it for me the joy and importance – it will come, there will be no way that I can stop it, and my life and death will become problems that I know and can try and take for a life and death. Amen.

Annie

At last I have found the time to add my own contribution to Ramsey's Diary and even more important to find time with Ramsey, just talking or not talking. Ramsey is weary and ready to die, but as he says himself, God doesn't seem to think that way just now. His visitors are becoming fewer and more select. Ramsey became quite tearful today just thinking about how dedicated Jill has been to him when she has so many opportunities she could pursue and so much to do. We decided he was a 'lucky man' and then he became quite excitable.

I am still amazed by Ramsey's state of mind. He is still so lucid and rational, and yet so peaceful. He never loses his temper or gets annoyed except with himself occasionally and he certainly isn't losing any of his personality.

Each day I wonder if we will write the diary again and each day that we do I'm more amazed at the sense it all makes (sometimes in a nonsensical way!). It's just a matter of time now.

*   *   *

They didn't write the diary again. Ramsey died five days later, having confirmed that Cicely could use his diary as she saw fit.

14

MARIAN

Heaviness may endure for a night, but joy cometh in the morning.

Ps. 30.5

Cicely sometimes likens her personal life to Hans Andersen's story of the Ugly Duckling. As the ugly duckling became a swan, so did the plain girl become a handsome, fulfilled woman: as the ugly duckling had to endure a long cold winter before the spring brought his transformation, so did she. But eventually spring came for Cicely too. In her middle age not only was she showered by professional honours, tributes and awards – reaching a climax when she was made a Dame in 1980 and awarded the £90,000 Templeton Prize for progress in religion in 1981 – but her private life was crowned by meeting the man she was eventually to marry. Her happiness shines from her. He was worth the long wait.

Not only was it a long wait, it was filled with pain and loneliness. As a girl and as a young woman, Cicely did not relate easily to men. A girl who has ambivalent feelings for her parents seldom has an easy passage in her emotional life, but Cicely had the additional problem of her size. She was not only big physically, she was big in every way. 'I seemed to spend so much of my life falling over myself because I'm too big,' she laments. Her father didn't help by telling her she looked like a 'cock-a-rooster'. This comic figure from a children's story was a gawky bird with a long neck and a large beak who was always putting his big feet into things. However affectionately such a remark is made, it is hardly likely to give confidence where it is lacking.

Cicely's abilities, her ambition, her perfectionism all set

her apart. So too, did the depth of her feelings. Her father, more kindly, would say, 'The trouble with your feelings is that they need so much relieving. You can't keep them controlled like a well-behaved race-horse.' There was a very passionate, feminine woman trapped inside the lanky body.

Unable to release these feelings naturally, Cicely developed a brusque manner that would not stoop to what she saw as the 'feminine wiles' that were, at that time, expected from women of her social background. The result was that she frightened men; they could not see through the abrasive exterior. In the words of one man who knew her when she was young, 'she was not the sort of girl you chose for hanky-panky in the gooseberry bushes.' The irony was that at least part of her longed to be such a girl. To make matters worse, during her vulnerable teens there was the constant comparison with her mother's companion Lilian – a glowing young woman surrounded by admirers.

Deeper than her physical disadvantages, deeper even than the family tensions, was the abiding wound that Cicely received as a tiny baby. Before she was a year old she had been rejected twice, first when her mother had given her into the care of her Aunt Daisy, again when, jealous of her baby's affection for her aunt, Chrissie had sent Aunt Daisy away. It was a hard way to start life. Cicely does not like psychological explanations of behaviour, but it is impossible to believe that this double loss, at such an early age, did not affect her. The inexplicable rejection, the feeling of total abandonment, must have caused a deep unconscious anger, a primitive sense of isolation and failure. Does one ever quite recover from such a deprivation?

At one level, of course, one does. The hurt is pushed aside, the irresistible urges of growing up take over. A plant can flower when its roots are damaged, even if it does not flower so profusely. From her teens Cicely loved, and she loved with passion. When she was in her last term at school she wrote to a friend about her feelings for a young air force officer. 'I love him – as I never dreamt of loving anyone else – as I knew I should one day love the right person. There is no doubt anywhere in my mind and I don't care how long I may have to wait, or what I may have to go through. I believe he loves me, anyway a little, but he is young and shy and I didn't expect him to say very much on the first meeting after all that time. If I'm unlucky, and he hasn't or doesn't fall really in love with me, then I shall have a dreadfully broken heart. But as long as there's a chance of its working out, then I don't care, I'll risk it. And if it doesn't work out, or anything happens to him, then there'll never be anyone else.'

These strong emotions were not to be allowed easy satisfaction. For years she was tormented by what she refers to as 'longings for love'. Socially too, she hated the single state, feeling that it put her at a permanent disadvantage. When she qualified as a doctor her great delight was that now she would never have to be 'Miss' again.

Cicely does not indulge in self-pity. She rejoiced with her friends as, one by one, they got engaged; she went to their weddings, became godmother to their children. She has a great capacity for enjoyment and she filled her life with activity – singing in choirs, going to concerts, bird-watching, entertaining, going on holiday with her single friends. She feels she is guilty of dropping her friends when she no longer needs them, but if they feel neglected, they do not, for the most part, admit it. In fact Betty Read remarks on her loyalty and how she 'stays put' in friendship and Rosetta Burch is amazed at what a supportive friend she is, despite leading such a busy life. Betty West, however, points out that St. Christopher's is her life and her child 'and she has the ruthlessness which all great people have to drop people – I know that's a cruel word – when they're no more use to her child. This is probably necessary, you can't keep too big a circle going, but it's a hard thing. People do get hurt, though I am one of the fortunate ones.' A clear-sighted judgement, made with great affection and probably true. But people *do* grow out of their friends. Cicely, growing and changing more than most, needs different people at different times. With most friendships this ebb and flow is a natural process, friends lose touch with each other. It is only when one of them is famous that it becomes a cause of criticism.

How did Cicely survive her long winter? She looks back at her life through two pairs of glasses, one rose-tinted, the other grey. The grey pair reveal rejection, bereavement, loneliness. This loneliness, which worries and perplexes her friends, is deep-seated, deeper than the single state she so disliked, deeper even than the solitude forced on her by the path she was destined to follow. It is manifested in her constant need for company, a characteristic she inherits from her father and which, surprisingly in one to whom prayer is so important, makes her unwilling to spend much time alone. Perhaps its roots lie in those very early years and the loss of both mother and aunt as the centre of her child's world. It remains a mystery.

But when she looks through the optimistic pair of glasses, rejection fades into insignificance; relationships appear in their joy rather than their sorrow; activity, achievement and companionship oust loneliness.

Each of her relationships were, in their own way, complete. Though she had to wait until she was thirty before she experienced, with David Tasma, a shared love and a real communication, she recognises, at least with hindsight, that fate had its reason. 'Kicking and screaming I was dragged to where I ought to be. There is no way I would have done what I have if I'd been married.' As a result of that relationship she knew something about the love between a man and a woman, she knew also what she had to do with her life. Her energy, frustrated and fragmented in her longing to be married, flowed eagerly into her long medical training and the building of the Hospice. Partially fulfilled, no longer so anxious for relationships, she was able to work hard and enjoy the companionship of both men and women.

At medical school she went around 'in the sort of gang

that doesn't distinguish very sharply between boys and girls'; she had her work and the activities of her keen Christian life; there too, she met her life-long friend Tom West.

It is not hard to see what drew Tom and Cicely together. They shared their profession, their religion and their interest in music. Tom's sensitive intelligence matched her own, his companionship took the edge off her loneliness. As Cicely was called to the dying, so Tom's calling was to the mission field. Soon after he qualified he went to Africa and was there all through the sixties when she was planning and building the Hospice. This geographical separation and the difference in their ages (he is twelve years younger than she) left them free to enjoy each other's friendship without the threat of a more serious involvement. Though Cicely might sometimes have wanted more from the relationship neither of them were ready for marriage.

So her state of involuntary celibacy left her free. Free to enjoy the friendships she would otherwise not have had time to develop – Tom, Mrs. G., Alice, Louie, Gill Ford, Madge Drake, Betty West, Rosetta Burch; free to work for the dying.

Antoni was a gift, a surprise. She was not, when she met him, seeking relationships as she had been in her twenties. And indirectly he was to lead her, at last, to marriage.

It was December, 1963. Antoni had been dead for three years, but still Cicely was mourning him. She was thinking sadly of him as she drove back from the public library, 'window shopping as any good woman driver can do' when her eye was caught by a picture in the window of the Drian Gallery. Magnetically drawn to it – a blue Crucifixion in oil – she parked the car and arrived at the gallery just as they were closing. It was the last day of the exhibition. She went from picture to picture, entranced, moved and eager to possess one. She had never bought a picture before, but such was her enthusiasm that the gallery sold her the one

of her choice, 'Christ Calming the Waters', at half price.
The artist was a Pole, Marian Bohusz-Szyszko.

The next day she wrote to him.

Dear Professor Bohusz,

I bought your picture 'Christ Calming the Waters' at
your exhibition at the Drian Galleries. I would like to
thank you very much indeed for the inspiration that lies
behind it, and to tell you how glad I am that I was
attracted by what I could see in the windows of the
gallery and went in and found it. It seems to me a most
exciting and inspiring work and to have so much to
convey on more than one level.

She went on to tell him that it was for the Chapel of a
Hospice for patients with terminal cancer.

The message of your picture is so fundamental to what
we are going to try and do that I am certain that it was
no mere chance that made me attracted by your pictures
and drew me to the gallery, the last evening before it
closed.

A few days later she received a reply.

Dear Doctor Saunders,

I received your letter three days ago – and I did not
reply immediately because I was too much moved by it
and I wished to have time to think it over.

Look, my exhibition was a kind of 'success' in the
sense of a 'prestige' and even financially. But, believe
me, the most important moment in all my artistic career
during forty years of my activity as a painter has been,
without any exaggeration, your letter, Doctor Saunders. Because nothing is more important for the artist
than feeling that he might be necessary for his brethren
and serve them by his art. Specially those of them who
need more help than others.

You have bestowed upon me the greatest honour in

buying my picture and thinking that it is equal for the purpose.

I ask you for a favour, Doctor Saunders. Be kind enough to visit my studio and discuss with me which of my pictures (the big ones) would be suitable for giving as a present for the new Chapel in the St. Christopher's Hospice. The right of giving it as a present I shall consider as my greatest privilege.

Just before Christmas they met. At last her long mourning for Antoni was over. She had been attracted by Marian's paintings at a very deep level. Now she fell in love with their creator.

Marian Bohusz was born of an aristocratic, wealthy family near Wilno in Poland in 1901. He studied at the Faculty of Fine Arts in Cracow and he was already an accomplished painter when, in 1939, he joined the ranks of those defending Gdynia and was almost immediately taken prisoner by the Germans. An artist to the depth of his soul, being a prisoner of war did not stop his creative work; he started courses for his fellow prisoners and made some 400 oil paintings and pencil drawings on scraps of paper, some of which he managed to preserve as he was moved from camp to camp. He was also a first class mathematician and taught some of his fellow prisoners up to university standard. On his release in 1945 he went first to Rome, then a year later to England, where he became Principal of the Polish School of Art and where he has remained ever since.

He is considered to be one of the leading Polish painters living abroad and he has exhibited widely. His paintings, mostly in oil, mostly expressing themselves as much in colour as in design, are vibrant, passionate and technically accomplished. A French critic describes the physical texture of his painting as 'thick, plentiful, broken-up, laid upon the canvas with a kind of controlled rage'. Marian is essentially a religious artist of extraordinary visionary power, his technique always his servant rather than his master. In a sense he is an expressionist painter, but the passion lies in the idea behind the painting rather than in the medium itself.

The more one considers these two exceptional people, the more appropriate it seems that they should be together. In Marian Cicely had met someone who, in his own way, is as big as she is. He is confident, in his manner as in his judgement – 'Just because this is painted by Rembrandt doesn't mean it's good. This one is rubbish.' He paints on the grand scale, he is his own man, not to be bossed around. Cicely has too many people prepared to play second fiddle to her – how refreshing to come home to someone who will, gently but firmly, stand up to her. As when, soon after they were married, she and Tom were at odds over the Good Friday three hour service. Cicely had been in the States, only returning a few days before. Thinking she would not have time to prepare, and would in any case be tired, Tom and the Chaplain arranged the service without including her. She was furious. 'This time you've gone too far. In my Hospice, you have not included me in the three hour service.' Tom offered her a part, his if she liked, but she would not be mollified. They were hard at it when Marian came in. 'Darling,' she said, 'Tom and I are having the most splendid row' (was she rather enjoying herself?) and told him about it. 'My darling, don't be silly,' he said, 'after all Good Friday is God's day, not yours.' Tom has had the greatest respect for Marian ever since. No doubt the incident increased Cicely's.

Marian knows, as few Englishmen know, how to treat women, how to bring out all that is feminine in them. It is deeply touching that Cicely, so deprived of masculine attention for so much of her life, should eventually find a man so gallant, so sexually aware, so very much a man.

It was a long haul for Cicely. She is quite prepared to say 'I fell for him at once, but it took me years to land him.' Even so, she was not immediately responsive. He was married, though he had not seen his wife since 1939, with a son in Cracow and a daughter in Italy. Though she met him during the 'swinging sixties' Cicely, in terms of social convention, was a product of the more restrained forties.

For a long time it was a tantalising relationship. Marian's wife was in Poland. He was a political refugee; she would not leave the country. Even more pertinently, the marriage had not been a success for some time. Marian is a devout Roman Catholic and there was no question of divorce. In any case, not being free to re-marry suited him quite well – he was enjoying his freedom and in no hurry to see it end. Further, the pride of the patrician Pole made him unwilling to put himself into the position of the poor artist befriended by the relatively rich woman. It was not until Cicely bought two more of his pictures that he was able to say, 'Now I can tell you that I love you. If I were younger and if I were free, I would offer you my hand.'

Despite his chivalrous manner, in the early days of their friendship, Marian was not considerate in his behaviour to Cicely. His desire for freedom and independence led to many uneasy situations for her. For instance when, after they had known each other for about three years, she flew back from America by way of Paris in order to meet him and see an exhibition of religious art, including some of his pictures. She had written to him asking where they should meet – no answer; she arrived at the airport – no Marian; she went on to the air terminal – still no Marian. All the hotels were full, she did not even know where the exhibition was being held. By pure chance she met the owner of the Drian Gallery in the air terminal and learnt that Marian was driving over with two of his pupils. She lit a huge candle in the Sacré Coeur for his safe journey (he is an erratic driver), spent the day helping to hang the pictures and found herself a room in a pension. The following day the exhibition opened and in bustled Marian. All was joy. He took her out to dinner, they spent the day in Paris together and she went back to London, content.

This state of affairs, with Marian alternately pressing and elusive, continued for nearly six years. Cicely waited, as she had waited when she was not sure of her next move in the planning of the Hospice – she is good at waiting.

Life was a great deal richer, she was obviously happy to have found him and delighted in his company. Tom West, writing from Africa in response to hearing of her new friendship, wrote 'Your professor sounds terrific. He also sounds good, lovable, loving and exciting. And so nice to hear he is *fun* as well.' She had clearly given a good account of him.

But patient as she was, Cicely was very aware of Marian's age; she wanted to be able to look after him whether they eventually married or not. In 1969 – he was by then sixty-eight – she persuaded two of his Polish friends, Hanka and Wladek Jedrosz, to share a home with them. She bought a house near the Hospice and the four of them lived there together, Hanka doing the cooking. Eventually – predictably? – there was a row. 'I felt Hanka was being interfering and possessive and she thought I was ungrateful and bossy – all of which were true.' They split the house so that the Jedrosz's lived upstairs and she and Marian had the ground floor. The four them have lived together happily ever since.

In 1975 Marian's wife died, but still they did not marry. 'By then I was too rich and too famous for a noble proud Pole.' Another excuse – was he never going to let go of his pride or his need for independence? It was a splendid arrangement for him; he came and went as he liked, he was totally confident of Cicely's love for him. But he came to realise that Cicely needed to be married more than he needed his freedom. He could not expect her to risk losing someone for a third time without having the official status she so craved. At last, in 1980, after they had been together for seventeen years, it happened.

Cicely had come home late one evening after giving a lecture. She didn't wake him as he was so deeply asleep, but at one o'clock in the morning he padded into her room and asked her to marry him – 'as long as it's secret.' She wasn't going to let this moment go. They applied for an archbishop's licence and were married two weeks later – in secret. They both wanted to keep it quiet. Marian couldn't rid himself of the fear that his Polish friends would think he was marrying for money; Cicely did not want 'Dame Cicely's Pole' splashed all over the South London press. It was only when, as the news leaked out and was greeted with delight, that they felt free to admit it. His family and friends could not have been more welcoming to her, nor hers to him.

Why is Cicely so continually attracted to Poles? The question is always being asked, never satisfactorily answered. Cicely herself quite simply does not know, nor does she seek an explanation. Neither does Marian. 'I do not know, Madame, what it is. All I know is that she loves us.'

Though Betty West says that even the word 'Polish' on a tin excites her, Cicely is drawn to the people and things of Poland even before she knows their origin. Just as she was moved by the Blue Crucifixion without knowing it was the work of a Pole, so she instantly loved and bought the statue of a kneeling woman (it is now in the front hall of St. Christopher's) before she knew it was the work of Witold Kawalec. Poland calls to something in Cicely at a level which defies rational explanation.

Cicely once referred to her connection with Poland as 'a link that was there from the beginning and was forged again and again.' Is there a sense in which her love for Antoni and Marian developed from her love for David Tasma? That fate drew a pattern in which, through loving one Pole, she was drawn to others? The effect of first love should not be under-estimated, but there is at least one reason why this explanation does not hold water – David was not the first Pole in her life. When she was a child, one of her favourite people was her father's friend Herman Diamant, a Polish doctor. Mrs. Diamant, who knew Cicely well as a child, says that her husband was the only one who could do anything with Cicely when she was naughty. Already she had an affinity with Poles, or at least with one Pole.

Could it be that the passionate, romantic side of Cicely, repressed by her very English upbringing, finds a resonance in the fierce nationalism, the proud suffering, of a country whose very existence as a nation is continually under threat? The great romantic poet Julius Slowacki, called Poland 'The Jesus Christ of Nations'. Drawn as she is to suffering and to courage, could she be drawn equally by this great symbol of heroism, this country that breeds martyrs?

Even if this were true on a broad, collective level, there is also a more personal way in which the Polish character must appeal to Cicely; that is in their attitude to women. Marian says 'We esteem very much women. Even our peasants appreciate that his wife is the mother of his children. When they go into church in Poland it is always the woman who enters first. Afterwards the children, the husband comes last. In Germany first goes the man, after goes the children, behind them goes the wife.'

The balance of male and female, in herself and in her life, is delicate and crucial to Cicely, with her strong, masculine drive and her femininity, so hidden, so strong, so little gratified. Herman Diamant cared for her as a girl, a potential woman. He would say to his wife, 'If she were my daughter I'd send her to the best dressmaker in London and have clothes specially designed for her. She could look so much better.' Cicely must have sensed this concern.

Even in David and Antoni, both dying when she met them, one senses this chivalrous attitude towards women. In Marian Cicely has found a man who loves women; who tells his wife she is lovely over breakfast; who wakes her in the middle of the night to say 'As light is to the world for the artist, so love is to life'; who at eighty-two can say to her that he has never been so happy in his life. No wonder she looks fulfilled.

They are very happy, very companionable – in Marian's words 'very cosy'. They give each other freedom to pursue their separate paths – Marian with his small school of painting, his devoted pupils, his Polish friends and his own painting, Cicely with the Hospice and all that follows from it, but every year they are more fused. Marian no longer comes home when he feels like it, leaving Cicely to imagine every sort of accident while the dinner gets cold; Cicely's foreign trips have become less and less frequent; now she will not spend so much as a night away. Marrying when he was seventy-nine, she sixty-one, they realise they cannot have very long together; Marian enjoys being cosseted just as Cicely enjoys having him to cosset. 'We're so happy just the two of us together, just watching the box and me working with one eye of an evening, that we don't need anything else. In a way it's the kind of marriage you don't encounter when you're young. You have to look at the world together rather than looking at each other – we've got such a short time, perhaps it's an excuse, perhaps we're allowed to do it.'

They enjoy each other's success and Cicely feels it very appropriate that she should have been drawn to the paintings before she met the man. She gives him very practical support, not only by publishing a book about his work, but by providing him with a permanent gallery. His pictures radiate from every corner of St. Christopher's and woe betide anyone who dares object to them. Richard Lamerton, referring to them (to Cicely) as 'violent, inappropriate for a hospice, more like scrambled eggs than pictures' must surely be in a minority. The light and energy Marian's pictures bring to St. Christopher's has become part of its atmosphere, part of its healing, welcoming quality. Not least, they are somehow symbolic of the ideals of St. Christopher's in that they are *real*. How many hospitals or hospices have original paintings of such calibre on their walls?

Sister Mary Eleanor's rather incoherent, ecstatic response to a painting that Marian and Cicely had given to her convent gives an idea of the effect his work can have on people. 'At first I covered my eyes and said, No, never. But *now* . . . how did we ever do without it? You have to look at it with the inner eye. The shapes are all wrong, only what they say is all *right*. I spent some time with it and next day I woke with it shining in my head and could not wait to get to it again – it speaks to God, and yet it doesn't because there's no need of speech in the Godhead, but it expresses, it *pours* forth the love in the Godhead to God. I suppose I'm saying that it expresses the Holy Spirit? And of course by the same token the love of the Godhead for man, it's all there . . . there is that shining joy in it, shining through the total agony even.'

Like any good artist Marian speaks through his painting; Cicely speaks through her work for the dying. Their communication with each other lies in being together more than in words. Marian's spoken English is fluent but inaccurate (it is his fourth language) and Cicely is not good at languages. For all her love of Poland, its language defeats her and she has only two phrases, 'I love you' and 'I am an obedient wife.' Surprisingly, she is. Lucie Wallace, Jack Wallace's widow, was entranced when Cicely and Marian came to dinner soon after they were married. 'Cicely changed from being the high-powered Medical Director of St. Christopher's to really being Mrs. Bohusz. She didn't dominate the evening at all and when he said he thought it was time to go she just said, "All right, darling, we'll go now." This was another side of Cicely we've seen late in life.'

Cicely is *so* happy with Marian that she sometimes wonders, guiltily but hardly able to contain her joy, whether her spiritual life is not being neglected. She still does her 'rather scrubby spiritual reading in the bath', goes regularly to the Chapel and says the Jesus Prayer in bed, but finds her prayer life is meagre in comparison to the richness of the dark days. How long can she live on the spiritual capital she acquired so painfully? Is she neglecting, in her fulfilment, the God who sustained her in her suffering? 'I know when Marian dies I'll be on my knees again, but I can't screw myself down there.'

Marian insists that every night they kneel down and pray together. And as they go to sleep Cicely says, 'Look after him tonight Lord, and please let me have him a little longer.'

15

EVOLUTION

Do not look back. Do not dream about the future either. It will neither give you back the past, nor satisfy your other day dreams. Your duty, your reward, your destiny – are here and now.

Dag Hammarskjöld, *Markings*

Cicely did not intend to start a movement; she had seen something that needed to be done and she had done it. It was to her great surprise that St. Christopher's and all that it stood for was the beginning of a movement that was, in a very short time, to become world-wide. 'Why was she so successful?' asks Dr. Richard Hillier (the Medical Director of the Continuing Care Unit at Countess Mountbatten House, Southampton) 'What was so special about 1967 that made the mustard seed grow to the tree we see today – the development of a handful of hospices into the hundreds that exist all over the world and hundreds more in the planning stage?' Cicely's answer to this question is that she was 'the right person in the right place at the right time.' It is hard to improve on this deceptively simple explanation.

The international spread of Cicely's ideas on terminal care began, as these things so often do, in a small way. It was in the spring of 1963. She was working hard at St. Joseph's, the site at Lawrie Park Road was being acquired though the contract was not yet signed. Negotiations were at a crucial stage and those involved were relieved when she took an opportunity to go to the States – she had a travelling fellowship from St. Thomas's, and, through an introduction from her brother Christopher, another from the Ella Lyman Cabot Trust. While she was there a doctor friend invited her to speak to the medical students at Yale

221

University. She showed her audience pictures of patients on admission to St. Joseph's, told them about the medical treatment they were receiving – in particular the regular giving of drugs – then showed them pictures of the same patients, alert and very much happier, after a few days of this treatment.

The students were enthralled. Medical students at Yale are notoriously sophisticated and hard to please, yet they gave her a standing ovation, something no one present had ever witnessed there before. Carleton Sweetser, Chaplain at Memorial Sloan Kettering, who heard her a few weeks later in New York, 'couldn't believe how happy and comfortable the patients were looking. She bowled us over with her presentation of what she was doing.' Reports of the talk reached Florence Wald, who at the time was Dean of the Yale University School of Nursing; she persuaded Cicely to give another talk to the nurses and anyone else she could assemble at short notice. Once again Cicely scored a bull's eye. Florence likens her impact to the Scotchman's in Thomas Hardy's *The Mayor of Casterbridge*. 'They began to view him through a golden haze, which the tone of his mind seemed to raise around him. Casterbridge had sentiment, Casterbridge had romance, but this stranger's sentiment was of a different quality . . . he was to them like the poet of a new school who takes his contemporaries by storm. Who's not really new, but he is the first to articulate what all his listeners have felt, though but dumbly till then.'

Though there were individuals and small groups of people in the States who were trying to improve the care of the dying and though Herman Feifel's important book *The Meaning of Death* had been published four years earlier, the widespread feeling on the subject of terminal care was of a helpless concern. In the desert of indifference there were a few who realised that the care of the dying was inadequate, but no one knew what to do about it. Now here was someone who had the key. As Carleton Sweetser says, 'She had a message of hope to those who were ready to hear.'

These two talks at Yale were the highlights of an extensive eight-week tour in the United States, during which Cicely visited eighteen different hospitals and discussed terminal care with doctors, psychiatrists, nurses, social workers and hospital chaplains. She had come primarily to learn, and her ideas for St. Christopher's were confirmed and clarified by the experience. What she had not anticipated was how much she would also give. She proved to be not only a success, but a catalyst, eventually bringing together and inspiring people from all over America and Canada; people who had been working in the same cause but who did not know each other. She has since been invited back virtually every year; her impact on the American medical scene – or at least that part of it concerned with terminal care – came to be enormous.

She did not, at first, stress the spiritual side of her message. Though Sam Klagsbrun, who was one of the first Americans to hear her speak, found her 'the closest embodiment to a person of faith I have ever known – almost to a scary degree,' – she wanted to be received first as a doctor. Florence Wald, who became a close personal friend, says it was not until she came to know Cicely personally that she realised how important the religious side of the work was to her. It was Cicely's clinical knowledge of the control of pain and her wish 'to turn tender loving care into efficient loving care' that first impressed people who met her.

Dr. Robert Fulton, Professor of Sociology at the University of Minnesota, feels that it was her pharmacological contribution that was the most significant. He likens her revolution in pain control to that brought about by Queen Victoria when, by insisting on having an anaesthetic for the birth of her sixth child, she shook the foundations of Christian teaching. Queen Victoria was in effect saying that women do not have a moral obligation to bear children in pain, a statement which, for the Christian fundamentalist, does not sit easily with Genesis, 'In sorrow shalt thou bring forth thy children.' Dr. Fulton feels that 'this second revolution, that people needn't die in pain as they needn't be born in pain, hasn't shaken the religious community as the first one did, the revolution has shaken the medical community – in America particularly.'

Dr. Fulton points out that the three major world prizes for work with the dying have all gone to women. The Nobel Prize to Mother Teresa of Calcutta, the Teilhard de Chardin Prize to Elisabeth Kübler-Ross, who alerted American society to the question of death and dying, and of course the £90,000 Templeton Award to Cicely. He feels that these women are making an important feminist statement. 'It has to do with a revolution in ethics, with the distinction between cognitive and a gut feeling response to life. More feeling, more concern, more empathy – that is an integral part of the whole hospice message.'

Cicely herself is no feminist and does not stress this aspect of her work; she is far more concerned with being medically sound, with making sure people do not see hospice work as a soft option, but as the tough clinical challenge that it is. Nonetheless she met resistance, or at best indifference, from the medical profession in America as in England. Why should there be a resistance to lessening pain and easing death? Surely such an advance would, in the twentieth century, be met with unqualified approval? Dr. Fulton feels that much of this resistance is accounted for by the Victorian attitude that still, at least subliminally, pervades Christian cultures. Cultures that have been taught that it is an honour to identify with Christ's suffering; that one should not interfere with God's plans for our salvation by avoiding the purifying experience of pain, which is, the teaching goes, a way to God.

Another explanation comes from Dr. Feifel, who suggests that people become doctors to master their own fears of death and that Cicely's wish to use medicine to care for patients, once cure is impossible, shows up the limits of their profession and arouses the doctors' above-average fears of death. 'So you're doing two things. One, you're kicking the hell out of their professional knight's armour and, more importantly, you're telling them – "hey, you too are mortal, you too are vulnerable." With this combination the reaction was – take your professional skills and resources somewhere else.'

But Cicely did not. She stayed her ground and took on the medical system in Britain and in the States. Those who understood just what this involved admired her for having the courage of her convictions, for persisting in the face of tribulations and vicissitudes, for being a fighter. And after St. Christopher's was built and her ideas had concrete expression, they respected her achievement without reservation. Dr. Balfour Mount who runs the Palliative Care Service at the Royal Victoria Hospital in Montreal and is the first Professor in the field says, 'What separates Cicely from everybody else who went before was first of all she had the vision and then she had the strength of will and leadership ability to produce the first centre focusing in an academic way on terminal care. And by academic I mean equal emphasis on patient care, research and teaching. Others had concerned themselves with patient care before but St. Christopher's unique contribution was on all three – that's what makes St. Christopher's historically significant. Her amazing contribution has been to take an academic model and apply it to terminal care.'

The Americans took Cicely to their hearts. To them she was a classic example of an upper-class English woman – visionary, dignified, enterprising and mildly eccentric. They found no difficulty in forgiving the way she tends to 'cut people off at the knees' – on the grounds that this is how Americans expect upper middle class English women to behave. They not only liked her, they respected and honoured her. In 1969, by which time the New Haven Hospice was already being planned, she was made an Honorary Doctor of Science by Yale University – the first of many such awards and the one that meant most to her. She still treasures the citation.

Your work with those who face death has become an inspiration to patients and their families. You have

combined the learning of science and the insight of
religion to relieve physical pain and mental anguish,
and have advanced the awareness of the humanistic
aspects of patient care in all states of illness. First as a
nurse, then as a social worker, you saw the special need
of the dying patient, and as a physician you founded St.
Christopher's Hospice. To it have come doctors, nurses,
social workers, and clergy from nations around the
world to work and study with you. Yale University, in
admiration of your contribution to science and humanity, confers upon you the degree of Doctor of Science.

Cicely would be less than human if she did not enjoy this
affection and admiration. She enjoys America and its
people; in fact in American Jews she finds something of
the mysterious quality that attracts her to Poles. Since her
first visit she has crossed the Atlantic many times, most of
America's leading hospice workers have come to learn
from St. Christopher's and some of St. Christopher's staff
have visited the States. Soon the second generation was
coming into its own and, says Cicely, 'when you start
something new it's the second generation that really
matters.'

How then, would the second generation of hospice workers
handle their inheritance? Cicely has never wanted St.
Christopher's to be used as a model, a prototype for others
to imitate; she is not enthusiastic about an indiscriminate
spread of hospices. People who have wished to build a
hospice and have consulted her about their plans, must be
surprised and disappointed at her ambivalent reaction.
What she does want – passionately – is that the ideas that
have been shown to work should be fed into general
medical practice.

The word 'hospice' has a long history. It derives from a
Latin root meaning both host and guest; it implies inter-
change, hospitality, giving and receiving. The concept is
nearly two thousand years old. Fabiola, a disciple of St.
Jerome, opened a place of refuge in the time of the Emper-

or Julian the Apostate; the monastery based hospices of the middle ages were likewise places of refreshment for pilgrims and travellers – all were welcomed and sheltered till they were ready to continue their journey, the sick and wounded cared for, the dying tended.

The word was not equated primarily with the dying until the late-nineteenth century, when the Irish Sisters of Charity opened Our Lady's Hospice in Dublin. Though they included long-stay patients, their special concern with the dying gave the term a special meaning. In founding Our Lady's Hospice and, sixteen years later, St. Joseph's in London, they were continuing a tradition of caring, but shifting the emphasis. Cicely's arrival at St. Joseph's in 1958 brought a greater concentration on pain control and more understanding of relatives' responses to pain and bereavement. 'The focus of the modern Hospice Movement thus began with attention to the nature of terminal pain, to its better understanding and therefore more effective treatment. Alongside this came a revival of the old concept of a "good death" and more attention to the achievements that a patient could still make in the face of physical deterioration.'

Today the movement is often referred to simply as 'Hospice' – an umbrella word covering a number of expressions. Its development does not depend on buildings, still less on institutions, but on the communication of ideas and attitudes. Within a very few years of St. Christopher's opening, the movement began to evolve in just the kind of organic way in which Cicely had hoped it might. The principles having been defined, they were now being interpreted – on both sides of the Atlantic and eventually all over the world – in different ways to suit different needs. Control of pain, alleviation of symptoms and support for the family can be practised anywhere, a separate environment is not essential; the point must always be the needs of the local community and the wishes of the patient.

During the seventies four different models began to emerge, all in one way or another influenced by St. Christopher's. They are identified most easily by the geographical base of the caring team.

Most direct in the line of succession was, of course, the separate hospice, modelled on St. Christopher's and built, sometimes with financial help from the National Society for Cancer Relief, by the energy and initiative of small and dedicated groups of people. First in this category was St. Luke's, Sheffield, opened in 1970 and planned by Professor Eric Wilkes; this was followed by St. Anne's Hospice, Manchester, and St. Barnabas, Worthing. There are now some seventy free-standing hospices in the United Kingdom and Eire. Many more are at the planning stage.

The separate hospice has the clear advantage of being solely orientated towards the need of the dying patient, but building and commissioning a hospice is expensive and Professor Wilkes, who was Chairman of the 1980 Report on Terminal Care for the Department of Health and Social Security, feels that the nature of the need has changed in the ten years since he founded St. Luke's. 'We do not consider that there would be any advantage in promoting a large increase in the number of hospices at present and we recommend the way forward is to encourage the dissemination of the principles of terminal care throughout the health service and to develop an integrated system of care with emphasis on co-ordination between the primary care sector, the hospital sector and the hospice movement.' Cicely agrees with Professor Wilkes, nevertheless she does feel the free-standing hospice has something special to offer – the community atmosphere that some patients need so badly, the freedom from external authorities hovering in the background, research and teaching facilities dedicated solely to terminal care, undistracted by other fields of medicine. The first three independent hospices were all built with her encouragement and she spoke at their inaugural meetings.

The second model is known variously as a Palliative Care Unit or a Continuing Care Unit. It is a unit on a hospital campus, sometimes incorporated into the hospital itself as a special ward, sometimes – like Sir Michael Sobell House in Oxford – in the grounds of a general hospital. In either case its proximity to the hospital is one way of developing the integrated system of care that Professor Wilkes recommends.

The first such unit was set up in Canada by Dr. Balfour Mount, a surgeon/oncologist, after a visit to St. Christopher's. He is proud to be known as 'one of Cicely's boys' and recalls his first contact with her with affectionate admiration, feeling it says much about her. 'I phoned her on impulse one day after I'd seen a reference to her work. I said I had some funding and I'd like to come and look at her work.' He suggested he would bring his wife over, spend a day or two at the Hospice, see London and have a bit of a break. Cicely's reaction to this leisurely scheme was 'Oh yes, I know you, you can come. But leave your wife at home, come by yourself, be prepared to work hard and stay a week. It'll take at least that long for you to learn what you have to learn.' Dr. Mount was very impressed. He returned for a longer visit and put what he had learnt into practice at the Palliative Care Unit in the Royal Victoria Hospital in Montreal.

The first Continuing Care Unit opened in Bournemouth in 1975, with money from the National Society for Cancer Relief. It was headed by an anaesthetist, Dr. Ronald Fisher, and included one of St. Christopher's nurses on the staff. This unit differs from Dr. Mount's in that it is housed in an independent building and so has more separation from the hospital.

There are considerable practical advantages to this system. Costs can be reduced by sharing facilities – for instance staff accommodation and kitchens – with the parent hospital; there is easy access to any medical investigation that might be thought necessary. Dr. Robert Twycross became Medical Director of Sir Michael Sobell House, one of the early Continuing Care Units in this country, when he left St. Christopher's. He writes in the *Journal of the Royal Society of Medicine*, 'At least ten per cent of the patients in a hospice or Continuing Care Unit require further investigation to determine appropriate treatment. Blood counts, bio-chemical estimations, X-rays and bacteriological studies are the most commonly required. Occasionally more sophisticated tests will be indicated. It is far easier to arrange for such tests if the unit is part of a larger hospital in which facilities for such tests are readily available. Likewise, the patient in the integrated unit can be seen far more easily by another doctor when specialist help is indicated.'

On this point Cicely is mildly defensive, pointing out that patients in a separate hospice can and do have any investigation or treatment necessary and that travelling to another hospital is very little more trouble than crossing a hospital campus.

Home Care will always be wanted by people who are able to remain at home and who prefer to do so. This third model, which began at St. Christopher's in 1969, reached the States five years later. Dr. Sylvia Lack, who had worked at both St. Christopher's and St. Joseph's, went to New Haven at Cicely's suggestion and became Medical Director of a Home Care Team known as Hospice Inc., first planned by Florence Wald. This was run from a two-storey house, once a private home, and was the first home care team without any back-up beds of its own. In a very short time they had reached seventy per cent of their people dying at home and received Federal funding as a research project. The idea has now spread widely in the States and has also been taken up in Scandinavia and Australia and of course in the United Kingdom.

Cicely's greatest enthusiasm is for the fourth model – hospital support teams. The first such team was started in 1975 at St. Luke's, New York, by Carleton Sweetser, who had spent a sabbatical at St. Christopher's. A similar group calling itself a Support Team began operating at St. Thomas's Hospital, London, two years later.

These groups, which like many of the Home Care Teams have no beds of their own, function like any consulting service – they are called in to see individual patients. Here again the principles of terminal care are being integrated into general medical practice. This sort of co-operation has the great advantage of providing continuity of care. The patient does not have to be separated from the environment with which he has become familiar when it becomes clear that he is not going to get better. He need not feel abandoned, but can know that everything possible is being done. 'There is no decision "to treat or not to treat" but a recognition by all concerned that there has been a shift in the type of treatment that is appropriate. The stance remains active, problem-solving and concerned. The patient is left with hope based in reality.'

There is no absolute policy on terminal care, nor should there be. Cicely has transformed the face of death throughout the world. 'I have met people in Japan, in New Zealand, in Australia, South Africa, Zimbabwe, Bermuda, all over the United States and all over Europe, who regard Cicely as their teacher, the person who originated all that they are doing,' says Richard Lamerton. She has brought about this revolution by the effective use of drugs and by changing attitudes to the one certainty of life and its greatest mystery. Through her, dying has lost something of its sting.

One might expect that at sixty-five, with such achievement behind her, Cicely would be content to sit back and enjoy retirement. This is far from the truth.

She is ambivalent about her position as the doyenne of the hospice movement. On the one hand she is genuinely self-effacing, she doesn't think she should be the lynchpin of the movement and is not even sure that there should be a 'movement' as such; she resists becoming a cult figure and much of her wants to disappear into the work and watch her ideas become incorporated into general medicine – she has never forgotten the dream in which she was warned that she was 'too visible'. On the other hand she has the natural human desire to be appreciated and recognised; she is pleased by the honours that are heaped upon her, she takes great personal pride when her staff are appointed to jobs in hospice work; she is very conscious that it is she who was first in the field and in most ways is still the most experienced.

She has said both publicly and privately that she is never going to retire and that she has no intention of giving up St. Christopher's. The question of her future concerns those who love St. Christopher's and the Hospice Movement and are involved with its work.

People who feel that it is time that she should leave the field to others could perhaps enter more sympathetically into her position. St. Christopher's has been her life, her child, until very recently it has filled the role of her husband too. She has given it all her very considerable energy and talents: even if these personal issues were to be disregarded, it is certain that she still has a very great deal to offer. It is a hard decision for anyone to make, harder still for someone of Cicely's temperament.

Now of course, she has Marian. She is deeply happy with him, happier than she has ever been before. Meeting so late in life, they do not take this happiness for granted, they appreciate it daily and treasure each extra month they have together. As Marian needs her more and as St. Christopher's can run quite effectively without her, there is little doubt where, in a crisis, her loyalty would be.

Cicely is gradually becoming more ready if not to retire, at least to change her role. The years have made her a more skilled and tolerant administrator and it is a tribute to her management of the hospice that it can do without her, even if she does not always wish that it were so. Sam Klagsbrun thinks she is 'an outstanding example of the executive officer concept. The staff reflect the president's wishes but can run the ship by themselves if necessary.' He compares her achievement in being dispensable with an American hospice that deteriorated rapidly within months of its founder's death. He may have had many strengths, but he did not have Cicely's ability to let his staff stand on their own feet.

Nevertheless Sam, who understands her international significance very well, is concerned that in the 1980s the world sees less of her. He wrote to her recently, 'Your travels in the past have done a number of things for you and for St. Christopher's. You have stirred people all over the world to experiment with hospice care and you have been a major source of support, both as a person with whom people wish to identify, and as a role-model for doing what seemed to have been impossible in the minds of many people. The movement has been launched across the world because of that constant presence that you offered at various meetings internationally. Without that presence, one of the results will most likely be a less unified, consistent approach to hospice care and a greater degree of individualisation of styles in different continents and countries. That may certainly turn out to be a good thing, though probably confusing for people.'

The change of role that Cicely is considering moving into is one that would leave her free of day to day activity, but still involved in the overall running of the Hospice. She has already done this to some extent by leaving the wards more and more in the care of Tom West, while she concentrates on administration and fund-raising. St. Christopher's is rarely free of financial worries and it is her imagination and personal reputation that ensures a regular income and protects those who work close to the patients from having to shoulder this burden. Though she cannot, because of Marian, travel widely and fulfil expectations as a world leader, she does respond to invitations in the United Kingdom whenever possible.

She is coming to be fairly content with the role of elder statesman and derives much pleasure from seeing other people have ideas and carry them out, but it would be very out of keeping with her character for her to cease to want to have a finger in every pie – or at least most of them. Her main work is done, and she knows it, but she has not stopped thinking creatively about the care of the dying. Her concern now is to spread the teaching through writing and speaking in public; to find new ways in which hospice ideas can be incorporated into the Health Care Systems, both here and in the States; and to complement this care with the continuing development of St. Christopher's and fresh areas of research. For instance, she wants to look at some of the common clinical syndromes that cause distress, such as breathlessness and obstruction; she has plans for a Centre for families, both before and after bereavement; she wants to take the holistic approach she has introduced into terminal care into the field of other mortal and long-term illnesses; she is concerned with the training of nurses in all these fields.

Already the explosion of the Hospice Movement is spreading beyond the care of the dying to the care of all. Dr. Fulton feels, 'It is dignifying the least of us. It dignifies the leper in Calcutta, the elderly person. It is a countervailing force to the disregard that we generally express towards the elderly.'

Cicely's role in encouraging a view of people in their totality, seeing their medical needs, but also seeing them in their emotional, spiritual and social context, is not over. She has not stopped, nor will she.

Why has Cicely devoted her life to the dying? Her answer is: 'Because of David. It's very simple. When I first became a Christian I asked God what I should do with my life and three years later he told me. Then when I went as a volunteer to St. Luke's I had the immediate certainty – these are my people and this is where I am meant to be.'

Cicely has put the whole of herself into her work. Mind, energy, faith, compassion and suffering. Her magnificent achievement is to have turned the pain and loss of her life into one of the most creative undertakings of this century. The early deprivation of mother and aunt, the pain of feeling she was 'a gawky, unattractive teenager', the tensions between her parents, the unsatisfied longings for love, the loss of David and Antoni and so many patients who had become friends – all these by virtue of her courage, her hard work and her vision, have become gold.

She does not think very much about her own death, believing you cannot come to terms with death in the abstract and preferring to deal with things as they arise. But she does believe that by learning to let go, even of little things – 'like not being able to sing a top B flat anymore' – you can prepare for the last and ultimate loss of death.

She has had more than her share of bereavement and knows that 'bereavement makes you cry out against it. You can either draw in or you can go out.' Cicely's cry echoes the cry of suffering humanity. 'Death is an outrage. It is terrible that people who deeply love each other, who prop each other up, are suddenly parted. You spend a whole lifetime becoming two into one and then one half is taken away. It is an outrage that a young mother should leave her children, who perhaps are going to have real problems because they haven't had her. It is an outrage that people should have pain and problems, in one sense. Anyone who works in our field and has no questions shouldn't be there. But it's all right.'

Cicely's concern to make death more tolerable, to help people 'to live until they die', is a reflection of her love of life. And underlying it all is the conviction that 'it's all right'. She most deeply believes that death is not the end.

In 1976 she was in Jerusalem, praying in front of the tomb in the Church of the Holy Sepulchre. When she got up the waiting monk came over and talked to her. Cicely said, 'I work with the dying, I'm always seeing resurrection.' The monk took a flower from the tomb, blessed it and gave it to her.

AFTERWORD

Cicely seems to have an endless capacity to grow and develop, so her creation, St. Christopher's, approaching its twenty first birthday, is never static.

1985 saw several changes at the most senior level. Dame Albertine Winner retired as Chairman and became President, succeeding Lord Amulree, who had died in 1984; Tom West has taken Cicely's place as Medical Director and Cicely herself has become Chairman.

These decisions had been preceded by endless heart-searching, and the initial period of the hand-over was a difficult time for Cicely. Not only did she suffer the inevitable pain of feeling excluded, a pain which had moments of sheer agony, but she was worrying over Marian, who was seriously ill, spending some time in hospital and needing her constant care and attention. But eventually it proved an easier evolution than many had at first thought possible. Dame Albertine has less regular work and a broader canvas; Tom finds the greater responsibility suits him a great deal better than he had thought it might, and the staff are becoming accustomed to his style – a consensus leadership with all senior staff involved in decision-making. Cicely herself has fewer day to day worries, though she is still very much involved and is consulted on all major decisions. She is now finding excitement in the changes and seeing new challenges in her role as Chairman.

Staff troubled by tensions in the Hospice can and do find release in talking to Dr. Sam Klagsbrun, who has become Visitor, continuing the tradition started by the Bishop of Stepney, Evered Lunt, in 1967. The shift from an Anglican priest to a Jewish psychiatrist reveals an interesting development. It is not that the spiritual dimension has become less important – far from it – but that after eighteen years' experience with patients, the theology is more safely embedded. In choosing Sam Klagsbrun, the staff of St. Christopher's have chosen someone they know and trust, someone familiar with their problems and someone who is prepared to come over from the States at least once a year for a week at a time, feeling it is a privilege to do so.

Another close friend of Cicely's to join the staff is Dr. Gill Ford, who has been involved with St. Christopher's, one way or another, since its conception. It says something for the standing of St. Christopher's that the Department of Health and Social Security have temporarily released Dr. Ford from her job as Deputy Chief Medical Officer and seconded her to St. Christopher's for three years as Director of Studies. Her experience is already helping Cicely to fulfil her long and deeply held wish to spread hospice education through the entire medical system.

A change which will further this aim is the acquisition of the house standing between St. Christopher's main building and the Study Centre. This has been affectionately known as 'Naboth's Vineyard,' because Cicely has been casting an envious eye on it for years; now it is part of the Hospice complex and will house a Family Centre. The extra building will enable the work already being done for patients' families to be developed, expanded and taught in the relaxed and friendly atmosphere of a home. There will also be space for modern teaching methods like audiovisual aids, video tapes and one-way glass, a well tried method proved in other fields, that enables students to learn about counselling by watching, without disturbing. It need hardly be said that permision will always be asked of the families before this is used, but Cicely has found that people are so keen to help others that a refusal is rare.

Cicely never imagined, when she started building St. Christopher's, that she would one day be called 'the founder of the modern hospice movement.' That movement is now well established and Cicely is continually delighted at the work being done by the second generation of hospice workers. Recent developments include an Association of Hospice Physicians, started by Dr. Derek Doyle, Dr. Richard Hillier and Dr. Robert Twycross and plans for a journal, to be called *Palliative Medicine*. This will cover the treatment and support of patients with terminal illness together with their families; it will also keep informed the ever growing network of people interested in hospice work, and more widely, all those working with patients where the underlying disease is no longer amenable to treatment.

With every year Cicely becomes happier, more secure, more relaxed; she enjoys her new role a step-mother to Daniela and Andrew and step-grandmother to Maxie, who lives in San Francisco, and Ala and Isa from Cracow. Ala has recently been working as a volunteer at St. Christopher's, and Cicely had the pleasure of seeing her put on her pink uniform and set out for the wards, where she was a great success. But her constant joy is Marian. He is becoming increasingly frail and Cicely spends more and more time with him, coming off several committees and refusing invitations to give talks – a change of lifestyle she regards as a privilege rather than a sacrifice. As Marian's studio is in the Hospice Cicely is able to be near him while she is working and she still does her monthly week-end on duty in the wards; her chief regret is that she can no longer arrive at the Hospice early enough to attend morning prayers in the Chapel.

Marian's creativity is undiminished and he is still experimenting with new techniques, still seeking to express a new vision. He is completely happy and without fear. Their relationship is loving, harmonious and refreshingly honest. 'I could hit him sometimes when he will talk Polish and take his hearing aid out, but after six years of marriage, Marian has taught me that perfection can go on getting better, and that's also a marvellous thought about heaven.'

REFERENCES

Chapter 1

17 A-L Leprard, *The True Alchemy of the Rose Cross*; in
    Sedir: Histoire et Doctrines des Rose-Croix, Bihorel-Lez-
    Rouen, 1932. (Quoted in *A Treasury of Traditional Wis-
    dom*, ed. Whitall N. Perry, Allen and Unwin, London,
    1971.)

Chapter 2

31 John V. Taylor, *The Go-Between God*, SCM, 1972.
32 *The Ship*, Journal of the Society of Home Students.

Chapter 3

43 Alan Ecclestone, *Yes to God*, Darton Longman and Todd,
    London, 1975.

Chapter 4

54 Kahlil Gibran, *The Prophet*, Heinemann, London, 1926.

Chapter 5

60 William Blake, 'Opportunity', ed. by W. B. Yeats, Rout-
    ledge and Kegan Paul, London, 1905.
61 *Thirteenth annual report*, St. Luke's House, 1905.
61 Grace Goldin, 'A Protohospice at the turn of the century,
    St. Luke's House, London, 1893–1921', *Journal of the
    History of Medicine and Allied Sciences*, Vol XXXVI No 4,
    October 1981.
70 *Nursing Mirror*, February 14th, 1964.
71 *Current Medicine and Drugs*, July 1960, Vol I No I.
72 *Anniversary Volume*, Cancer Institute, Madras, 1964.

Chapter 6

81 *Report on a national survey concerning patients with can-
    cer nursed at home*, Pub. by Marie Curie Memorial Found-
    ation, 1952.
81 Brigadier Glyn Hughes, 'Peace at the last' – a report to the
    Calouste Gulbenkian Foundation, Pub. London United
    Kingdom and British Commonwealth Branch, 1960.

82   John Hinton, *Dying*. Penguin Books Ltd, 1967.
82   J. H. Sheldon, Report to the Birmingham Regional Hospital Board, 1961.
83   Cicely Saunders, 'Long-term Illness and its Implications', Report of a one-day conference held at the Royal Commonwealth Society, London WC2, 1962.
84   Cicely Saunders, 'The Need for Institutional Care for the Patient with Advanced Cancer', Reprinted from *Anniversary Volume*, Cancer Institute, Madras, 1964.

Chapter 7
97   Letter from Jack Wallace to Cicely Saunders.

Chapter 9
117 Srimad Bhagavatam, *The Wisdom of God*, III 2, Hollywood, California, Vendanta Press, and New York G.P. Putman and Sons, 1943. (Quoted in *A Treasury of Traditional Wisdom*, Allen and Unwin, London.)

Chapter 10
135 Bruno Bettelheim, *Home for the Heart*, Thames and Hudson, London, 1974.
137 Cicely Saunders, 'A Medical Pioneer' (Tape), Charles Press Publications.
138 Colin Murray Parkes and Jennifer L. N. Parkes, *'Hospice versus Hospital Care: Re-evaluation of Ten Years of Progress in Terminal Care as seen by Surviving Spouses'*, *Postgraduate Medical Journal*, awaiting publication.
139 Cicely Saunders, *In the Service of Medicine*, A Quarterly Paper, July 1965, No. 42, p. 2.
140 T. S. West, *St. Christopher's Annual Report*, 1976–7.
142 Cicely Saunders, 'And From Sudden Death', *Frontier*, Winter, 1961.
143 Colin Murray Parkes, *op. cit.*
145 Elisabeth Earnshaw-Smith, *St. Christopher's Annual Report*, 1980–1.
149 Samuel C. Klagsbrun, *Man and Medicine*, Vol. I. No. 3. Spring 1964.
154 The Bishop of Stepney, St. Christopher's Day Meeting, November 28th, 1964.

Chapter 11
155 Frank Zfeiffer, *Meister Eckhardt*, Leipzig, 1857. (Quoted in *A Treasury of Traditional Wisdom*, ed. Whitall N.

Perry, Allen and Unwin, London.)

156 Cicely Saunders, *Living with Dying*, Columbia. 1974.
158 Cicely Saunders, *Beyond All Pain*, SPCK, 1983.
158 Ed. Cicely Saunders, *The Management of Terminal Disease*, Edward Arnold, 1978.
159 Cicely Saunders, 'Faith', A Sermon, Guildford Lectures. 1974.
160 Message with First Newsletter, Bishop of Stepney, 1964.
160 Letter to Bishop of Stepney, July 26th, 1967.
161 & 163 Cicely Saunders, 'Watch with Me', *Nursing Times*, November 26, 1965.
162/3 Letter from Dr. Ford to author, January 10th, 1983.
163 Ted Holden, 'Patiently speaking', *Nursing Times*, June 12th, 1980.
164 Cicely Saunders, 'I was sick and you visited me', *In the Service of Medicine*, A Quarterly Paper, July 1965, No. 42, p. 2.
166 Letter from Cicely Saunders to Sister Mary Eleanor, November 9th, 1967.
166 Letter to author.
168 The *Lancet*. August 5th, 1967.
170 Cicely Saunders, 'Telling patients', *District Nursing*, September 1965.
170 *Annual Report of St. Vincent's Hospital*, 1962, Dublin.
171 Cicely Saunders, St. Christopher's Day Talk, 1964.

Chapter 12
174 Cicely Saunders, BMA Congress Talk, 1964.
175 *Annual report of St. Vincent's Hospital*, 1962.
179 Colin Murray Parkes and Jennifer L. N. Parkes, 'Hospice v. Hospital Care: Re-evaluation of Ten Years of Progress in Terminal Care as seen by Surviving Spouses', 1982, *Postgraduate Medical Journal*, awaiting publication.
180 T. S. West, *Journal of the Royal Society of Medicine*, Vol. 72, June 1979.
181 The Rt. Hon. Lord Justice Lawton, *Journal of the RSM*, Vol. 72, June 1979.
182 Cicely Saunders, 'Questionable dogma', *World Medicine*, September 20th, 1978.
186 Ed. Cicely Saunders, *The Management of Terminal Disease*, Edward Arnold, London, 1978.
190 *St. Christopher's Annual Report*, 1974–5.

Chapter 15
221 Dag Hammarskjöld, *Markings*, Faber and Faber Ltd, 1964.
221 A. Corr and D. Corr, *Hospice Care – Principles and Practice*, Springer Publishing Co., New York, 1983.
227 Cicely Saunders, 'Hospices' in *The Dictionary of Medical Ethics*, eds. A. S. Duncan, G. R. Dunstan, R. B. Wellbourn. Darton, Longman & Todd Ltd, London, 1981.
228 Terminal Care – Report of a Working Group. 1980. A committee sponsored by King Edward's Hospital Fund for London.
229 Robert Twycross, 'Hospice Care – Redressing the balance of medicine'. *Journal of the Royal Society of Medicine*, Vol. 73, July 1980.
231 Ibid.
235 Cicely Saunders, 'A Medical Pioneer' (Tape), Charles Press Publications.

FURTHER READING

Sr. Zita Marie Cotter, 'Institutional Care of the Terminally Ill', reprinted from *Hospital Progress*, June 1971

A. L. Crockford, 'Medicine as a Career', *St. Thomas's Hospital Gazette*, Vol. 51, 1953

Kristina Fabibanska-Przbytko, *Marian Bohusz-Szyszko z Londynu*, Gdansk 1981

Ed. Herman Feifel, *The Meaning of Death*, McGraw-Hill Book Company 1959

G. R. Ford and G. Pincherle, 'Arrangements for Terminal Care in the NHS (especially those for Cancer Patients)', *Health Trends*, 1978, Vol. 10

G. Gorer, *Death, Grief and Mourning*, Cresset Press, London 1965

John Hinton, 'Comparison of Places and Policies for Terminal Care', The *Lancet*, January 6th 1979

Elisabeth Kübler-Ross, *On Death and Dying*, Tavistock Publications 1970

Balfour M. Mount, 'Hospice Care', *Journal of the Royal Society of Medicine*, Vol. 73, July 1980

Colin Murray Parkes, *Bereavement*, Pelican Books 1972

Colin Murray Parkes, 'Terminal Care: Evaluation of In-Patient Service at St. Christopher's Hospice', *Postgraduate Medical Journal*, 1979

Colin Murray Parkes, 'Terminal Care: Evaluation of an Advisory Domiciliary Service at St. Christopher's Hospice', *Postgraduate Medical Journal*, October 1980, No. 56, pp. 685–9

Colin Murray Parkes, 'Evaluation of Family Care in Terminal Illness' (Alexander Ming Fisher Lecture), *Social Work with the Dying Patient and the Family*, ed. E. R. Prichard et al. Columbia University Press, New York 1977

Colin Murray Parkes, 'Home or Hospital? Terminal Care as Seen by Surviving Spouses', *Journal of the Royal College of General Practitioners*, 1978, No. 28, pp. 19–30

Henri J. M. Nouwen, *The Wounded Healer*, Doubleday and Co., New York 1972

Lily Pincus, *Death and the Family*, Faber and Faber 1974

Sandol Stoddard, *The Hospice Movement*, Jonathan Cape 1979

Robert G. Twycross, 'Euthanasia – A Physician's Viewpoint', *Journal of Medical Ethics*, 1982, Vol. 8, pp 86–92

T. S. West, 'Approach to Death', *Nursing Mirror*, October 10th 1974

T. S. West, 'Good Care or Bad Law?', *Journal of the Royal Society of Medicine*, Vol. 72, June 1979, pp. 461–4.

E. Wilkes, 'Terminal Cancer at Home', The *Lancet*, 1965

E. Wilkes, *The Dying Patient*, MTP Press, Lancaster, 1982.

Helen Willans, 'Selecting Staff for Hospice Work', *Nursing Times*, December 6th 1979

David Winter, *Living Through Loss*, Marshalls Paperbacks 1982

Max Wykes-Joyce, *The Art of Marian Bohusz,* Drian Gallery 1977

Rosemary and Victor Zorza, *A Way To Die*, Andre Deutsch 1980

'Care of the Dying', *Canadian Medical Association Journal*, July 17th, Vol. 115

On Dying Well, An Anglican Debate on Euthanasia, Church Information Office, 1975

Report on Services for the Elderly in the Metropolitan Borough of Lewisham by a committee sponsored by King Edward's Hospital Fund for London, 1964

CICELY SAUNDERS'
DEGREES AND AWARDS

1960   MA
1967   Awarded OBE in New Year Honours
1968   MRCP (Elective)
1969   Hon Dsc (Yale)
1974   FRCP
1977   Lambeth Doctorate of Medicine from Archbishop of Canterbury
1978   Hon Doctorate from The Open University
1979   Hon Doctorate of Law (Columbia University, New York)
       The first woman to receive the Worshipful Society of Apothecaries' (London) Gold Medal in Therapeutics
       Hon Doctorate of Humane Letters, Iona College, New York
1980   Awarded DBE in New Year Honours
1981   Awarded the Templeton Prize for Progress in Religion
       FRCN
       Hon Doctorate of Humanitarian Service, Creighton University, Omaha, Nebraska
       Hon Doctorate Marymount Manhattan College, New York
1982   Hon Doctor of Humane Letters, Jewish Theological Seminary, New York
1983   Hon Doctor of University, University of Essex
       Hon Doctor of Laws, University of Leicester
       Hon Doctor of Science, University of London
       Hon Fellowship, Sheffield City Polytechnic
1984   Hon Doctor of Medicine, Queen's University of Belfast
       Hon Doctor of Civil Laws, University of Kent
1986   Hon Doctor of Law, University of Cambridge
       Hon Doctor of Civil Law, University of Oxford
       FRCS (Elected)

PUBLICATIONS
BY CICELY SAUNDERS

1957   'Dying of Cancer', *St. Thomas's Hospital Gazette* Vol.
        56(2).
1959   'Care of the Dying', *Nursing Times*.
1960   'The Christian and Healing', *Portman Review*, January.
        'The Management of Patients in the Terminal Stage'.
        Chapter in *Cancer*, ed. Raven, Butterworth, London.
        'Drug Treatment in the Terminal Stages of Cancer',
        Current Medicine and Drugs 1.16.
1961   'A Patient', *Nursing Times*, March 31.
        'And From Sudden Death . . .', *Frontier*, Winter number.
        'The Care of the Dying', *Better Health*, May.
        Lonely and Fearful, Booklet for Church Union, Frisby
        Sons & Whipple Ltd.
        Why Does God Allow Suffering? Booklet for Church
        Union, Frisby Sons & Whipple Ltd.
1962   'Working at St. Joseph's Hospice, Hackney', *St. Vincent's
        Gazette*, Dublin.
1963   'The Treatment of Intractable Pain in Terminal Cancer',
        Proceedings of the Royal Society of Medicine, 56, 195.
        'Care of the Dying', *Current Medical Abstracts for Prac-
        titioner*, Edinburgh 3, No. 2.
1964   'The Symptomatic Treatment of Incurable Malignant
        Disease', *Prescribers' Journal* 4. 68.
        'The Need for Institutional Care for the Patient with
        Advanced Cancer', Reprint, *Anniversary Volume*, Can-
        cer Institute, Madras.
        'Death', *The Living Church*, USA, July.
        Review of *Pain, Its Meaning and Significance* by F.
        Sauerbruch and H. Wenke, *Medical News*, p. 16, July.
        'Care of Patients Suffering from Terminal Illness at St.
        Joseph's Hospice', *Nursing Mirror*, February.
        'Drugs in the Treatment of the Dying', *Drugs and Thera-
        peutic Bulletin,* Volume 2, No. 26, December.

1965   'Light at the End of the Road', *In the Service of Medicine*,
       Christian Medical Fellowship Quarterly, No. 42, July.
       'Watch With Me', Reprint, *Nursing Times*, November
       26th.
       'Telling Patients', *District Nursing*, September.
       'The Last Stages of Life', *American Journal of Nursing*,
       Reprint, March.
1966   'The Care of the Dying', *Guy's Hospital Gazette*, Reprint
       80. 136.
       'The Role of Social Medicine in Teaching in Gerontology',
       Paper for the Pre-Congress Colloquium of the 7th Inter-
       national Congress of Gerontology, Vienna, June.
       'Death and Responsibility', from *Psychiatric Opinion*,
       Vol 3. 28.
1967   *The Management of Terminal Illness*, Hospital Medicine
       Publications Ltd, London.
       'Care of the Dying', *Gerontologia Clinica*, 9. 385–390.
       'St. Christopher's Hospice', *British Hospital Journal*, Vol
       LXXXVII, 4047.
       'The Care of the Terminal Stages of Cancer', Reprint,
       Annals of the Royal College of Surgeons, Vol. 41, Supp.
       Issue.
1969   'The Moment of Truth – Care of the Dying Person', Con-
       tribution to *Death and Dying*, Edited by Leonard Pear-
       son.
       'The Management of Fatal Illness in Childhood', *Pro-*
       ceedings of the RSM, June, Vol. 62.
1970   'Nature and Management of Terminal Pain', Contribu-
       tion to *Matters of Life and Death* – London Medical
       Group, Ed. E. F. Shotter.
       'Training for the Practice of Clinical Gerontology', *The*
       Role of Social Medicine. Interdiscipl. Topics Geront., Vol.
       5, 72–8 (Karger, Basel/München/NY).
       'An Individual Approach to the Relief of Pain', *People*
       and Cancer. The British Cancer Council.
1971   'Patients' Response to Treatment', *Proceedings of the 4th*
       Nat. Symposium 'Catastrophic Illness in the Seventies',
       Cancer Care Inc. NY.
       'Care of the Dying Patient and the Family', LMG Re-
       print from *Contact*.
       'Death in the Family', DHSS Symposium, November.
1973   'Patient and Doctor', East European Conference on Can-
       cer Control, May.

'Need for In-Patient Care for the Patient with Terminal Cancer', *Middlesex Hospital Journal*.

'Research into Terminal Care of Cancer Patients', Reprinted from *Portfolio For Health 2*, DHSS.

1974   'The Working of St. Christopher's, Chapter contributed to *Medical Care of the Dying Patient*, Foundation of Thanatology, New York.

A Therapeutic Community: St. Christopher's Hospice in Psychosocial Aspects of Terminal Care, ed. B. Schoenberg et al., Columbia University Press, New York.

'Care for the Dying', Chapter contributed to *The Hour of Our Death*, ed. S. Lack and R. Lamerton, Geoffrey Chapman, London.

'A Place to Die', *Crux*, A Quarterly Journal of Christian Thought and Opinion, Toronto, Ontario, Vol. 11, No. 3.

'Faith', Guildford Lectures, Seven Corners Press Ltd., Guildford.

Sermon in Bristol Cathedral for the Fellowship of the Road Silver Jubilee, March.

1975   'The Challenge of Terminal Care', Chapter contributed to *The Scientific Foundation of Oncology*, ed. T. Symington and R. Carter, William Heinemann Medical Books Ltd, London.

'Terminal Care and the Relief of Pain'. Chapter contributed to *Medical Oncology*, ed. K. D. Bagshawe. Blackwells, Oxford.

On Dying Well. An Anglican Contribution to the Debate on Euthanasia, Chapters contributed to *On Dying Well*, Church Information Office, London.

The Nature and Management of Pain in Terminal Malignant Disease, Script of a tape for the Medical Recording Service, 3rd Edition.

'Dimensions of Death', Chapter contributed to *Religion & Medicine*, SCM Press Ltd, London.

1976   'Care for the Dying', *Patient Care*, Vol. 111, No. 6, June.

'A Window in Your Home', *The Light of Experience*, BBC Publication.

1977   'Care of the Dying', *Nursing Times*, 1977 series of articles.

'This House believes some form of Voluntary Euthanasia should be legalised.' *World Medicine*, September 20.

1978   'The Need for In-Patient Care for the Patient with Terminal Cancer', Reprint in *St. Thomas' Hospital Medical School Gazette*. 3rd Edition.

The Management of Terminal Disease, ed. C. Saunders. Edward Arnold (Publishers) Ltd., November.

'Hospice Care', *The American Journal of Medicine*, Vol. 65, 726–728, November.

1979 'The Care of the Dying', *Murmur* (Cambridge University Medical Society Magazine) p. 14–16, January.

'The Nature & Management of Terminal Pain and the Hospice Concept', *Advances in Pain Research & Therapy*, Vol. 2, ed. J. J. Bonica & V. Ventafridda. Raven Press, New York.

'Hospice Care', *The Indian Journal of Cancer*, Vol. 16, No. 3–4, December.

1980 'Caring to the End', *Nursing Mirror*, September 4th.

1981 'Hospices'. *The Dictionary of Medical Ethics*, eds. A. S. Duncan, G. R. Dunstan, R. B. Wellbourn, Darton, Longman and Todd Ltd.

Hospice, The Living Idea, eds. C. Saunders, D. Summers, N. Teller. Edward Arnold Publishers (London) Ltd.

1982 'Principles of Symptom Control in Terminal Care', *Medical Clinics of North America*, Vol. 66, No. 5, September.

1983 *Living With Dying*, eds. C. Saunders & M. Baines. Oxford University Press.

'Living With Dying', *Radiography*, Vol. 49, April.

'Terminal Care', Chapter in *Oxford Textbook of Medicine*, eds D. J. Weatherall, J. G. G. Ledingham and D. A. Warrell, OUP.

Beyond all Pain, SPCK.

DIRECTORY OF HOSPICES AND HOMES, HOME CARE TEAMS AND HOSPITAL SUPPORT TEAMS IN THE UNITED KINGDOM AND THE REPUBLIC OF IRELAND

AVON

Dorothy House Foundation
162 Bloomfield Road
Bath
Home care (0225) 311335
In-patient (0225) 318368

St. Peter's Hospice
St. Peter's Lodge
Tennis Road
Knowle
Bristol BS4 2HG
(0272) 774605
Home care also available

BEDFORDSHIRE

Sue Ryder Home
St. John's
Moggerhanger
Nr. Bedford
(0767) 40622

BERKSHIRE

The Paul Bevan Foundation
50 High Street
Sunninghill
(0990) 24721
Home care only

Macmillan Service
East Berkshire Health Authority
Health Clinic
Burlington Road
Slough SL1 2JS
(2) 820833
Home care only

Macmillan Service
West Berks Health Authority
25 Erleigh Road
Reading RG1 5LR
(0734) 61471
Home care only

BUCKINGHAMSHIRE

Hospice of Our Lady and St. John
The Priory
Willen
Milton Keynes MK5 9AB
(0908) 663636
Home care also available

CAMBRIDGESHIRE

Arthur Rank House
Brookfield Hospital
351 Mill Road
Cambridge CB1 3DF
(0223) 245926
Home care also available

The Hospital at Home Scheme
The Health Department
Midgate House
Peterborough
(0733) 51634
Home care only

CHESHIRE

St. Ann's Hospice
St. Ann's Road North
Heald Green
Cheadle SK8 3SZ
(061 437) 8136/7
Home care also available

St. Roccos' Hospice
86 Orford Avenue
Warrington
(0925) 573105
Home care also available

Macmillan Service
The Health Centre
Garven Place
Sankey Street
Warrington
(0925) 35961
Home care only

Macmillan Service
Community Nursing Service
St. Martin's House
Princess Street
Chester CH1 2BA
(0244) 27161
Home care only

CLEVELAND

Macmillan Service
Guisborough Health Centre
Bar Street
Guisborough TS14 7AA
(0287) 35436
Home care only

The Macmillan Nurses
Hartlepool Hospice
Alice House
13 Hutton Avenue
Hartlepool
(0429) 221503
*Home care only – day care/in-patient
unit to follow*

CORNWALL

Mount Edgcumbe Hospice
Porthpean Road
St. Austell PL6 6AB
(0726) 65711

Macmillan Service (Cornwall)
3 St. Clement Vean
Tregolls Road
Truro
(0872) 77876
Home care only

CUMBRIA

Macmillan Service
c/o Mrs Margaret Dowling
Laybarrow
Gallowbarrow
Hayton
Nr. Aspatria CA5 2PH
(0965) 20352
Home care only

DERBYSHIRE

Nightingale Macmillan
Continuing Care Unit
Trinity Street
Derby
(0332) 385012
Home care also available

DEVON

St. Luke's Hospice – Plymouth
Dean Cross Road
Plymstock
Plymouth
(0752) 41172
Home care also available

Torbay & South Devon Hospice
Rowcroft House
Avenue Road
Torquay
(0803) 211656

Macmillan Domiciliary Service
Castle Circus Health Centre
Abbey Road
Torquay
(0803) 62951
Home care only

Hospiscare
Mowbray Cottage
Victoria Street
Exeter EX4 4NS
(0392) 54281
Home care only

Tidcombe Hall
Marie Curie Memorial Foundation
Home
Tidcombe Hall
Tiverton EX16 4EJ
(0884) 252181

Hospice Care Trust
(North Devon) Ltd
7 New Buildings
Vicarage Street
Barnstaple EX32 7BT
(0271) 44248
*Opening Autumn 1984 for home care
only*

DORSET

Macmillan Unit
Christchurch Hospital
Fairmile Road
Christchurch BH23 2JX
(0202) 486361
Home care also available

ESSEX

Macmillan Home Care Service
Central Clinic
East Lodge Court
High Street
Colchester
(0206) 79411
Home care only

St. Helena Hospice
Myland Hall
Eastwood Drive
Colchester
(0206) 845566

Southend Terminal Care Support
Group
34 Priory Avenue
Southend-on-Sea
(0702) 610598
Home care only

Macmillan Service
Southend General Hospital
Prittlewell Chase
Westcliff-on-Sea
Southend (0702) 48911, ext. 2537
Home care only

St. Francis' Hospice
The Hall
Broxhill Road
Havering-Atte-Bower
Romford RM4 1QH
(0708) 753319
Home care also available

GLOUCESTERSHIRE

Sue Ryder Home
Leckhampton Court
Leckhampton
Nr. Cheltenham
(0242) 30199

HAMPSHIRE

Countess Mountbatten House
Moorgreen Hospital
Botley Road
West End
Southampton SO3 3JB
(0703) 477414
Home care also available

Sue Ryder Home
Bordean House
Langrish
Nr. Petersfield
(0730) 61005

253

HEREFORDSHIRE

Macmillan Service
Westfield Health Centre
Westfield Walk
Leominster
(0568) 4211
Home care only

St. Michael's Hospice
Bartestree
Hereford HR1 4HA
(0432) 851000

HERTFORDSHIRE

The Hospice of St. Francis
(Berkhamsted)
St. Francis' House
27 Shrublands Road
Berkhamsted HP4 3HX
(04427) 2960

Welwyn Hatfield Hospice Care
Service
Gooseacre Health Centre
Welwyn Garden City
(070 73) 24541

St Alban's & District Hospice Care
Team
Kimberley Rehabilitation Unit
City Hospital
Normandy Street
St. Alban's
Herts
(56) 661222, ext. 450

HUMBERSIDE

Macmillan Domiciliary Service
North Humberside Hospice Project
Dove House
Beverley Road
Hull HU6 7NH
(0482) 446782
Home care only

ISLE OF WIGHT

Earl Mountbatten House
Fairlie Hospital
Newport
(0983) 529511/529536
Home care also available

JERSEY

Jersey Hospice Care
Gloucester Lodge
Stopford Road
St. Saviour
(0534) 73915
*Home care only – day care centre to
follow*

KENT

Pilgrims' Hospice
56 London Road
Canterbury CT2 8JY
(0227) 459700/457766

The Wisdom Hospice
St William's Way
Rochester ME1 2NU
(0634) 812571
Home care also available

Hospice at Home
Michael Tetley Hall
Sandhurst Road
Tunbridge Wells TN2 3JS
(0892) 44877
Home care only

South Bromley Hospiscare
c/o Orpington Hospital
Orpington BR6 9JU
(66) 29010
Home care only

LANCASHIRE

East Lancashire Hospice
Park Lea Road
Blackburn
(0254) 63555, ext. 493

Macmillan Liaison Nursing Services
Park Lee Hospital
Blackburn
(0254) 63555 ext. 408
Home care only

Hettinga House
(St. Joseph's Hospice Association)
Dark Lane
Ormskirk
(0695) 72942
Home care also available

Wigan Hospice
Poolstock Lane
Poolstock
Wigan WN3 5HL
(0942) 496092
Home care also available

Trinity – the Hospice in the Fylde
Low Moor Road
Bispham
Blackpool FY2 0BG
(0253) 58881
Home care also available

LEICESTERSHIRE

The Leicestershire Hospice
Groby Road Hospital
Leicester LE3 9QE
(0533) 313771

LINCOLNSHIRE

St. Barnabas' Hospice
17 Lindum Terrace
Lincoln LN2 5RT
(0522) 24145
Home care also available

LONDON

The Continuing Care Unit
Pembridge Wing
Paddington Community Hospital
7a Woodfield Road
London W9
(01) 286 6669

St. Christopher's Hospice
51/53 Lawrie Park Road
Sydenham SE26 6DZ
(01) 778 9252
Home care also available

The Catherine McAuley Unit
Hospital of St. John and St.
Elizabeth
60 Grove End Road NW8 9NH
(01) 286 5126

Edenhall
Marie Curie Memorial Foundation
Home
11 Lyndhurst Gardens
London NW3 5NS
(01) 794 0068

St. Joseph's Hospice
(Irish Sisters of Charity)
Mare Street
Hackney E8 4SA
(01) 985 0861
Terminal cancer/chronic sick
Home care also available

Macmillan Home Care Service
St. Joseph's Hospice
Mare Street
Hackney E8 4SA
(01) 985 6422
Home care only

Trinity Hospice
30 Clapham Common
North Side
Clapham SW4 0RN
(01) 622 9481
Home care also available

Brent Terminal Care Team
Primary Health Care Unit
Wembley Hospital
Fairview Avenue
Wembley
(01) 903 1323
Home care only

The West Ham Central Mission
The Stanley Turl Wing
409 Barking Road
Plaistow E13 8AL
(01) 476 5065
Medical day care centre

Ealing Continuing Care Team
Block C, Clayponds Hospital
Occupation Lane
South Ealing W5
(01) 568 4743
(After 10.30 a.m. 579 7371, ext. 68)
Home care only

North London Hospice Group
c/o 76a Wilton Road, N.10
(01) 444 2146
*Home care available early
1984 – in-patient unit
to follow*

The Continuing Care Unit
The Horder Ward
The Royal Marsden Hospital
Fulham Road, SW3
(01) 352 8171, ext. 483

MANCHESTER

St. Anne's Hospice
Peel Lane
Little Hulton
Worsley
Manchester M28 6EL
(061) 702 8181
Home care also available

MERSEYSIDE

St. Joseph's Hospice Association
Jospice International
La Casa de San Jose
Ince Road
Thornton
Nr. Liverpool L23 4UH
(051) 924 3812/3

Macmillan Nursing Service
Pensby Clinic
Pensby Road
Bebington
Wirral
L63 7RX
(051) 645 7661
Home care only

St. John's Hospice
Mount Road
Bebington
Merseyside
(051) 334 2778

Macmillan Home Care Service
Community Nursing Office
St Helen's Hospital
Peasley Cross Wing
Marshalls Cross Road
St Helen's
(0744) 26633, ext. 278
Home care only

Macmillan Service
2 Church Street
Southport
(0704) 40911
Home care only

Sunnybank
Marie Curie Memorial Foundation
Home
Speke Road
Woolton
Liverpool L25 8QA
(051) 428 1395/6

256

MIDDLESEX

Michael Sobell House
Mount Vernon Hospital
Northwood
(01) 652 6111, ext. 302
Home care also available

NORFOLK

Priscilla Bacon Lodge
Colman Hospital
Unthank Road
Norwich
(0603) 28377, ext. 7214
Home care also available

NORTHAMPTONSHIRE

Cynthia Spencer House
Manfield Hospital
Northampton NN3 1AD
(0604) 491121
Home care also available

NOTTINGHAMSHIRE

Hayward House
City Hospital
Hucknall Road
Nottingham NG5 1PB
(0602) 608111
Home care also available

The Nottingham Hospice
Fernleigh
384 Woodborough Road
Nottingham NG3 7JD
(0602) 606265
Day care facilities and home care only

OXFORDSHIRE

Helen House
37 Leopold Street
Oxford OX4 1QT
(0865) 728251

Sir Michael Sobell House
The Churchill Hospital
Headington
Oxford OX3 7LJ
(0865) 64841, ext. 7088
Home care also available

Sue Ryder Home
Nettlebed
Near Henley-on-Thames
(0491) 641384
Home care also available

SHROPSHIRE

Shropshire Macmillan Service
Wellington Cottage Hospital
Wellington
Nr Telford
(0952) 51155, ext. 271
Home care only

SOMERSET

St. Margaret's Hospice
Flook House
Station Road
Taunton
(0823) 79465
Home care only – in-patient unit to follow

STAFFORDSHIRE

Douglas Macmillan Home
Barlaston Road
Blurton
Stoke-on-Trent ST3 3NZ
(0782) 317118
Home care also available

St. Giles' Hospice
Fisherwick Road
Lichfield WS14 9LH
(0543) 432031
Home care also available

SUFFOLK

St. Nicholas' Hospice
Turret Close
Westgate Street
Bury St Edmunds, Suffolk
(0284) 66133

SURREY

Phyllis Tuckwell Memorial Hospice
Trimmers
Waverley Lane
Farnham GU9 8BL
(0252) 725814

Sam Beare Continuing Care Service
Weybridge Hospital
Church Street
Weybridge KT13 8DY
(97) 52931
Home care also available

Harestone
Marie Curie Memorial Foundation
Home
Harestone Drive
Caterham CR3 6YQ
(0883) 42226

SUSSEX

Copper Cliff
74 Redhill Drive
Brighton BN1 5FL
(0273) 504842

Douglas Macmillan Unit
King Edward VII Hospital
Midhurst GU29 OBL
(073081) 2341
Home care also available

Jerusalem Hospice
22 Buckhurst Road
Bexhill-on-Sea TN40 2JA
(0424) 223460

Tarner Home
Tilbury Place
Brighton BN2 2GY
(0273) 604665

St. Barnabas' Home
Columbia Drive
Worthing BN13 2QF
(0903) 64222
Home care also available

St. Wilfrid's Hospice
Millgap House
2 Millgap Road
Eastbourne
(0323) 644500
Home care also available

St. Peter's and St. James'
Wivelsfield Green
(044 484) 598

Symptom Control Service
Community Nursing Office
13a Holmesdale Gardens
Hastings TN34 1LY
(0424) 714805
Home care only

St. Catherine's Hospice
Malthouse Road
Crawley RH10 6BH
(0293) 547333

TYNE & WEAR

St. Oswald's Hospice
Regent Avenue
Gosforth
Newcastle NE3 1EE
(091) 285 0063
*Home care only – in-patient unit to
follow*

Conrad House
Marie Curie Memorial Foundation
Home
Bentinck Terrace
Newcastle-upon-Tyne
(0632) 737931

St Benedict's Hospice
Havelock Hospital
Hylton Road
Sunderland SR4 8AE
(0783) 656256

WARWICKSHIRE

Myton Hamlet Hospice
Myton Lane
Myton Road
Warwick CV3 6PX
(0926) 492518
Home care also available

Macmillan Service
Stoke Aldermoor Clinic
Aldemoor Lane
Coventry
(0203) 452473
Home care only

WEST MIDLANDS

Compton Hall
4 Compton Road West
Wolverhampton WV1 3HH
(0902) 758151
Home care also available

St. Mary's Hospice
Raddlebarn Road
Selly Park
Birmingham 29 7DA
(021 472) 1191
Home care also available

Taylor Memorial Home
76 Grange Road
Erdington
Birmingham 24
(021) 373 5526

Warren Pearl House
Marie Curie Memorial
Foundation Home
Warwick Road
Solihull B91 2AG
(021) 705 4607/8

WILTSHIRE

The Prospect Foundation
Prospect House
5 Church Place
Swindon SN1 5EH
(0793) 481458
Home care only

Salisbury Hospice Care Trust
Salisbury General Infirmary
Fisherton Street
Salisbury SP2 7SX
(0722) 336212, ext. 681
*Home care only – in-patient unit to
follow*

NORTH YORKSHIRE

Macmillan Domiciliary Service
Monkgate Health Centre
31/35 Monkgate
York YO3 7BB
(0904) 30351, ext 30
Home care only

Macmillan Service
St Catherine's Hospice
Macmillan House
137 Scalby Road
Scarborough YO12 6TB
(0723) 351421
*Home care only – in-patient unit to
follow*

SOUTH YORKSHIRE

St. Luke's Nursing Home
Little Common Lane
Off Abbey Lane
Sheffield
(0742) 369911
Home care also available

WEST YORKSHIRE

Ardenlea
Marie Curie Memorial Foundation
Home
Queen's Drive
Ilkley
(0943) 607505

Sue Ryder Home
Wheatfields Hospice
Grove Road
Headingley
Leeds LS6 2AE
(0532) 787249
Home care also available

Sue Ryder Home
Manorlands
Oxenhope
Nr. Keighley
(0535) 42308

St. Gemma's Hospice
329 Harrogate Road
Moortown
Leeds LS17 6QD
(0532) 693231
Home care also available

Macmillan Service
Overgate Hospice
30 Hullen Edge Road
Elland HX5 0QX
(0422) 79151
Home care also available

SCOTLAND

St. Columba's Hospice
Challenger Lodge
Boswall Road
Edinburgh EH5 3RW
(031 551) 1381
Home care also available

Strathcarron Hospice
Randolph Hill
Fankerton By Denny
Stirlingshire FK6 5HJ
(0324) 826222
Home care also available

Roxburghe House
Tor-Na-Dee Hospital
Milltimber
Aberdeen
(0224) 867307
Home care also available

Roxburghe House
Royal Victoria Hospital
Jedburgh Road
Dundee DD2 1UB
(0382) 66246
Home care also available

St. Margaret's Hospice
(The Irish Sisters of Charity)
East Barn Street
Clydebank
Glasgow G81 1E9
(041 952) 1141

Macmillan Home Care Service
Dedridge Health Centre
Nigel Rise
Dedridge
Livingston
West Lothian
(0506) 414586
Home care only

Fairmile
Marie Curie Memorial Foundation
Home
Fairmile Head
Edinburgh EH10 7DR
(031) 445 2141

Hunters Hill
Marie Curie Memorial Foundation
Home
Belmont Road
Glasgow G21 3AY
(041) 558 2555

Prince and Princess of Wales
Hospice
The New Glasgow Hospice
71/73 Carlton Place
Glasgow G5
(041) 429 5599

WALES

Ty Olwen Hospice
Morriston Hospital
Swansea
West Glamorgan SA6 6NL
(0792) 703361
Home care also available

Paul Sartori Foundation
Paul Sartori Foundation Room
County War Memorial Hospital
St. Thomas' Green
Haverfordwest
Dyfed
(0646) 600742
Home care only

St. David's Foundation
Cambrian House,
St. John's Road,
Maindee,
Newport NPT 8GR
(0633) 281811
Home care only

Macmillan Service
Ogwr Health Office
Maesteg Road
Tondu
Bridgend
Mid Glamorgan CF32 9HG
(0656) 720121
Home care only

Colwyn Bay Community Hospital
Hesketh Road
Colwyn Bay, Clwyd
(0492) 515218
Home care only

Macmillan Service
Maelor General Hospital
Wrexham, Clwyd
(0978) 353153
Home care only

Macmillan Service
Community Health Authority
Royal Alexandra Hospital
Rhyl
Clwyd
(0745) 55188
Home care only

Holme Tower
Marie Curie Memorial Foundation
Home
Bridgeman Road
Penarth
South Glamorgan
(0222) 709353

MACMILLAN MINI UNITS IN WALES
(Two-bedded wards attached to
community hospitals in Wales. Built
and equipped by the National Society
for Cancer Relief during 1976–7 and
run by the National Health Service)

Denbighshire Infirmary
Ruthin Road
Denbigh
Clwyd
(074571) 2624

Groeswen Hospital
Margam Road
Port Talbot
West Glamorgan SA13 2LB
(0792) 703361
Home care only

Monmouth General Hospital
15 Hereford Road
Monmouth
Gwent NP5 3HG
(0600) 35223

Oakdale Hospital
Blackwood
Gwent NP2 0JH
(0495) 225207

South Pembrokeshire Hospital
Fort Road
Pembroke Dock
Dyfed
(0646) 682114

Treherbert Hospital
Treherbert
Rhondda
Mid Glamorgan
(0443) 771202

Amman Valley Hospital
Folland Road
Glanamman
Ammanford, Dyfed
(0269) 822226

Brynseiont Hospital
Caernarfon
Gwynedd LL5 2YO
(0286) 3371
Home care also available

NORTHERN IRELAND

The Northern Ireland Hospice
Somerton House
74 Somerton Road
Belfast BT15 3LH
(0232) 781836
Home care also available

Beaconfield
Marie Curie Memorial Foundation
Home
Kensington Road
Belfast BT5 6NF
(0232) 794200

REPUBLIC OF IRELAND

Our Lady's Hospice
(Irish Sisters of Charity)
P O Box 222
Harold's Cross
Dublin
(0001) 972101/972839

Marymount Hospice
St. Patrick's Hospital
Wellington Road
Cork
(010 353 21) 501201

Little Company of Mary Hospice
Milford House
Castletroy
Co Limerick
(010 353 61) 43303
Home care also available

CHANNEL ISLANDS

Guernsey Home Care
c/o Grange End Medical Practice
St Peter's, Guernsey
(0481) 64185
Home care only

SYMPTOM CONTROL /
HOSPITAL SUPPORT TEAMS

HAMPSHIRE

Macmillan Service
Basingstoke District Hospital
Park Prewett
Basingstoke RG24 9NA
(0256) 473202
*Advice, support and
teaching only*

KENT

Macmillan Service
Queen Mary's Hospital
Sidcup DA14 6LT
(01) 302 2678

LONDON

Pain Relief Team
Pain Clinic
Second Floor
Doyle House
Guy's Hospital SE1
(01) 407 7600, ext. 3673/3680

Macmillan Support Team
Hither Green Hospital
Hither Green Lane
Lewisham SE13
(01) 698 4618 (or via Sister's bleep)
Home care only

The Terminal Care and Support
Team
(University College Hospital)
The National Temperance Hospital
Hampstead Road NW1
(01) 387 9300, ext. 553 (or 387 0608)

The Support Team
Hart Ward
The Royal Free Hospital
Pond Street
Hampstead NW3 2QG
(01) 794 0500, ext. 3861 (or Sister's
bleep 892 889)

The Macmillan Continuing Care
Team
St. Giles' Hospital
St. Giles' Road SE5 7RN
(01) 703 0898, ext. 6257

The Support Team
St. Thomas's Hospital
Lambeth Palace Road SE1
(01) 928 9292, ext. 2876

Greenwich Support Team
Greenwich Hospital
Devonport Annexe
King William Walk
Greenwich SE10
(01) 858 8090

The Support Team
St. Bartholomew's Hospital
Smithfield
London EC1
(01) 600 9000, ext. 2159
Support and advisory service

MERSEYSIDE

Whiston Hospital
St. Helen's and Knowsley
Health Authority
Prescot L35 5DR
(051) 426 1600

SURREY

Macmillan Continuing Care Team
Averill Lodge
Kingston Hospital
Galsworthy Road
Kingston KT2 7QB
(01) 546 7711, ext. 435

YORKSHIRE

Wakefield Hospital Support Team
Pinderfields General Hospital
Aberford Road
Wakefield WF1 4DG
(0924) 375217, ext. 2290

The Macmillan Support Nurse
Royal Hallamshire Hospital
Glossop Road
Sheffield S10 2JF
(0742) 26484
Support and advisory service

INDEX

Index

Index